AN INTRODUCTION TO A
CHRISTIAN PSYCHO-THERAPY

AN INTRODUCTION TO A CHRISTIAN PSYCHO-THERAPY

J. A. C. MURRAY, B.D.

Minister of Tolbooth-St. John's Parish Church, Edinburgh

" Canst thou not minister to a mind diseas'd
Pluck from the memory a rooted sorrow,
Raze out the written troubles of the brain,
And with some sweet oblivious antidote
Cleanse the stuff'd bosom of that perilous stuff
Which weighs upon the heart?"

("Macbeth.")

Edinburgh: **T. & T. CLARK, 38 George Street**

PRINTED IN GREAT BRITAIN BY
MORRISON AND GIBB LIMITED

FOR

T. & T. CLARK, EDINBURGH

FIRST EDITION . . . . . *September* 1938
SECOND EDITION . . . . *October* 1947

TO

E. M.

MY INSPIRATION AND MY GUIDE

PREFACE

THIS book seeks, very humbly, to address itself to what the writer feels to be one of the greatest needs of the world. The more we ponder over the swift and cumulative disorders of the day, the more do we realise that in combating them, we wrestle, not against flesh and blood, but against the principalities and powers which, in the mind, impel that flesh and blood to strange and warlike things. These disorders are, in the last resort, mental disorders ; and just when we seemed to need it most, a whole new strategy of approach and attack is put into our hands, by the recent advances in our knowledge of the baffling kingdoms of the mind. The study of psycho-therapy becomes, therefore, one of the most practical, as one of the most imperative, requirements of the age.

There is no necessary divorce, as some think, between such psychological study or therapeutic practice, and the work of the Christian in the cure of souls ; that has been directly brought home to the writer, both in intimate personal experience, and in the pastoral office, through consultative and curative work. Out of that conviction, he has written what is, after all, but an introduction to a twofold science, of mind and of spirit, a science which, by God's blessing, will be greatly used in the reconciliation of His creatures to Him, and to each other.

J. A. C. MURRAY.

THE MANSE OF KERSE,
  GRANGEMOUTH,
    STIRLINGSHIRE,
      September 1938.

PREFACE TO SECOND EDITION

THIS reprint would have appeared much sooner, had it not been for war-time conditions and paper restriction. I am most grateful for the many tokens of appreciation which I have received from readers of this book in all parts of the world. That it has done good, fulfils my dearest hope in sending it out : and I am glad that conditions now permit a reprint to be made.

J. A. C. MURRAY.

14 RAMSAY GARDEN,
    EDINBURGH, 1.

CONTENTS

CONTENTS

AN INTRODUCTION TO A
CHRISTIAN PSYCHO-THERAPY

CHAPTER I

THE CURE OF SOULS

> The scope of this book; ministerial education does not include therapy of the mind; the present world-wide overstrain; its connection with irreligion; a materialist psychology insufficient; its low concepts of reality ; its incomplete therapy ; a Christian psycho-therapy the only complete one ; pioneers in this research ; links with credal revision and spiritual healing ; plan of our survey.

THE thesis of this book can be simply stated. It is an endeavour to bridge the gap between the great structure of Christian doctrine, and the epoch-making discoveries of recent psychological research ; and specifically, it sets out to buttress that which has always been the work of the servant of Christ, namely, the care and cure of souls, with the support and certitude of our new knowledge regarding the nature, structure, and functions of the mind. During the last forty years more has been elucidated and written down of the dark geography of the mind, of its warfares and rebellions, its disorders and maladjustments, than at any other period of time. Yet though some attempt has been made, here and there, to synthesise the new-found laws and the Christian system, there has been surprisingly little attention given to the clamant necessity of outlining a Christian psycho-therapy which will mediate this new knowledge to the drifting and the overstrained, and which will point out a clear pathway to spiritual unity and health—a pathway known in part before, but one which is now more fully revealed in the new light thrown upon the shadowy continents of the mind. And it cannot be too strongly emphasised at the outset, that though much land has still to be explored, yet in mapping out the troubles of the mind, and the paths of their healing, we are not groping, but treading assured ground ; and it is more than time that part, at least, of this new territory were annexed to the Empire of Christ.

In this regard, a great task no doubt awaits the Christian theologian, for our knowledge of the behaviour of the mind cannot but profoundly affect our judgment of those doctrines which, although divinely inspired, have yet reached us through the media of many frail minds. Many of these may have to be restated and readjusted, and certain moral standards revalued, when this science of behaviour takes its place as a handmaid of the Gospel. Guilt, for example, assumes new proportions, redemption becomes far more manysided, the content of Sin will need to be re-examined, and new depths charted in some little-heeded parts of the Gospel. The present work has, however, no such purpose, save incidentally, as and when these things impinge upon its specific purpose, namely, the therapy of the mind ; a therapy which, as we shall see, binds up wounds of every kind, including such as are made by abuse of the spiritual, and abortion of the religious instinct in man. Its endeavour will rather be to examine first, the content and function of the mind, as now shown to us by the new psychology ; then to survey and correlate the major mental and spiritual disorders, again guided by the principles of that psychology ; thereafter to state certain therapeutic methods of proved avail, with special concentration upon the analytic method ; and throughout, to emphasise the intimate bond which may be forged between all these truths, these disorders, and these

instruments of healing, and the Christian Gospel. Incidentally, it firmly denies the exclusive right of such exposition
and correlation, to that profession which has hitherto claimed
it, namely, the medical profession ; and it seeks to put into
the hands of ministers in especial, but also of Christian
students in general, certain directions which, if wisely and
carefully used, cannot fail immeasurably to enrich their
ministries, and to increase their powers as mediators of healing and cure to the souls of men.

I

By ancient and truthful usage, the Ministry is said
to be vested with the Cure of Souls—an honourable and a
fearful office. The academic training for it is long and
elaborate, devised to equip the student with knowledge of the
Scriptures, and knowledge of the structures, ecclesiastical and
theological, that have been built thereon, but curiously barren
of guidance concerning the troubles and the needs of the
soul, to which his own life in the future is to minister. Greek
and Hebrew are given him ; he is led through the labyrinths
of Systematic Theology ; Church History and Moral Philosophy are his also, together with some training in the exegesis
of Scripture, and the conduct of worship ; and his own
spiritual life is often wisely and rightly guided by older men.
When he advances into his ministry, that knowledge, and his
own youthful spiritual experience, are his equipment for the
cure of souls, and at once he discovers their inadequacy.
The very first impact of the world on a Christian mind so
educated and sensitised, is the poignant need of lives disordered and souls inhibited, and at the outset, such contact
must reveal to him the great gulf between his ordered and
theoretical knowledge of Theology, and the need which cries
for help. He finds, with heart-searchings, that even his

consecrated desire cannot bridge it, simply because he has no means of diagnosis, of " getting at " the sick and bewildered mind. Certain rare souls there are, gifted from the start with a spiritual intuition which enables them to minister spiritual strength direct to the broken in mind ; but the average novice in the cure of souls, when faced with a life in obvious and inexplicable distress, too often finds himself unable to relieve it. It is true that as years go on, his own deepening experience of life and of God give him a certain technique and knowledge in such cases, but it is won at the cost of many needless failures, and, at the best, it is casual and haphazard. It is equally true that he frequently finds anodyne for his conscience in the multitudinous organisations of the modern Church, and makes escape and substitute—unconscious perhaps—in committee and conference, for the personal dealing and healing he knows he cannot undertake. The twofold accusation so often made, that the Church is divorced from the needs and the life of the world, and that the Ministry has forgotten how to shepherd the individual soul, may find its justification exactly here, and correspondingly may find its negation in a Church and a Ministry which has become expert in probing the wounds of humanity, and has learned the Christian therapy of the mind.

Now mental disorder and nervous tension, though as old as humanity, have never been so frequent as they are at the present time. The all-too-familiar troubles of the day, national and international, have their repercussions on every part of our public and private life, repercussions which economist and politician endeavour in vain to mitigate. But underneath all the visible upheavals, and the surface currents of the storm, another and a far more ominous tide is at work, disturbing the very foundations of Being itself ; for the stresses and the pace of modern life are producing dire confusions in the mind, and that to an extent which is at once more serious and more widespread than most men know. The willingness to be regimented—the responsiveness to propaganda regardless of its truth—the mass hysteria that finds outlet in the blind adulations and hates of the hour, these are not in themselves symptoms so threatening as the fundamental instability in the minds of men that they reveal. When, therefore, we witness, as we do, the uprush of primitive instincts of lawless self-assertion and anger from the subliminal consciousness of the race, it begins to be evident that if the structure of civilisation is being threatened, it is largely because the minds which are incorporated therein are being so attacked and weakened, that they can no longer support its burdens. It is not that the merely economic disorders of the age are producing an aftermath of spiritual wreckage ; it is rather the truth that successive forces are being let loose upon humanity with such repetitive strength, that men's minds, habituated for centuries to quieter things, are unable to withstand their shock. These forces have been, and are, so catastrophic, so apparently independent of the will, that the mind has simply no categories in which to place them, no precedent to which to relate them, and thus no knowledge of whither they are driving it, or what their future power of attack will be.

II

That shadowy continent of the mind, to which we referred, is therefore being subjected to earthquake, and landslide, and fissure ; and the process of defining the affected areas and the depth of their disturbance, is sufficiently far advanced to be called a science. That science knows, as we shall see, with fair accuracy, most of the causes of this over-strain, but there is one cause in especial which is relevant here, which is overlooked by all the medical protagonists of the psychological faith save one or two, and which indicates

the proper domain of the Christian psychologist. The
nervous breakdown may be, and often is, attributed to the
strain of life ; but its increase in our midst has coincided with
a very noticeable loosening of religious belief. Here is the ripe
experience of one of the greatest of all psychologists in this
connection :

> " During the past thirty years . . . among
> all my patients in the second half of life (that is to say,
> over thirty-five), there has not been one whose problem
> in the last resort was not that of finding a religious out-
> look on life. It is safe to say that every one of them fell ill
> because he had lost that which the living religions of every
> age have given to their followers, and none of them has
> been really healed who did not regain his religious outlook.
> It is indeed high time for the clergyman and the psycho-
> therapist to join forces to meet this great spiritual task." [1]

That is a consummation devoutly to be wished, for
a testimony so impressive as his shows that the dimming of
the flame of religion in a man has results even more far-
reaching than the teachers of the Faith have yet realised.
It is a truism to say that many forces to-day have united to
drive man from his anchorage in religion, that he is therefore
at the mercy of the currents of the world, and that to his
aimless state are attributable most of the sins and ills of
society. But this is only half the truth, and the whole is
graver far. Our preaching in every age has always been that
to turn from God means spiritual death, a fate which may yet
leave the man *compos mentis* ; he is in much more urgent peril,
if, as we now know, his rebellion is a root cause of neurosis
and complex, and an undermining of the seat of reason. If
faithlessness rots so deep, and produces a sickness in the

[1] Jung : *Humanity in Search of a Soul*, p. 264.

mind itself—makes a man not only anchorless, but holes and staves him, what a vista opens up for the Christian minister who understands the mechanisms and defences of the mind. He can indeed magnify his office, for he, almost alone among men, will be able to minister to a mind diseased, by first understanding its symptoms and the illness to which they point, and then using the laws of psychology to mediate Christian spiritual healing with an exactitude and skill, till now unknown.

Psychological research and psycho-therapy have so far been carried on mainly by men who were not consciously animated by the religious motive, and whose views are far removed from those of the Christian. It is to them that we owe the advances of the last fifty years, and the discovery of the fundamental laws of the structure and behaviour of the mind. Yet it cannot be regarded as outwith the providence of God, that just when the need of the mind threatens to become overwhelmingly acute, this new light of healing has come ; and to that extent, the materialist psycho-therapy which at present holds the field, is a thing for which to thank Him, and not men only. Unfortunately, however, Christian psychological research has till now lagged far behind, and this neglect has caused the tremendous assumption to gain ground, that the mind can be dealt with, and cured, without regard to spiritual issues, and even that God and Faith are projections and sublimations, higher in degree, but in essence the same, as other escape mechanisms of the ailing mind. That assumption, for example, dominates all Freudian psycho-analysis, but it is being increasingly challenged from many quarters, and its weaknesses displayed, as we shall see. It is regarded as axiomatic here, at least, that apart from religion, this great new science is truncated, and that only by giving due place to the values and standards of the Christian system, can the newly discovered laws be fully

understood and used. Modern medical psychology can
indeed unveil the shadow side of life, and explicate the
complex, but only a religious psychology can give meaning
and unity to life, and explain man's deepest desires to
himself.

III

There emerges, therefore, a double need. On the
one hand, the minister, student, or social worker needs for
the " cure of souls " all the light which this new knowledge
of psychology has shed on the dark workings of the mind.
On the other, the scientist needs to be reminded that if his
own personal life be such as to exclude God, and if the
spiritual powers of his own mind be atrophied, his views on
life and other men must necessarily be incomplete and pre-
carious. It is an immeasurable enrichment of the pastoral
experience to be able to understand, though very partially,
how to ease and direct the thwarted instinct or the wounded
mind. It is also necessary for, say, the Freudian and the
Adlerite, to realise that the religious instinct is as legitimately
a part of humanity as any other, and that psychology must
fall into line with the rest of science which is more and more
finding it impossible to rest in the former definitions of matter
and of man. If, in the case of matter, a revolution in thought
has taken place, and our new conceptions and definitions are
as immaterial as anything there is, so also in regard to man,
science and religion should find their common ground at last,
and together investigate the real man, who is spirit as well as
body and mind, giving each element its place, shirking no
issue because of preconceived materialist limitations, and
letting spirit crown the whole.

It has to be acknowledged, however, that this
common ground is far from being explored. There are
impediments in the path of joint research, and what is per-

haps the chief of these confronts us at the very outset, in a fundamental distortion of the scientific spirit itself. Broadly speaking, both religion and psychology deal with the re-actions of man to Reality, and both seek to correct those reactions where man's frailty makes readjustment necessary. Psycho-analysis and analytical psychology (for the two are different, as will be seen) profess to rid the mind of fantasy and complex, and bring the man back to proper contact with what they term reality ; but it must be confessed that the reality on which medical psychology lays stress, and which its writings envisage, is a limited affair, based on purely intellectual premises, and taking no cognisance of spiritual certainties. It is a very myopic view of the world and of man's potentialities which ignores the supreme realities of God, and of His contacts with the minds He made, and this lack of vision from the first has done disservice to true psychology. While, therefore, medical psychologists have staked this claim, and worked it very thoroughly, and while they are undoubtedly right in deprecating, as they always do, the interference of what they term the amateur, they are wholly unjustified when they ignore in their investigations the religious instinct, and the spiritual powers of the mind. These have a life and certainty which are as valid and creative as any other (to put it at its lowest), and the very carefulness with which such workers limit their concept of reality to material things, and the almost ostentation with which this is paraded as the true scientific spirit, are symptomatic, to say the least, of the fact that they themselves are not fully equipped for their subject, when they are unwilling or afraid to test and examine powers and experiences to whose validity the best minds of humanity bear emphatic witness. Such an omission may, it is true, be partly an unconscious one—there are none so blind as those who will not see—but it implies none the less an insensitiveness alike to the deeper needs and the higher powers of the mind, as these are revealed in religion, which is very serious, and sufficient to disallow their claim to scientific impartiality.

Now, the immovable claim of religion is that it deals with Reality, a Reality in whose comprehension all others are embraced, and that it gives life contact with, and experience of, truths which are as verifiable empirically as, say, those of botany or biology. The irrefragable witness of the millions who have lived the Faith and not looked on at it, is, that they have moved in planes not attainable by unspiritual understanding, and that they have been made aware of an overshadowing Truth, which transcends all other experience. Who is to judge the value of their testimony ? Certainly not the scientist whose own inner life has never touched even the hem of such phemonena. He can only categorise that of which he is already aware, and accordingly, when faced with a prodigal son, or a converted Saul, he follows his only gambit, eludes the issue completely, and uses the procrustean and hoary device of labelling all such witness as abnormality, distorted sex or fear, or the like. His values are proportionate to the height of his experience, and if that stop short at the threshold of the spiritual, his perspective is meaningless.

IV

Here, therefore, right of entry for another type of investigator can be claimed. The whole question is one of the correct measuring-rod to be applied to human life. Is it to be measured by its minimum or its maximum realities ? Is it to be reduced to its lowest common denominator—a series of rather vulgar fractions—as a matter of common sense, and the connotations of the five senses, or is it to be measured by the highest that we know ? In other words, what is the content of the word " normal " ? The " abnormal " who seeks cleansing and readjustment at the hands of the psycho-therapist, discovers in the process that the norm to which he is asked to remould his life is scaled well down to the average unimaginative specimen of the race, to whom vision is a fantasy, and conscience an encumbrance. Life is to be lived with the soft pedal on ; the treatment purges him, certainly, of his morbidities, but too often at the cost of erasing unease and discontent which have no relation to these, and its goal is reached when the man is lapped in the contentments of ordinary life, and thoroughly at ease in an earthly Zion.

That measuring-rod will not do ; it is not tall enough. It is not sufficient to know with reasonable accuracy the border lines which divide, say, paranoia from harmless fantasy, or libido from lust. We have learned to grub among the roots and the mud well enough, but there is urgent need of research at the other end of the human scale, till we know more fully where vision ends and fantasy begins, where innocence fades and guilt possesses, where spiritual healing and faith degenerate into auto-hypnotism and quackery. There is no unhealthiness in divine discontent, and that life is truly normal, which is not only freed from the subhuman and the animal, but incipiently linked with the superhuman also.

If, as Freud tells us, the discords of life are produced simply by the wrongful co-ordination of certain known functions of the mind, then all that is needed for their re-solution is a sublimated piano tuner. Such an one will achieve a certain harmony, but only at the cost of silencing part of the instrument, and even then, the overtones refuse to be stilled. You cannot deal with the mind in sections, and while it is convenient to dispense with hope, and sacrifice, and con-science, the constant immediacies of life refuse to leave those strings alone, but pluck them again and again, and only

another Hand can complete the chord, and restore real
harmony within. You cannot tune the middle octave only,
and label that the normal instrument for living. Normality is
achieved when the man is rightly adjusted to God as well as
to life, wholly attuned, not only to the still, sad music of
humanity, but also to the echoes of eternity.

And it is not only in its premises, but in the actual
process of its therapy, that a psychology which ignores the
religious hierarchy of values seems to fail. It is a conflict of
motives, conscious and unconscious, which produces the
discords to which we have referred, and the whole aim of
psycho-therapy in resolving that conflict is, as we shall see,
to establish one dominating motive as overlord of the rest,
so that the mind is no longer the prey of civil warfare, but
keeps the peace under a self-elected king. Clearly, as Christ
profoundly said, some new affection of expulsive power must
be instilled when the house of life is swept and garnished, lest
the former occupant return with seven others worse than
himself.

In this regard, it is an illuminating experience to
study the methods of the medical psycho-therapists. With
real skill (the result of their researches in the ground floor and
the basement of life) they track the elusive symptom to its
remotest lair, and, subject to the above limitations, they label
it, and prescribe. But there it ends, and " finis non coronat
opus," for their constructive power is simply non-existent ;
they dig, but cannot build ; they destroy, but cannot fulfil.
Ask of them what is to cement the pieces they have readjusted, and fill the gaps of the dear illusions they have
abolished, and they will offer a little mild philanthropy, or
an open air life, splinted with Art, and bandaged with
Literature. It will not work, and they know it. These are
pinchbeck inducements to continue in the united life ; stop-
gap is indeed their true description. And be it noted that the

very eagerness with which such therapists slam and bolt the door against the powers of religion, is their disappointment in another guise. They have nothing to offer, and this exacerbates, unconsciously perhaps, their desire to exclude those who have.

There is but one flame hot enough to weld, and having welded, to supply heat and light and life, and only a Christian psycho-therapist can apply it. Only one psychology has a future, and that is the psychology which *has* a future. We are so constituted that we must have a rationale of the universe and of life, and no system can satisfy save that which can give meaning to the past, and hope for the future ; and of these two, the latter is the more necessary. Once more, therefore, the conclusion is forced upon us that the overstrain and disorientation of life to-day have their cause and their cure alike, just here ; and that all roads lead to what, for the Christian, is the central truth, " Thou hast made us for Thyself, and our hearts are restless till they find their rest in Thee."

V

There are not wanting signs of hope, for there are rebels in the camp of orthodox psycho-therapy. Freud himself, so profound, yet so curiously limited of vision, exclaims " I prefer the pastor to the doctor " ; and although he is not in the least animated by desire to acknowledge or help the Faith, that saying is a sign of grace. And Jung, who stands alone among the leaders of psychological research in the place he gives in his system to the spiritual powers of the mind, says quite definitely :

" Although the theories of Freud and Adler come much nearer to getting at the bottom of the neuroses than does any earlier approach to the question from the

side of medicine, they still fail, because of their exclusive
concern with the " drives," to satisfy the deeper spiritual
needs of the patient." [1]

And, picturing the doctor confronted with the task of con-
veying to the patient the meaning that quickens life, of
giving him something that will take possession of him, Jung
continues :

"Is the doctor equal to his task ? What
will he do, when he sees only too clearly why his patient is
ill ; when he sees that it arises from his having no love,
but only sexuality ; no faith, because he is afraid to
grope in the dark ; no hope, because he is disillusioned by
the world and by life ; and no understanding, because he
has failed to read the meaning of his own existence ? . . .
We can hardly expect the doctor to have anything to say
about the ultimate questions of the soul. It is from the
clergyman, not from the doctor, that the sufferer should
expect such help." [2]

Of the three greatest figures in this realm of
psychology, Freud, Adler, and Jung, the last is by far the
most delicately sensitive to every echo in the chambers of
the mind, for he has allowed no materialist presupposition
to blunt the acuteness of his hearing. Though himself far
from orthodox, he has yet had sufficient spiritual experience
to make him truly catholic in outlook, and constructive in
ideals ; and among his followers, there is fortunately a growing number of students and psychiatrists, for whom the truths
of religion are as necessary as those of material science, and
who do not wish to dissociate that Faith, of whose powers
they have had experience, from the great mass of relevant

[1] Jung : *Humanity in Search of a Soul*, p. 259.
[2] *Ibid.* p. 260.

scientific truth. Their new course avoids the Scylla of
antiquated Theology and the Charybdis of materialism, and
they have stated that for them at least, there is no gap
between the laws which govern the workings of their minds,
and those ethereal yet well-authenticated laws which move
the psyche, or spirit of man, and that their creed embraces
assent to both codes.

And there is a small band of ministers, of all
denominations, who are working tentatively, yet accurately,
towards just such a synthesis of the laws of the psyche. They
feel that that synthesis can and will be achieved without any
trespass on the rightful domain of the medical man, or any
rash meddling that would make the last state of the patient
worse than the first. They are convinced that Christ was the
great Psychologist, and that the New Testament contains
much which waits to be unfolded and fulfilled in the fresh
light which psychology has shed on the dark labyrinths of
the mind, on the accepted moral values, and on the capacities
and gifts of man. They believe that the impact of the Gospel
on the mind of humanity has hitherto been studied by men
whose minds were ignorant of many of the laws of their own
inner workings, and whose view of other minds was thereby
distorted ; by men oblivious too, of the subtle interweavings
of body and mind—that co-partnership whose mystic title-
deeds are but now being brought to light. In fine, they hold
that the knowledge we now possess is God-given, for the
especial end of bringing mind and Maker nearer to each
other.

It is obvious, therefore, that we have here a field
which deserves much fuller investigation than it has hitherto
had. The subject needs careful and continuous study, not
only in academic circles, by men who are expert in the origins
and implications of the New Testament, but clinically, by
men who are daily dealing with the depths and heights of

human experience. Such research, in our Universities, is yet in embryo, but there are one or two Christian clinics, of which the writer has had knowledge, where invaluable data are being accumulated, and where skilled therapists are all too few. It is perhaps indicative of the helpfulness of such clinical work, that had it not been for the vision there obtained of immeasurable need, and the strength there verified of Christian psycho-therapy, this book could never have been even begun.

VI

In addition to its therapeutic work, which is the main preoccupation of this book, a Christian psychology will also, in the first instance at least, serve a twofold end. It can ally itself with the widespread call for a restatement of Christian faith and values, and it can clarify some of the much-debated problems of Faith healing.

The fierce light of many sciences — historical, archæological, and comparative—has been concentrated on the little handsbreadth of time that holds the earthly lives of Jesus of Nazareth and the Apostles. They have led us into His very presence-chamber, freed the glory of His Gospel from the mists of time and error, and have made necessary a restatement of the things most surely believed among us. But since Christianity proceeds down the ages from mind to mind, borne on the unseen wings of perception and emotion, no such restatement can be proportionate, except it be influenced by true knowledge of the mind and its laws. Accurate information, therefore, of mental errors and fallibilities, empirically obtained through sheer case-work, can make a contribution of great value to the work of clarifying the creed, and so linking us with the mind that is in Christ Jesus. And while such revision is no part of the purpose which this book attempts to serve, the bearings of psychology on Christian doctrine will be abundantly evident in its course.

Concerning Faith healing also, its avenues, its vehicles, and its results, a Christian psychology will have much to say. In such a process the unseen power of God is mediated to man, and in its course, crosses from eternity into time, and from Spirit through spirit into the flesh. Such an incarnation, in the last resort, transcends description, and can but be recorded, not explained. Yet if we know the channels of the mind through which it passes on its way, and the grooves of suggestibility and instinct and habit which it may use to effect the inscrutable alchemy of God, and work a miracle of healing in the flesh, then a corner at least of the veil of mystery is lifted, and we have advanced in knowledge. If we have learned that the lower processes of disappointed self-love, or sex, or any other hunger, can so work on the body as to maim and paralyse its activities, and that the unconscious mind with all its ferments, is a potent dictator to the functions of the body, then it must be in response to similar laws of reaction that the body answers, when thrilled by the influence of the highest to which its mind can reach. That body which is to be healed, lies midway between the subconscious and the superconscious ; its mind ministers both of these to it, through avenues which now are partly known ; and thus we can hope that since medical psycho-therapy has shown us the subconscious working through those avenues to heal or to destroy, so will a Christian psycho-therapy shed light on the hitherto mysterious approaches of the healing power of God, which flashes through the mind of man, on its way to the ailing flesh it seeks to mend. Once more, natural law in the spiritual world will be discerned, and even the complex and the repression and the neurosis can indirectly be made to redound to the glory of God.

When, therefore, that twofold purpose which we

2

envisaged is accomplished, Christian psychology will enter its Kingdom, and take its high place with the other glories of the Faith. Psychology, " sub specie Eternitatis," will be a noble science indeed.

VII

It has become obvious in the course of this introduction that the first postulate of a Christian psycho-therapy is that the mind of man must be mapped out as in the sight of God, and that no system can for a moment be entertained which ignores His voice, and the inner ear to which it speaks. If catharsis be our primary aim, any instruments we may use to effect it are weak and ineffectual beside the spiritual fires that can vivify, as well as cleanse ; and if, after catharsis, we are to build and restore, we shall fail, unless we be fellow-labourers together with God.

In trying to expound such a system, we have a fourfold task. (1) We shall need, as our foundation, to survey something of the structure and content of the mind itself. The Christian student has a right to share the new knowledge that is now possessed of these, and an equal right to refuse what does not square with his own fundamentals.

(2) We shall need to know something of the disorders of the mind, and its wayward flights from reality, and to delimit the extent of our field in dealing with them.

(3) We shall need to clarify our aims and ideals in dealing with the maladjusted mind, and to make explicit from the Christian point of view what we mean by mental health.

(4) We shall need to set in order the various therapeutic methods which have proved their worth ; and not least among them, one that is often overlooked, namely,

the direct influence of the character of the psychiatrist
himself. He can succeed only when he is himself linked on
the one hand to God, by living personal experience, and on
the other, to the minds he seeks to heal, by hard-won
technical skill.

CHAPTER II

THE HUMAN MIND

THE CONSCIOUS MIND. THE UNCONSCIOUS MIND: (1) ITS CONTENT
AND (2) ITS CHARACTERISTICS.

Need for self-examination ; recent psychological research ;
definition of psychology ; content of the conscious mind ; preconscious
region ; vastness of the unconscious mind ; other states of consciousness ; (i) Contents of the unconscious mind ; its perfect record of events ;
this record discoverable in analysis, hypnosis, dream-analysis ; the unconscious the home of the instincts ; the storehouse of racial experience ;
(ii) Characteristics of the unconscious mind.

I

IN order properly to understand the misbehaviours,
the aberrations, and ultimately, the health of the
mind, it is fundamentally necessary to know something of
its nature and content, and to examine the mechanisms and
store-houses of that which is at once the vehicle of sensation,
and the reservoir of experience. Our task is a complex one,
for that which we survey has the multiple function of being,
at one and the same time, the apparatus of reception, the
mediator of energy, and the recorder of what it perceives ;
and each of these functions colours and modifies the others.
The absence of experience in any one department of life, for
example, must obviously inhibit the range of perception of
the whole, and energy misused, or repressed into a complex,
will, as we shall see, warp the entire instrument. The student
therefore of the mind has a task of the utmost delicacy, for he

must ever keep in the foreground the fact that his own instrument of observation, namely, his mind, must be shaped by his own presuppositions—as witness the limitations of the physicist approach to psychology, which we have already noted—and that while it is humanly impossible to achieve, here above all, an impartial survey, yet the approach to it must be made with a mind that is willing to turn to every point in the compass of human experience. Two men, working in this field, side by side, but operating widely differing instruments, will work in different worlds, for each reaction will be different for each ; it is axiomatic that the student whose mind is in tune with spiritual reality has, *ipso facto*, a better instrument with which to think, and that his record will be more balanced and inclusive. The study of psychology, it must never be forgotten, is, in this respect, a most wholesome discipline, since it imposes on the student the constant necessity of self-examination at every point, for if he allows his prejudice or unwillingness to blur his lens, he stultifies his work.

Those who approach the study of psychology from the religious point of view need perhaps a special reminder of this initial need for self-examination, and the unbiased mind. The material scientist is not alone in taking short-sighted views concerning psychology. A similar myopia is sometimes evident in the reported sayings and writings of Christian thinkers ; and it is but right that they should know that the new psychology has suffered a threefold wrong. It has suffered much at the hands of the half-instructed and of those who have tried to make it a fashionable cult of the day ; they have degraded its concepts into a jargon, and their journalese has made us all-too-familiar with the inferiority complex, and the sex instinct. It has equally, as we shall see, been wounded in the house of its founder and his friends, who have given to certain of the terms they use, a connotation found nowhere else in psychology, and have robbed them of their universal meanings. And it has been stunted of its full growth by the swaddling bands in which the medical profession has enswathed it, for hardly one psychiatrist in a hundred allows the validity of the religious instinct, or has himself added faith to his knowledge.

When, however, the science is approached with a mind that refuses to rest content with half-truths, a mind freed from the fear of what religion may do when " let in " on a man, its vital importance, and the magnitude of the advances it has made within the last two generations, are at once obvious ; for it is not too much to say that the last forty years have transformed the science of psychology, and that the transformation dates from the epoch-making work of one pioneer, Sigmund Freud of Vienna, who, as Professor William McDougal says, " has done more for psychology than any one student since Aristotle." One or two writers had indeed foreshadowed in part some of his findings, notably Janet the French psychologist, and Charles Creighton, whose book, *Unconscious Memory in Disease*, published in 1886, has not received the attention it ought to have had. But, broadly speaking, before him, the only advances which psychology had made were the very limited ones rendered possible by our improved knowledge of the physical nervous system in health and disease, and of the structure of the brain, and by our better classification, in the field of experimental psychology, of the nature of sensation, and of reaction to stimulus. It had been content to tread the well-worn paths of many generations of academic psychologists, and its concepts had become lifeless, and its results negligible. But Freud, finding it thus " a sterile compromise between neurology and metaphysics," quickened and fructified it with new and daring thought ; and to-day, though there are many schools of psychology, they all derive from him, and if their systems differ on many vital points from his, yet his basic hypotheses remain, in spite of challenge.

A vast literature has grown round these systems, embodying a vast amount of research, which in the names of three protagonists stand out, those of Freud, Jung, and Adler, each of them, especially the first, endeavouring to make his own system absolute to the exclusion of all others. For us, the outstanding feature of all this work, with the exception of that of Jung and his followers, is that none of them find any place in their systems for the spiritual capacities of man. God, for the Freudian, is but a projection of the " Father imago," an illegitimate creation of the mind itself, and religion and conscience, but distortions of the " libido," or life force ; while the Adlerite expects his cures to run their lives on strictly business lines ; and both Freudian and Adlerite seem to regard not only religion, but creative imagination in art and poetry, as slightly regrettable excrescences which the normalised man can well do without. Jung alone is not afraid to speak of the soul and the spiritual, and for that, is freely castigated as a philosopher and no psychologist by both rival camps. Yet, though far indeed from the Christian point of view, he is the most understanding of them all, and the most sensitively attuned to the vibrations of the superconscious ; and his works ought to be first on the bibliographies of the Christian student of psychology. Notwithstanding this, within the limits of the five senses, and on the plane of the physical world, the work, especially of Freud, is fundamental, and ought to be approached, as he himself suggests, with a mind " benevolently neutral." Bias shuts the doors of understanding, and even though we cannot go all the way with some of the leaders of the science, yet, if we approach the whole subject with reverence and readiness, we shall assuredly be convinced that here is a science which makes in the end, for the enrichment of the personality, and the dignity of life. When allied, as we hope to see it allied, with the forces of the Christian gospel, it brings new hope as well as new light, where all was dark before.

II

There are many definitions of psychology, but that which defines it as the science of Behaviour, is at once simple and sufficient.

It is the study of man's bodily and mental reactions to the world in which he is set. And when we thus define man as a " behaving animal," and begin to observe his dealings with the stimuli which come at him from the outside world, we at once perceive that these dealings are not haphazard or fortuitous, but that all his responsive behaviour is dictated by conscious or unconscious Purpose, and that Purposive is the first attribute that we must postulate for man. All the energy with which he cleaves his way through the world, whether mediated in thought, speech, or act, is purposive, or Hormic, as it has been called ; this last deriving from the Greek word HORME, indicating Force, Impetuosity, Drive, Attack, Zeal. He bears, and has borne for countless generations, the impact of his environment on a plastic structure of mind and body, and to that impact he reacts along the path of more or less conscious instinct and desire, but always with inherent purpose. Right at the beginning, it is thus possible to ally the concept which is of the essence of religion, and which, as has been stated, has frequently denied entrance into the domain of psychology, namely, that man is here *for* a purpose, to this one, that man is here *with* a purpose ; the purposive being is set in a purposive creation.

The whole aim of curative psychology is therefore seen to be the education, and where necessary, the re-education of man's purposive activities, so as to enlarge his personality and life. Every neurotic may be regarded as suffering from thwarted purpose and all that psycho-therapy does, is aimed at releasing and properly redirecting his Hormic urge. Its whole teaching is, that that man is truly normal, whose energy is rightly harnessed to his instincts and desires ; its great value is that this process is being, for the first time, scientifically mapped out, and can be, for the first time, traced in actual operation during the course of analysis and cure ; but where psychology has to leave off, religion can step in and enfold the newly purposive life within the larger purpose which God has for it, thus providing it not only with its most assured means of continuing in its new health, but also with the only power which can build it up from strength to strength.

Now, if man is a "behaving animal," the first question which emerges is : What is the instrument of his behaviour ; what is it which mediates his power to do ; through what channels do his purposive reactions make themselves evident ? It is in its answer to this simple primary question that recent psychology is most revolutionary against all older hypotheses ; for it is its determination of the structure of the mind as the vehicle of behaviour, which is fundamentally new.

In that structure of the mind, materialist psychology has now discerned two levels, one conscious, the other unconscious, and between the two, a zone which can be called the preconscious.

The conscious mind is that part of the instrument which make us aware of the world around us, and which rationalises our experience of that world. Its avenues of perception are the five senses, its rationalisations are effected by means of conscious will and desire, and it can focus at will along any of these avenues, by means of its ever-changing,

ever-shifting " focal point." At every instant of conscious
life, that focal point is played on some part of the field
around us, the impulse which directs it, and the purpose
served, varying infinitely. While there is this bright central
spot of consciousness always in the forefront of the waking
mind, there is also round it, like a nimbus, the impression of
a number of other facts, of which we are simultaneously
aware. Thus, at the moment of writing this, I hear my
daughter practising, I am aware of the noise of traffic, I feel
a rheumatic pain ; all which are on the verge of consciousness, and are less vividly apprehended, though at any moment
the focal point can leave this writing, and attend to them.

Slightly farther back in the mind, we are also
conscious of a tract from which, at will, we can summon up any
fact we desire, with more or less effort. It is the reservoir of
those memories and experiences which are sufficiently vivid
to be more or less available at will. It is called the preconscious, its upward limit being the field of consciousness,
its lower shading downwards into the unconscious.

These two are simple ideas, already partly understood by every thinking man. Till the advent of Freud,
these two levels of consciousness were the only two with
which psychological investigation concerned itself ; and the
unconscious mind, if regarded at all, was regarded as a mere
limbo, filled with the unwanted and discarded rubbish of the
mind, and without function or importance. His work,
however, and the thirty years of research which have followed
it, have utterly changed that view. It is now firmly established
that even the conscious mind, richly educated as it is, and
able at will to survey with its focal point the whole finite
world, able also to rationalise the results of such survey into
the majestic fabric of the sciences, and the preconscious,
with its great stores of available experience, are inferior to the
unconscious mind in extent, in power, and in profound

influence on the personality and life. It is the home of the instincts, which can, and often do, override will and reason at their pleasure ; it is the seat of those unconscious desires which motivate half our life, and which, as we shall see, can defeat and rout any conscious desire when the unconscious mind so wishes ; it is the repository of incredible stores of memory, and those, racial as well as personal : it is the dwelling-place of all those unconscious bodily controls which dictate our processes of digestion, respiration, and the like, and from it, issues every atom of life-force and energy which we possess : it is the habitation of the complex, which issues sometimes so disastrously from its lair as to wreck the personality. It is independent of reason, owes no allegiance to the will, and often utterly disobeys our conscious desires and tendencies, always winning when it does. Its nature is even yet very partially understood, yet enough is known to make us very respectful in our approach, for it is no sleeping partner with whom we deal, but an active, functioning, and energetic entity ; indeed, the senior of the whole firm.

With the explication of these levels of consciousness, psychology has largely so far been content ; but if it teaches, as it often does, that these be the only avenues through which apprehension of the universe is mediated to the mind, it is but half a science. Overwhelming evidence exists, that in certain circumstances the mind is capable of expanded receptivity, and finds itself functioning, with amazed awareness, in regions so alien to the plains of ordinary consciousness, as to deserve the name of superconscious. Call them mystical states, inspirational, transcendental, visionary, what you will ; for the moment leave aside the question of the power that on occasion so imperiously opens unsuspected doorways in the mind ; the unchallengeable fact remains that these states are the universal experience of the race. They can be traced from primitive levels in the savage, where they manifest half-apprehended (as, for example, the surprising poetic life and output of the Aborigines of Australia, till recently considered as lowest in the human scale), continuously, without a break, to the liberated communion of the Christian saint with the unseen. Side by side with these intimations, in their innumerable variety, are the allied phenomena of inspiration, of genius, of anæsthetic experience and the like, to reinforce them, and to drive us irresistibly to the conclusion that on the upward side, the mind of man opens out into worlds of consciousness which hold the loftiest experiences and the sublimest truths which life can give ; that our ordinary consciousness is divided from them by the thinnest of veils ; and that, in obedience to certain laws, whose workings we cannot as yet fathom, that veil is sometimes partly rent, and we may step through. And it simply will not do, to label this mighty consensus as pathological ; to cast it aside as an unhealthy condition of the " normal " consciousness ; to lump it with wilful hysterias, and hallucinations and deceits, in one all-embracing blind classification, as materialist psychology has hitherto done. If we are to survey the whole mind of man, these too must be included ; they are states of consciousness as valid, and as evidential, as any others.

III

Of the levels of the mind, thus briefly indicated, two need no more explanation, namely, the conscious and the preconscious. But our next step must be an investigation of the nature and function of that unconscious mind whose empire is so wide, and of how its powers reach out from the shadows to mould our conscious acts. The work devoted to its understanding has been enormous, and the conclusions drawn therefrom have been varied, but in order to grasp its functions and capacities, it may be convenient to group the facts under three heads :

       A. What are the contents of the unconscious mind ?
       B. What are its characteristics ?
       C. What are its powers ?

A. WHAT ARE THE CONTENTS OF THE UNCONSCIOUS MIND ?

While at first sight it may seem impossible to classify that which does not enter into the conscious, yet research has revealed in it what may be called strata—differing layers of deposited material from different sources. Through the entry of certain elements in this material into consciousness during normal or abnormal states, we can determine their nature and origin, and the extent of the deposits from which they sprang.

(1) First and most obvious, it holds the record of all that has ever happened to the individual. Nothing he has once possessed is ever entirely lost, for there, stored away and laid down, is all that he has ever said or seen, thought or done. What penetrates to the memory, and is available there, is obviously only a fraction of the total experience of the individual ; and all that mass of material which is outwith the range of normal recall, and therefore not accessible to normal consciousness, forms part of the content of the unconscious mind. Older psychologists had allowed this thought without grasping its profound significance ; for apart altogether from its effects on the personality, the mere fact that all experiences are meticulously registered is a most impressive one. Every impression, even the most insignificant, leaves an ineffaceable mark on the individual, and is capable, under certain conditions, of being recalled to the light of day. It is an overwhelming thought ; but it is of the first import-

ance for the understanding of the mind, to realise that man is his own recording angel, that he has within him a power so perfectly retentive, and so absolutely comprehensive, that conscious memory is but a pale shadow of it, and that while in his own researches, this power is but faintly known, for the purposes of God, this infallible record is the inevitable determinant of the nature of man's immortal life.

In normal life, these deposits remain undisturbed ; but when any of them have associated with them an unusual force of emotion, they become one of the causes of the complex, and upset the balance of life, acting in the mind like a festering point. When necessary, there are three ways in which this great tract can be excavated ; buried memories are recoverable to a great extent under hypnosis, or can be traced in dream analysis, or can emerge in abnormal states of the mind. Three or four examples of these, taken from very many, must suffice for the present.

To take the last first, one of the classical examples is the case of the servant girl, an illiterate, who was removed to hospital in high fever. In her delirium, she was heard to speak for long periods in a tongue unknown to any of the staff ; but a Rabbi, passing through the ward, overheard her ravings, and found to his amazement, that she was reciting in Hebrew, long passages of the Old Testament. On investigating her history, it was found that once, years before, she had been in service in the house of a minister who was a great Hebrew scholar, and who had been in the habit of reciting to himself Psalms and other passages aloud in his study. She had been busy on her duties outside in the hall, had often overheard him, had unconsciously registered it, and in her delirium, it reappeared in its entirety ; an impressive proof of the involuntary accuracy of a power quite outside her conscious mind. It is a power which can also be seen at work in cases of dissociated or split personality, where one personality can recall detailed memories of childhood, for example, which are totally forgotten by the other.

This is no abnormal power, or gift given to the few ; it is, on the contrary, an universal human endowment, whose relevance to human experience is only now being explored, and whose irruptions into consciousness are but newly discerned. Its characteristic is its colourlessness ; will or desire have nothing to do with it ; it is an impassive automatism, a clock-work mechanism of the mind. The energy of emotion which surrounds any part of it may profoundly affect and disturb the conscious life, but the record itself is dispassionate, and its completeness is a proof of the awe-inspiring width of the powers and functions of the unconscious mind.

In the second place, it frequently happens in dream analysis that one element which the dream is endeavouring to represent, is an experience which is quite obliterated from the conscious memory. The dream, as we shall see, is one of the voices of the unconscious, and among the means at its disposal for securing the attention of the conscious to its message, is its command over the contents of the tract we have been observing. It has the power of recalling, and of reproducing in its own peculiar language, remote and forgotten events associated with the earliest periods of life, events which are frequently without any discernible emotional significance in themselves, but which are detached, and worked into the structure of the dream, to serve the ends of its message. There are thousands of recorded cases of this kind, and here is one that is typical.

" Maury records that as a child, he often went from his native city to a neighbouring town, where his father was superintending the construction of a bridge. One night a dream transported him to that town, and he was once more playing in the streets there. A man approached him, wearing a sort of uniform. Maury asked him his name, and he introduced himself, saying that his name was C., and that he was a bridge guard. On waking, Maury, who still doubted the actuality of his reminiscence, asked his old servant, who had been with him in childhood, whether she remembered a man of this name. ' Of course,' was the reply. ' He used to be watchman on the bridge which your father was building then.' "

It is obvious from this, and from other examples, that the dream has at its disposal, abundant material which is quite forgotten in ordinary life, but which is nevertheless there, laid away in the treasury of the unconscious. It is one of the lesser powers of the dream, but it is one which reinforces the evidence we are now examining.

In the third place, there is abundant evidence to be gained through hypnotism, of these inexhaustible records of the unconscious mind. This method is used in psycho-therapy mainly for the recovery of repressed memories which are injuring the personality, and frequently these memories are exceedingly remote. In hypnotism, it is found that resistances can be discounted, and the very deepest roots of the particular complex, however embedded in the unconscious and defended by unconscious resistance, be brought to light. Once again, that will in a later chapter be more fully dealt with ; at this point, however, this one result of it can be observed. Here are two instances typical of many :

" A lady teacher, aged 31, had suffered for ten years from an intense craving for alcohol, which, however, she had always successfully resisted. I saw her twice. On the first occasion, I hypnotised her very lightly, and suggested that she would recall some incident of childhood, which was connected with drink or drunkenness, and which had distressed her greatly ; I told her it had probably occurred between the ages of three and five. However, she could recall nothing ; so I roused her, and told her to come again the next morning. Five minutes later, she returned, to tell me that she had recalled the incident. It appeared that, when she was about three years old, a man had told her mother in her presence about a woman who had got drunk and murdered her own child. The story had distressed her intensely for some days, and then seems to have been repressed. The craving was not really a craving at all, but a fear lest she should take alcohol and some tragic result should follow. When she had told me what she remembered, I said to her : ' Don't you ever feel afraid of injuring your pupils ? ' She replied ' Yes, and I can't think why.' This symptom was, of course, due to the murder of the child. The symptoms left her, and she has been well for some four years."

Or again : " A schoolboy, aged 12½, suffered from intense terror of the dark, which had commenced about two years before I saw him, and had become intolerable. There was a history that when he was five years old he had slept for a week in the same room with a governess who was then discovered to be insane. When he came to me, I found him quite unable to recollect anything about it, or even what his governess looked like. As it seemed more than likely that his fear of the dark was due to a repressed memory, of something that had then occurred, I determined to try to make him recall it. I treated him five times, and on the fifth trial, he recalled the cause of his terrors. The governess, who was a Roman Catholic, used to wake him in the night, put a Crucifix into his hands, and tell him to hold it tight, as the whole room was full of devils, who were going to attack them ; naturally, the unfortunate child passed through extremities of terror. His memories revived a little with

3

each trial, after the first, and the night after the fourth treatment, he suffered from frightful nightmare. He could not remember what it was in the morning, but told his mother he would recall it when I saw him ; and it turned out that the nightmare was a recollection of his week of terror. When I saw him the day after, his memory had been revived ; he said he felt quite different, and no longer felt the old fear. To use his own words, he now ' Likes the night as well as the day.' " [1]

Here then is evidence of what is indeed a lost continent, the seat of an experience as rich as that of the fabled Atlantis. For the present, we note but its extent ; its mass is variously conditioned, as we shall see, by emotion and energy ; earthquake and tremor and eruption sometimes move it, but for the most part it lies deep, without movement, below the peaks of consciousness which appear above the surface ; yet those peaks are, like their exemplars in the Atlantic, resting far down on unseen foundations, and their waters are fed by springs whose fountains lie very deep.

(2) The unconscious mind is the home of the instincts, and the seat of energy.

The former will have a chapter to themselves, but for the present we note that all men are born with certain simple ante-natal predispositions, as essential to life as eyes or mouth, through which their life-force finds its outlet. Man asserts his needs, cries for help, or defends himself, instinctively ; conscious of these needs, it is true, but moved to be thus conscious of them, by an inborn tendency called instinctive. What thus moves him is that elemental life-force, which, from the unconscious, and by means of its unknown faculties, keeps the body functioning, maintains the constancy of the heart and all the rest of the hierarchy of glands and organs, quite independently of

[1] Wingfield : *Introduction to Hypnotism*, p. 140.

conscious control; which pours through the channels of those elementary " Instincts," and their derivatives ; which supplies the power to conscious as well as unconscious motive and desire ; which activates and colours the emotional life, sometimes to an incredible intensity ; which in short is the driving force of that Purpose, which is the primary characteristic of man.

The effects of this Energy, Libido, Life-Force, Hormic Urge, or Elan Vital, as it has been variously labelled, are often conscious, as are the results of any instinct, but its dwelling-place is in the unconscious, far out of sight. Its nature and its quantity are alike mysterious, but its manifestation is the whole sum of human endeavour and achievement. To those who regard creation as teleological and expressive of a purpose of God, this explosive nature of man, expressing itself through his purposes, and through the whole of that evolution wherein, by means of experience, he can train and sublimate his life-force from the satisfaction of primitive instincts to the fulfilling of those that are higher and more creative, is a conclusive evidence of his link with the Divine.

(3) There is yet a third stratum to be distinguished, analogous to the last. Close analysis has revealed, that in addition to the equipment of instinct which we bring into the world, we possess what may be called a store of racial experience, an inherited predisposition to certain modes of thought, standardised through countless generations in certain universal ways. These are not revealed in any actual race memories of events (though analysis has uncovered some fascinating vestiges that might be described as such) but in symbols which approximate to the universal symbolism of primitive peoples, expressed in their myths and cosmogonies.

This last stratum is worked in with great skill by Dr. Jung, and is one of his especial contributions to the science.   He points out the parallelism which exists between this primitive imagery, and what he has found in analysis ; and proceeds to show how these archaic modes of approach to the world are found to be universal, and are to be met with at every stage in man's development.   He says :

> " It is quite easy to discover intuitional activity in primitive peoples.   There we constantly meet with typical images and motives which are the foundation of their mythologies.   Those images are autochthonous, and of relatively great uniformity, as, for instance, the idea of magic power or magic substance, of spirits and their behaviour, of demons and gods and their legends.   We see the perfection of these images, and at the same time their envelopment by rational forms, in the great religions of the world.   The archetypes appear even in the exact sciences, where they are at the root of indispensible auxiliary concepts, as of the ether, energy and the atom." [1]

The word " archetype " which he uses to describe these primitive ways of apprehending things, he borrows from St. Augustine, and the thought is familiar to Platonists, though not the reality which analytical psychology has revealed.   Primitive man everywhere, it has been found, tends to cast his apprehensions of the outside world into certain standard " Moulds," while his symbols, and the intuitions they express regarding the impact of nature on him, are peculiar to no one nation, but are world wide. Underneath all our highly differentiated systems, and the conventions which advancing thought has taught us, our own intuitional life is found to conform to those moulds, or archetypes.

[1] Jung : *Contributions to Analytical Psychology*, p. 280.

" Just as every one possesses instincts, so he also possesses archetypes. The most striking evidence for the existence of archetypes is seen in mental derangements that are characterised by an intrusion of the ' collective unconscious ' into the conscious, as occurs in all paranoiac and hallucinatory processes. Here we can easily observe the occurrence of instinctive impulses associated with mythological images." [1]

We are accustomed to rationalise and exaggerate concerning the way we understand things, yet civilisation and education form but a recent and a thin crust, easily to be broken through, and underneath the newer processes, can be discerned the old moulds of thought which we all inherit from an archaic past, as part of our equipment for life. None of us create them, nor are they acquired empirically ; they are an universal endowment, a deposit from the totality of the past experience of the race.

IV

B. CHARACTERISTICS OF THE UNCONSCIOUS MIND

In addition to determining some of the content, many of the characteristics of the unconscious mind can now be postulated, as a result of observation of its reactions and habits. It comes with something of a shock to discover thus within the personality, a separate, and sometimes an antagonistic entity, whose desires and motives often cut right across those of the conscious mind, and which, in order to gain its ends, can inflict the body itself, with various ailments, and can disguise its motives very skilfully, in order to make them acceptable to that mind. Its characteristics are frequently alien from those of the conscious and more highly developed mind, being those of the child, the archaic, and the animal

[1] Jung: *ibid.* p. 281.

within us, but in their proper recognition, we find the clue to the diagnosis of many, if not all, of the disorders of the mind.

Some of these characteristics may be briefly put as follows :

(1) When we get into touch with the unconscious, and disentangle its blurred speech, it always tells the truth, not from any moral motive, but simply from incapacity to produce anything but the facts.

The unconscious cannot lie.

(2) It has no moral sense or values, its code being utterly self-centred, and its point of view, that of the infant and the primitive. It is quite incapable of distinguishing between good or bad, its only criteria being the pleasure or pain it receives, and even these are on the infantile level. All the elaborated structure of sin and guilt, belong to the conscious.

The unconscious does not sin.

(3) That highly energised desire known as the will is quite outside it, and has no power over it. It is suggestible, far more so than the conscious mind, but entirely wayward and uncontrolled ; and when the will and the unconscious desires are at variance, the unconscious, in devious ways, can always undermine the will.

The unconscious cannot be driven.

(4) Its desires are the primitive ones, and it has no language with which to present them save that of the symbol, the dream-picture, or the archetype. In addition, it can make its desires grievously felt by sheer pressure, as, for example, in the anxieties or phobias it can produce, and the neurotic habits it can effect ; but always silently, wordlessly.

The unconscious has no words.

(5) It desires the fulfilment of its purposes, and therefore has its motives, which are often quite different from those of the conscious mind ; and it displays enormous skill and perseverance in so insinuating and disguising them, that the unsuspecting conscious can accept them, and fit them in with its own more controlled ones.

The unconscious usually gets its own way.

(6) It is in opposition to, and compensatory of, its conscious partner. It resists giving up its content, and the defences which that resistance throws up, are among the most difficult things which psychology has to overcome. It censors rigorously what it chooses to let out ; and the censor is so consistent, obeying such highly individualised laws, that it is frequently difficult not to think of it as a " Him," a person within the person. It compensates for the moral code of its partner by an a-moral one of its own.

The unconscious is resistant.

(7) In it, emotion and energy are in a state of flux, easily moved from one idea to another. It is infantile in its emotional life, the energy of its emotions being freely transferred, and detachable from any one idea or constellation of ideas. This fact alone makes possible much of the work of psycho-therapy, an important part thereof being the detachment of buried emotion and energy from the complex, and its reattachment to conscious and more worthy ends.

The unconscious is emotionally infantile.

CHAPTER III

THE HUMAN MIND (*continued*)

THE UNCONSCIOUS MIND, (3) ITS POWERS. The SUPERCONSCIOUS, INSPIRATIONAL AND RELIGIOUS

(iii) Powers of the unconscious; unconscious processes; their purposive character; psycho-somatic unity; sense of time and number in the unconscious. Inspirational states; anæsthesia; contact with another world of values and experience; characteristics of this; near approach of this to religious experience; characteristics of the "mystical" state.

I

IT is an obvious consequence of contents and characteristics such as we have noted, that the unconscious mind is vested with powers that are vital and far reaching. The seat of energy, the repository of experience, the regulator of bodily function, it influences both body and conscious mind profoundly. For very many years, the influence of mind on body has been a commonplace, but it has been left for the new psychology to demonstrate conclusively, that this influence is so great as to justify us, in speaking of man, no longer as made up of mind and body, but as a mind-body, an entity, in which mind is the prevailing partner.

When men used to speak of the effect of mind on bodily function, it was usually the conscious mind of which they thought, and from their premises, which are abundantly verifiable, has grown all the edifice of mental healing, from spiritual healing downward through Christian Science and auto-suggestion to quackery. The insight which psychology has given us into the unconscious mind, however, enables us to say that we have within us a power whose all pervading influence in the body is at present but faintly understood, but which, as we come to know it better, will be capable of performing what we would now call miracles. Psychology has but begun the investigation of it, and we have as yet no indication of any means whereby we can harness or direct it, except by the little-known powers of suggestibility. When we have such means, we shall be able to modify or alter bodily function so radically, and to protect it from accident or disease so effectually, that His saying will be fulfilled, Whose miracles of this very kind science either looks on with contempt as legend, or else ignores, but Who, pointing to those self-same miracles said, " Greater works than These shall ye do."

Some such thing, Galen foreshadowed, when he wrote of a creative natural power resident in each of us, which used alike the faculties of the mind and the organs of the body for its own unwritten purposes, and so did Hippocrates, when he analysed the characteristics of the Physis, the innate unity of power we all possess. But we can now believe from evidence, that there *is* an unknown Intelligence (I use the word advisedly) within us, which guides and repairs the body ; and can say with Van Helmont and Groddeck that this inner ruler is not only the silent regulator of all the so-called automatic functions of the body, and the administrator of the " vis medicatrix naturæ," but that it can and does inflict on us sickness and disease at its desire and for its own ends. Look for a moment at each of these three, and gain an impression of the power of the unconscious in this one direction alone.

(*a*) Just as the conscious mind is only the surface layer of our whole mind, with a far greater unconscious beneath it, so the conscious and voluntary acts of the body are far less at any given moment, than the complicated and

subtle processes continually being carried on unknown to us.
It is wrong, for example, to speak of the beat of the heart or
the process of digestion, as automatic and involuntary, for
though it is true that they go on independently of the control
of the conscious mind, yet they are maintained and controlled infallibly by directive powers within, and to speak
of them as automatic or machinelike, is only part of the truth.
The seat of the energy which drives the heart and conducts
the regular chemistry of digestion, is the unconscious mind
that ceaselessly, and without sleep, directs from its unknown
place the whole hierarchy of circulation, glands, and organs.
It is the power-house of living, and this too-obvious fact is
sometimes overlooked when we speak of the drives and urges
that issue from the unconscious as if they were all, or even
the greater part of its force. Rightly viewed, the greatest
wonder of bodily life is that it *is* unconscious, and that all
those subtle and interwoven functionings are carried on
outwith our knowledge. The " unseen ruler " within us
deserves our homage for this alone, apart from all other
manifestations of his power.

(b) Not only so, but there is a very evident
expression of purposive character in the activities of this
inner power, when we regard the self-healing, self-repairing
work of the body. Here also, it is not enough to refer to,
say, the healing of a wound, or the abating of a disorder as
natural or automatic ; it begs the question, and to take a
thing thus for granted neither explains it, nor entitles us to
accept it. Why should a wound heal, except it be em-
powered to do so ? Why should the forces of the blood
mobilise to expel an alien infection, unless at a rallying call
from deep within us ? Deeper than any instinct of self-
preservation is this purposive drive towards health, which
we often thwart by our habits of self-neglect, but which,
given the least encouragement or help, will work such

wonders. The doctor, with all his equipment of laboratory and materia medica, aims now not so much at cure by drugs or by his own treatment, as at giving this " vis medicatrix naturæ " its chance by clearing its path of obstacles, and letting its unconscious energy have free play. It is the most fundamental of all hormic urges, and it only fails at last when the fountain of energy itself dries up, and the life force is exhausted.

Yet when its own purposes or desires have to be served or are being gainsaid, the unconscious can and does speak sharply and unpleasantly to the body, in the language of disease. A familiar example of this is seen in the ability of the neurotic, who dare not face reality, to produce on himself illnesses which are nothing more or less than means of defence or escapes, and who thus perpetuates his fantasies at the expense of infirmity. Repressive mental forces, acting through the unconscious, can and do bear directly on the body, producing not only such affections as hysterical and epileptic fits whose mental or nervous origin can be more or less easily seen, but also mutism, paralysis, or complete loss of memory ; as was abundantly seen in those cases that were lumped together as " shell shock " cases during the war. It is known too, that under hypnotism, suggestions may be made to the unconscious, which mark or otherwise modify the tissues of the body, and that emotions of anger, fear, and the like, can, through the unconscious, deeply affect the functions and the secretions of the glandular system.

(c) But what is not so generally acknowledged is the profound connection between the psychic and the physio-logical in *all* sickness and disorder. There is a growing school of medicine which, in diagnosis and treatment even of such things as broken limbs or pneumonias, begins from the psychic and not the bodily end, regarding them as declara-tions of the power of the unconscious mind, and endeavouring to see in them the message which the unconscious desires to send out. They find growing support for the idea, that the unconscious powers of the mind have their residence, not in the head alone, but in other parts of the body as well ; and that the ancient Greek idea of the organs as the seats of various emotions and powers, is beginning to be verifiable by modern knowledge. The usual clear-cut distinctions between mental and organic processes are going by the board, and while an enormous field of complicated relationships remains to be explored, enough has been done to make it clear that Physio-therapy and Psycho-therapy are one. This new orientation in the medical sciences can be but indicated here, yet its importance ought to be emphasised, since it not only reverses the traditional approach of the physician to disease, but opens a new and fascinating field for research, and broadens our appreciation of the powers of the unconscious mind. Here is a statement by one of the leaders of this new school :

"I take it that the Unconscious is always purposeful in its actions, and that every case of illness, therefore, expresses something. Disease for me is a kind of speech, the meaning of which I, as a doctor, must try to interpret, and then decide my treatment accordingly. The unconscious, when it wishes for any reason to be ill, chooses something from the mass of possible means in the world around, and this it uses to produce certain symptoms, taking this or that definite course, according to its purpose. For instance, it makes use of a bit of orange peel or a stone to slip over and get a broken leg, if it does not want to tread the path that lies before it, or it infects itself with some bacillus, in order to work off an inconvenient emotion in the form of high fever. It makes a man grow dizzy in looking down from a height, so that it

may warn him he is in danger of a moral fall, or it takes
advantage of some innocent article of diet to make him
vomit, and rid himself symbolically of a mental poison." [1]

In this connection, to enter into detail is outside
the scope and purpose of this book, but enough has been said
to reveal the strength and range of the powers of the Unconscious in this one field alone of its relations to, and sway over,
the body. We have that within us which can smite as well
as heal, which can even slay if need be, and of whose powers
over the body in sickness and in health, we are only now
beginning to be aware. We know enough, however, to make
us at least profoundly respectful towards it, and very careful
indeed of meddling rashly with its strength.

II

There is yet further evidence that complicated and
exact processes take place in the unconscious mind, and that
the results of these activities can issue into consciousness in
surprising ways. The Unconscious, has, for example, a sense
of time far more accurate than that of the waking mind.
What save that, is the explanation of the act of the man who,
under hypnotism, was instructed to make a mark on a piece of
paper 20,185 seconds after being wakened, and who, to the
instant, did so ? Or what the explanation of the fact that
if we really desire to waken at 4.15 a.m., we can usually do so?
Not only so, but the Unconscious can perform feats simultaneously, which the conscious mind cannot, except with great
difficulty, parallel ; as, for example, the case of the man told
on awaking from hypnosis to multiply $12/3\frac{3}{4}$ by eight, repeat-
ing meanwhile " God save the King " with every second
word left out, who did so without a falter. It can also solve

[1] Groddeck : *Exploring the Unconscious*, p. 211.

our problems for us, for who has not taken a knotty point to bed " to sleep on " and awakened with the knot unravelled, and the skein in order ? What agency answers our riddles, like an inner capricious Sphinx, and smooths our paths in sleep, if it be not that Unconscious which needs no sleep, and which seems to work best when the conscious mind will let it alone, as it does while sleeping, or under hypnosis ?

It is the working of these processes which explains also certain obscure disorders and thwartings in life, which the will cannot control, and which no conscious purpose can deflect. Our own experience is full of these interruptions and interferences from another sphere, as if an alien voice spoke to us and through us, and when these things happen, we say " I cannot imagine what possessed me to do it " ; a revealing phrase. We forget an important engagement, or make a slip of the tongue, or find the word we seek for vanished into thin air, simply because we were not wanted to do or say certain things, by an imperious inner necessity. How else explain the case of the blameless spinster who, writing to an unknown young man, was found to have signed herself " Yours passionately " ? These things are among the familiarities of experience, but their commonness should not blind us to their meaning. When our mood changes, or our desire vanishes, or we are suddenly consumed with anxiety for no apparent reason, or a thought possesses us for a whole day, and will not be exorcised, or (if we be neurotic) we are compelled to do senseless things whose stupidity we well know, it is just because certain strong and subtle processes are going on in the Unconscious, and our inner ruler sways us for his own determined ends.

Instances from experiment and experience may thus be multiplied to show that side by side with our conscious thinking, can and do go on, other thoughts of which we have no knowledge, some of which indicate that we possess faculties that are keener and stronger in many ways, than those of the waking mind. While too, we observe these faculties clearly working in obedience to post-hypnotic suggestion, or solving the conundrums we put to them before we fall asleep, we cannot suppose that these are the only exercises they have, or that they live and work only when we choose to call them before our conscious mind to amuse or help it. It is impossible to avoid the conclusion that they are always there, and that their operations may, all unknown to us, be very deeply modifying our conscious processes. This conclusion is strengthened by one specially noteworthy line of evidence which is not often given its due weight, and which, in the light of Christian experience, is of paramount interest.

III

For this line of evidence, our next step must be briefly to examine those states of mind previously referred to as states of expanded consciousness, or receptivity. Such states are of the essence of religion, but are also to be found behind much of the creative experience of the race in art, in literature, in music, and wherever that elusive quality which we label genius occurs. If we regard them for the moment simply as states of mind, two things are observed to be common to them all, in whatever realm they manifest.

They are, in the first place, so alien to ordinary consciousness, as to create a marked duality, similar to that already observed between unconscious and conscious, both of which frequently conflict in motive and in character. All inspirational life is lived at the beck and call of imperious and alien powers, which impel the man to leave his ordinary paths, and live for the moment in another region. His normal gifts and capacities either swell and surge up to undreamt-of levels, in obedience to the stimulus, or else every conscious gift is blotted out, and submerged, in the incandescent tide of powers unexercised and unknown in ordinary life. In either case, the man is, for the moment, a new creature.

In the second place, there is no constancy in such states ; they are not only unpredictable, but fickle. Whether they be regarded as commands from a power not ourselves, or as self-originated tidal waves of our own life-force ; whether they be bolts *from* the blue or bolts *for* the blue, they are alike sudden and evanescent. It is not till man comes to his highest in sainthood, that anything approaching stability in the inspirational life is attained, and even the saints tell us of their days of " dryness," when the ebb-tide of the spirit sets in, and the light is gone : as a rule, it is only momentarily that man can live at white heat.

Take first, that which is the commonest of all such states, the Inspirational. When we survey the field of human achievement, while it is true to say that much of it is accomplished by painstaking work, which has harnessed will and reason to man's capacities, and built stone on stone, here a little, and there a little, yet it is also true to say that its highest and best is the result of what we call inspiration, of that sudden upsurge from the inner deeps, which floods the conscious mind, and presents to it, independently of conscious effort, a creative idea, or a completed work of genius. The greatest works of man are done, not when he thinks, but when his thoughts think themselves. It is the universal testimony of the greatest minds of the race, that they are at their greatest and most creative, when thus invaded, when to them, as to the singer,

> " In the sudden glory of a minute,
> Airy and excellent, the pröem came,
> Rending his bosom, for a God was in it."

The pedestrian scientist, in psychology or any other field, whose pride it is that he deals with the " facts of life," finds

in the works of the artist and the saint, his most difficult
puzzle ; for poetic or religious genius fits into none of his
categories, yet its evidential results transcend them all.

While the achievements thus won differ widely
from each other in permanence and beauty, they all share this
inspirational nature. It is not sufficient to say that they are
clothed with, and energised by, emotion, for then the facts
of emotion could be called in to explain and rationalise them
all. Emotion, like a nimbus, surrounds and colours the light
of genius, but it is not that light. A sharp distinction must
be made between the two, and it is a distinction not always
made ; for even an acute observer like William James, when,
in his *Varieties of Religious Experience*, he enumerates the
characteristics of the inspirational states as ineffability,
noetic quality, transiency, passivity, fails to note that these
belong also to simple emotional states, and does not sufficiently
allow to the inspirational that added quality of contact with
a higher power, and of reality, which distinguish them from
merely emotional states.

They possess that " plus " quality which separates
them from all other states, and their universal characteristic
is, that they appear suddenly and unasked over the threshold,
full-fledged and vital, often exceedingly involved and many-
folded, always iridescent with life and power, and making an
instant appeal to the mind of the race, as supremely beautiful
and true. The mere fact that they so exist, as the crown of
all human achievement, and that they are not fully explicable
by any categories of emotion or instinct, is impressive evidence that here we impinge on higher levels of consciousness.
We need not argue at the moment, whether they are gifts
from an external source, revealed at moments of heightened
insight into another world, or whether they are products of
unknown capacities working in exceptional minds, and outside the realm of their normal consciousness ; what matters is,

4

that they prove the mind to be expansive, and that there is another plane of consciousness, to which it can attain.

There thus emerges that duality, to which reference was made. No processes of ordinary consciousness produce these results, and they stand apart from the reason and the will. Minerva-like, the work of genius or inspiration springs from the head, full-armed and unlooked-for, no constant visitor, but always fickle and evanescent, speaking no ordinary tongue, but ever imprisoned with the greatest difficulty within the bounds of sound or pen, and those in whom the visitant arises, are the least able to tell us how or whence it comes. Even the unconscious mind, so abundantly furnished in content and powers, cannot be called in to explain these things ; another region must be postulated in the mind, which is as far removed from the primitive and the instinctual within us, as genius is from lust, in which the mind moves upward, by means of its inspirational powers, towards the planes of the Faith, and to which the name of superconscious can, not unjustly, be given. Of all human experiences, these are the ones most closely allied to those of religion, since the high faculties of the mind, which thus emerge and speak to us in the language of great poetry, art, or music, move in the same plane, and breathe the same air, as the intimations which come to us from God.

IV

Another link in the chain of evidence for the superconscious, may here be briefly noted, for closely akin to such inspirational states, are the phenomena of youthful prodigy, and anæsthetic experience. In the former, gifts of mathematical genius, or gifts of transcendent musical and artistic technique, are displayed passively—note that—by otherwise ordinarily gifted children of three years

old, and upwards, fading before puberty is reached, into the
life of an ordinary individual, unmathematical and un-
musical, and persisting only in exceptional cases. Regarding them, only this need at present be said. Whatever
glandular distribution, or other physical peculiarity accom-
panies them, these gifts manifest from no earthly experience
or education. They are so adult, and so manifold, as to
be explicable only on the hypothesis of contact with another
plane of consciousness ; and one proof of this may be the
very fact, that, under pressure of developing "normal" life,
they are rapidly squeezed out of conscious existence, though
possibly recoverable under hypnosis. The inner knowledge
possessed by such beings is unacquired, and flows abundantly from some central source, through a channel precoci-
ously opened, but similar to that through which, in later
life, inspiration flows in on man. And as an interesting
footnote to such phenomena, the problem may be propounded ; why do "poltergeist" manifestations usually
occur in the near neighbourhood of a partly imbecile child,
or cretinous adult, and what plane of consciousness is
touched there ?

The problem of experience under anæsthetic, which
is sometimes closely akin to inspirational experience, can
be simply expressed in one question ; anæsthetics block the
five senses in normal use, but what do they set free ? They
set free, it is true, considerable buried and primitive material,
but they also enable some to share very exactly in the experience of the mystic, to such an extent as to modify all their
after-life. Ex-stasis—a man outside himself—is very real in
anæsthesia, and while no laws can yet be seen working here,
a sufficient body of experience is available, to prove that here
also, we have a pointer to that expansion of consciousness
which we are considering, and that in certain conditions of
abrogation of the normal consciousness through anæsthetics,

man can grope on another plane, and occasionally get a glimpse of the unspeakable. What is said of anæsthetics applies also partially, in the cases of alcohol and other drugs. It is their liberating quality which makes them so sought after, and the hunger which seeks satisfaction in them, is stepbrother to that vast instinct which seeks its freedom in ways more akin to the divine.

From one specific set of experimental experiences gathered under the influence of an anæsthetic known to excite such inspirational reaction, namely, nitrous oxide and ether, William James draws the following conclusions, which are capable of more than particular application :

"One conclusion was forced upon my mind at that time, and my impression of its truth has ever since remained unshaken. It is, that our normal waking consciousness, rational consciousness, as we call it, is but one special type of consciousness, whilst all about it, parted from it by the filmiest of screens, there lie potential forms of consciousness, entirely different. We may go through life without suspecting their existence ; but apply the requisite stimulus, and at a touch they are there, in all their completeness, definite types of mentality which probably somewhere have their field of application and adaptation. No account of the universe in its totality can be final which leaves these other forms of consciousness quite disregarded. How to regard them is the question—for they are so discontinuous with ordinary consciousness. Yet they may determine attitudes, though they cannot furnish formulas, and open a region, though they fail to give a map. At any rate, they forbid a premature closing of our accounts with reality." [1]

[1] James : *Varieties of Religious Experience*, p. 388.

V

That which unites all such states, by whatever cause invoked, is not only expanded receptivity, but the clear sense they bring of contact with another world of values and experiences. Without entering yet into the sphere of religion, it is possible to collate from this consensus of experience certain omnipresent characteristics of that world, and to observe how nearly they touch the borders of religion. Just as psychology has charted some of the dark regions of the unconscious mind, so also must a Christian psychology make straight the way for the Faith by adventuring a geography of the superconscious; always remembering the extreme risk of using words to crib, cabin, and confine, that which is ineffable.

(1) There is there nothing measurable by our measures, none of the proportions that are mediated to us by space and time. For example, points of space which are as the poles asunder, can meet there, provided they are linked by inner affinity or antipathy; and moments of different ages may touch one another, for events there, do not happen, but exist. Space and time coalesce in a four-dimensional world.

(2) In that world, the opposites and separates of our world meet, and are reconciled upon a higher plane. Our laws of reasoning do not apply, because reason separates, and discriminates and classifies, on premises that are seen to be partial. Divergence tends to be annihilated, and the highest experiences there, speak of the unity of the part in the whole, and of the inclusion of the whole in the part.

(3) That world therefore, includes the partial view which we call our world, as seen through the narrow avenues of the senses. The perception of the unreality of this present world, which is so marked in inspirational

experience, is part of that truth. So also is the knowledge given that lifelessness and matter are not categories which apply there ; that everything lives, and that spirit enfolds and includes what we call matter. There are not two worlds, but one.

(4) Perception of that world is impossible, if the approach be made to it on the level of the five senses. Intellectual processes, operating the will and the reason, have no prescriptive right of entry. We cannot yet approach it as and when we will, for the wind bloweth where it listeth, to clear the clouds, and make plain the path.

(5) Is there then a key ? Ask those who in thought or art or music, in inspirational experience of any kind, have pioneered and explored, and they will answer that of all known inducements of the state, the sense of wonder is the most potent ; it seems to be the key, at least to the outer doors, the instrument of expanded consciousness. What new depth, therefore, can we now perceive in His saying, who told men that unless they became as little children, they should in no wise enter the Kingdom ?

Plotinus, in his *Letters to Flaccus*, has foreshadowed with amazing exactitude a theory of knowledge, founded upon just such expansion of the conscious, as we have been considering :

" You ask, how can we know the Infinite ? I answer, not by Reason. You can only apprehend the Infinite by a faculty superior to Reason, by entering into a state in which you are your finite self no longer, in which the divine essence is communicated to you. This is ecstasy. It is the liberation of your mind from its finite consciousness. Like can only apprehend like : when you thus cease to be finite, you become one with the infinite.

" All that tends to purify and elevate the mind will assist you in this attainment, and facilitate the approach and the recurrence of these happy intervals. There are different roads by which this end may be reached. The love of beauty which exalts the poet ; that devotion to the One, and that ascent of science which makes the ambition of the philosopher ; and that love and those prayers by which some devout and ardent soul tends in its moral purity towards perfection—these are the great highways conducting to the height above the actual and the particular, where we stand in the immediate presence of the Infinite, who shines out, as from the depths of the soul."

VI

Such states of expanded consciousness are clearly nearest of all to that state, which is the especial property of religion, namely, the mystical consciousness of the unseen. On this, there is a body of evidence from every race, every age, and every creed of humanity, so colossal, that it is inconceivable that intelligent psychologists have neglected it as they do. No mental process of the unconscious, however powerful and moving, can be invoked to explain it ; that is a favourite gambit of the material scientist, but to do so, is to label, and not to explain. Nor is it upon mass alone that this consensus of humanity depends for its weight, for the qualitative results in truth attained, and unity of the personality achieved, and resultant character built, are unapproachable in any other realm of experience, and are explicable only on the hypothesis, that what religion claims is true, and that it alone points the Way, by which Truth and Life can be ministered to the mind of man.

No detailed treatment is possible here, but broadly

speaking, and keeping in mind always the psychological approach, these facts emerge :

(1) When analysed from the merely human side, the underlying impulse or motive which impels towards such states, has always two stages. First, there is revolt against the so-called certainty of all ordinary knowledge, the rebellion of the mind against itself ; and second, a yearning of the mind for contact with the unseen source of Truth, a " divine home-sickness for God " ; and every atom of testimony we possess tells us that from another side, this hunger is satisfied, and that the covenantal relationship is at once established, " Draw nigh to God, and He will draw nigh to you." Religion, however mediated, thus becomes the bridge between the finite and the infinite.

(2) With a unanimity which is amazing, and shared in few other fields of experience, those who unite in this particular type of experience, whatever their mother tongue, speak in almost identical terms of the emergence therein of the mind, upon a plane of consciousness where truth is approached in an unparalleled degree, and liberation experienced. In it, our normally limited personality becomes consciously continuous with a wider self, and this super-conscious experience is the root of all personal religion.

(3) The supremely important characteristic of all such states is, that they give knowledge unobtainable in any other way. Direct experience of them gives the perception of the unity of all things, and of the immediate presence and power of God in all creation, a perception apprehended with an authority and clarity which transcend all other means of knowing. Not only so, but those truths tally with certain others discoverable by the mathematics of the infinite, and through the theories of philosophy ; yet they differ in their quality of *livingness*, as a painted scene differs from the reality of living vision. In their wholeness, such truths

cannot be imprisoned in words ; and an infinity of argument and violence would be escaped by the realization that " truth cannot be expressed in our language."

(4) This experience has many grades of intensity, from the simple " moods " induced by encompassing Nature, through the beginnings of conscious Faith and the education of prayer, to the higher flights of which we have such abundant record. From beginning to end, the character of the experience, however, remains the same, and every evidence of it bears the imprint, more or less clear, of the superconscious.

(5) It is no occasional or sporadic gift, as is genius, but is part of the ordinary equipment of the race. The instinct to which revealed religion ministers, is common to all, and the changeless claim of religion is, that inspired goodness, through communion with the unseen, is possible to all. No antecedent gift or culture is required, but wherever any mind expands so as to find itself functioning fully on the plane of the superconscious, a new creative act of God takes place, as real as any on the material plane, and a Son of God is born.

(6) This vehement and universal phenomenon is shared by many of the established faiths of humanity, Mahommedanism, Brahminism, Lao-Tseism, and others ; but it is the irrefutable claim of Christianity, that in and through Christ alone (not through His Gospel only, but through Him) is that mystical state of union with God ministered to men in fullness and readiness beyond compare, and that in Christ, we touch the highest ever given to the mind of man.

VII

This brief survey of the range and powers of that instrument of behaviour which we all possess, in its conscious, unconscious, and superconscious levels, is amply sufficient to demonstrate its majesty, and its infinite variety. In these last two regions, much of the land has yet to be surveyed, but its features and resources are emerging from the mists ; and though its recesses are unknown, we know that all the springs of life flow from them, into the land of the conscious. And though attention has hitherto been preponderatingly given to the unconscious as the source of catastrophe, the Christian psychologist can nevertheless see that from unconscious and superconscious alike, if their inhabitant powers be abused or repressed, can come those storms and earthquake shocks which devastate a man's career. And in order to understand better how and whence they come, we have now to deal in greater detail with one especial part of these regions, and learn something about the instincts which dwell there. When these are rightly harnessed, and given their due place, life is normal and creative, while from the thwarted instinct come most of the troubles of abnormal psychology.

CHAPTER IV

THE INSTINCTS

WITH SPECIAL REFERENCE TO THE SEX INSTINCT, AND CHRIST'S TEACHING THEREON. THE RELIGIOUS INSTINCT

> Our store of energy; definition of instinct; the two fundamental instincts; (1) the Value instinct; its subsidiaries of self-preservation and self-assertion; (2) the instinct of Incompleteness; its subsidiaries, especially those of sex and religion; (a) the Sex instinct; reverence in its approach; its true proportion in psychology; its periods of manifestation; our errors in teaching it; proportions of masculine and feminine in each sex; the change at puberty; its constant urge; the need to face it on the highest level; a religious control the only possible one; the Christian attitude; Christianity dependent on a Person, not a principle; the key texts of the New Testament in this regard; directions in the teaching of Christ; (b) the Religious instinct; axiomatic in a Christian psychology; its thwarting disastrous to the mind; its twofold function; its receptivity of the intimations of God.

I

IN the unconscious, as we saw, there exists our store of mental energy, and this energy, from the very beginning of life, is directed along certain well-defined channels. As the mind grows, these channels increase in number and variety, and are, of course, different in each personality, according to the circumstances of his life. But there are certain elemental demands made by life on all of us, that are answered in invariable ways by the individual. Universal demands and invariable reaction to them, produce in each of us, certain equally universal and invariable channels through which energy flows, and these universal channels we refer to as instincts.

59

The deepest characteristic of our store or reservoir of energy is that it *must* be used. There is no such thing as stagnation there, for it has an outward drive, an imperative urge to make contact with its surroundings, which will not be denied. The twin ideas of energy and purpose cannot be separated in man, and our instincts are the first expressions of this hormic drive of our energy. They are the grooves it wears in the mind for its outlet, some of them inherited, some self-made. The seat of instinct is the unconscious mind, and the release of instinctive energy is quite independent of conscious control. Once released, it is incapable of recall, and must find an outlet; we may inhibit, but inhibition only diverts, and does not dam up energy which has once been released; we can only deal with an unwelcome and unwanted instinct, by raising its energies to a higher plane, and effecting what is called sublimation, such as occurs, for example, when a single woman finds her maternal instinct translated into child-welfare work, thus finding outlet for an instinct, whose legitimate expression has been denied her.

An instinct then is simply a mental reflex, comparable to the motor reflexes of the muscular system. It is to be distinguished from the obsession, which also, in the neurotic, is automatic, by the fact that an instinct is a thing universally possessed by all, while the equally unconscious and machine-like obsession is a highly individual thing. Only those things which are universally possessed, being the same reactions to the same stimuli of life, are to be called instincts.

Instinctive activity has a special interest for the man who studies psychology from the religious angle. It is, as Jung tells us, " a more or less abrupt psychical experience, a sort of intrusion into the continuity of conscious events," and as such, it arises not from motives of which we are fully conscious, but from a kind of hidden inner necessity. That will always be matter of interest to the psychologist as evidence of a faculty of the unconscious mind, but it is of especial interest when we ponder the nature of the religious instinct, its connection with the others, and its powers of sublimation. The hidden inner necessity which marks instinctive action, is nowhere more noticeable than in our response to spiritual stimuli ; and the religious instinct is seen, not as an afterthought, a piece tacked on to man's equipment by man himself (as many psychologists who have not felt its strength would have us believe) but as an instinct at one in this with all the rest, though dealing with matters infinitely higher. The fact of its unity with the rest of life, is also of great importance when we come to consider the thwarted instinct as a source of grave disorder in the psyche, because only that psychologist who can understand and use the powers of the religious instinct, can permanently heal the disorder, re-educate the instinct, and redirect the misused energy along the best lines.

In their estimates of the number and variety of the instincts, psychologists have differed widely, some putting it as high as forty or even seventy, others as low as two ; classifications which obviously spring from very various ideas of what really constitutes an instinct. When, however, the characteristics already noted are kept in mind, and when it is remembered that all the instincts are not there all the time, but that as the mind develops, new instinctual grooves are formed, the problem of their classification becomes easier, and it becomes clear that they can all be grouped under two main heads.

II

The two invariable and fundamental reactions of the individual to the stimulus of the outside world, may be expressed in the two statements :

(A) I am of value,
(B) I am incomplete,

and from these two, all the others can be discerned emerging at the varying calls of life, each at its own time and place in the developing mind.

(A) *I am of value.*—This has been called the instinct of self-love or self-regard, but in both these terms, there is an element of later rationalisation. Love and regard are words too highly coloured by later experience, to be used of the oldest of all instincts. The earliest, most primitive response to the outside world, at the dawn of life is simply " I *must* go on living," and in that " *must* " can be discerned the element of value, the instinctive perception of its worth by the unit. That perception is wordless, of course, but the statement " I am of value " embodies it ; and the word " value " is not coloured by later knowledge. It declares the instinctive push of the new life against the impact of the world, and from it come the two great subsidiary instincts ;

(a) I must preserve myself.
(b) I must assert myself.

These two are not primary instincts, as has been thought ; there is a deeper instinct antecedent to both, of which both are expressions, namely, the instinct of the value of life to its owner.

(a) From the first of these, Self-preservation, spring the secondary instincts of Food-getting and of fear. Both these are directly derivative, for the satisfaction of hunger is an instinct which cries aloud " I must preserve myself," and so too Fear is instinctive information to the individual of external danger that he may take measures of self-preservation. With Fear again, are to be grouped the subsidiary instincts of Disgust and Submission. Disgust being a compound of terror and recoil, always self-preservatory in intent, and submission being always, at its roots, the fear of being overwhelmed by a stronger power, and again self-preservatory.

(b) Similarly from the second, Self-Assertion, come those instincts through which the urge to power is gratified. In the early stages, there are only two of them, Hoarding and Anger. The infant soon realises the power it exercises by hoarding its fæces ; it is one of the simplest forms of self-assertion, and Hoarding is thus one of the earliest manifestations of that instinct, developing later into acquisitiveness and carefulness on the one hand, and greed and secrecy on the other. Anger is from the first the rush of energetic resentment at outside forces which belittle or resist the individual, and its main strand is always self-assertion.

Two subsidiary instincts may also be grouped here, namely, those of Construction and Laughter, both of which gratify the sense of power. When I make something, I clearly assert myself ; and (not so clearly) when I laugh at anyone, I must be above him in my own estimation in order to do so, and thus when I laugh, it is at the contrast between his inferiority and my power.

(B) *I am incomplete.*—Why does man possess the gregarious instinct and the mating instinct, and highest of all, the religious instinct, if not from this deep-rooted knowledge that he does not live unto himself alone ? The " Incomplete " instinct is traceable right from the start of life. It begins to manifest in the instinctive turning to the mother, as the source of the food and comfort which are needed to complete and continue the infant life ; it continues as the Play instinct develops from solitary play to team play ; it grows through the gregarious instinct, the sex instinct, and last in the religious instinct ; and it can be traced as a distinct unit throughout all these.

As in the case of the Value instinct, there are subsidiary instincts to be noted, which share the characteristic of incompleteness. Curiosity is one, for it says " I am drawn to this other life, to see what it is doing," but the *seeing* is secondary, the *approach* primary, and the Incomplete instinct dictates it. It is seen very easily in the Gregarious or Herd instinct, which is deeper than mere self-protection, and arises from man's intuitive feeling of being lonely and incomplete, apart from the presence of his kind. It is seen at its clearest in the sex instinct, and at its highest in the Religious instinct, which develops later in life, as man's mind begins to learn the insufficiency of material causes to explain the dealings of the world with him.

These instincts are not all equally primitive, not all manifesting from the earliest years. Instincts like the Herd instinct, and the Constructive instinct, obviously come later than those of Fear or Anger, while the Religious instinct, as has been said, emerges last of all. Most of them are explained by their names, and easily identifiable, by our own experience of them. Volumes have been written on their origin and interactions, and on the whole intuitive life of man, but the above short classification is enough to let us see the place and nature of the chief instincts, and when we come to investigate the complex, and the phenomena of repression, we shall have ample evidence of their power. But concerning two of them, those of Sex and Religion, more must be said, because the former is the most misused and feared of all our instincts, and because the latter is often denied the right to be called an instinct at all.

III

(1) THE SEX INSTINCT

The first thing the student has to do in regard to this instinct, is to define his own attitude towards it. In the first place, he must learn never to be afraid of it, but must observe it dispassionately, with reverence and purity of motive, as one of the deepest and most powerful and most mysterious things he possesses. He must be prepared to override all the taboos which ignorance and extremism have sought to impose, and to be absolutely frank in analysing the motives which have imposed them. Let there be neither disgust nor over-eagerness in his approach to this much misunderstood instinct, neither morbid curiosity about it, nor revolt from it, but a calm objective attitude, akin to that of the chemist or the anatomist in their own domains.

Only by adopting such an attitude, can the student of the subject realise the great dangers, as well as the beneficent powers, that lie within this sex instinct, for it is at once one of the strongest of physical urges, and the vehicle of a deep psychic need. Rightly apprehended and used, it can be made sacramental, an immeasurable enrichment of life, and a far greater thing than the mere blind procreative instinct of popular thought. No words can be too strong wherewith to reprobate the traditional attitude of taboo and repression towards sex and its powers. The extreme manifestations of that attitude in the last century have no warrant in either experience or true morality, and while they are happily transient, the real antidote to them is to be sought, not by rejecting all restriction whatever in the matter of sex, and ignorantly claiming, as some do, the sanctions of psychology for such misdeeds, but in the true and open understanding of what the function of this instinct really is. To these taboos are due directly not only most of the wreckages of married life, but also most of the disorders of the solitary life, and indirectly, as the experience of every psychiatrist of whatever school has shown, most of the worst perversions and aberrations of the neurotic. It is not the least of the achievements of the " new " psychology that it has, for the first time, given due recognition to the powers of this instinct, and freed it from the mistakes and fears with which it was encumbered.

5

Yet here a word of warning must also be said. This process has, to some extent, been distorted by the popular mind, and the idea is widespread that in the new psychology sex has been given a disproportionate place and emphasis, and that it has been alleged to colour the whole of life. The idea has been encouraged by the freedom used by Freud and his followers in giving to the words " sex " and " sexual " a meaning peculiar to their own school of thought, and one much broader and more inclusive than anyone else gives. In their writings, the words, and the instinct they connote, are made to include not only the manifestations of sex as ordinarily understood, but nearly all manifestations of energy, and all urges, however directed ; an arbitrary extension of meaning, which has led to confusion, and which must always be kept in mind whenever we think of Freud and his school. If, however, it *is* judiciously kept in mind, the work of Freud and his followers in disentangling the subject from taboos and misconceptions is seen as pioneer work of the utmost value.

" Most people give a little unpleasant shudder whenever Freud is mentioned, and they will tell you that ' sex ' is the foundation of all his theories, of all his teaching. That is a very exaggerated statement. One of Freud's fundamental concepts is based on the manifold manner in which *unexpressed* sex wishes or repressed sex desires may manifest themselves in our mental and physical reactions. His teaching is not a huge pornographic collection of the horrible things that sexually uncontrolled people *do* ; it is a study of what people do and think who have not been able to express themselves sexually at all. It is the things that people want to do, half consciously perhaps, the things they cannot or will not do, in which Freud is chiefly interested.

And no matter what your reaction may be to this whole matter of sex, you must admit that Freud and his pupils have done us all a great service in making it possible nowadays to discuss matters of great importance to humanity, openly and cleanly, instead of pushing the same matters into a dusty shadowy corner, relegating them to ' medical books,' and putting such a general taboo on them that their very existence was almost denied. Had it not been for the freedom of discussion induced by the Freudian theories, the sex inhibitions of the early 'sixties and 'seventies would have resulted to-day in an obsession of sex even greater, even more appalling than the obsession from which we are still suffering." [1]

IV

A right understanding of the thorny problems of sex is of paramount importance to the minister, and to all those whose work lies among young men and women. One much neglected side of the work of the ministry in this country, has been the " consultative " side ; and as the knowledge of Christian psycho-therapy increases, co-ordinating body, mind, and spirit in a new synthesis, this side of the office will be enormously developed. And since the universal experience of medical psychiatry has been that seven-tenths of the troubled minds that come for consultation and analysis, come because of disorders more or less directly caused by misuse of the sex instinct, it becomes obvious that the ministry has to devote much thought and research to it, in order to learn its psychic, as well as its physical rationale, its right place in the moral code, its relation to the teaching of Christ, and its Christian sublimations. While a great deal may be learned

[1] Oliver : *Psychiatry and Mental Health*, p. 180.

from the vast literature on the subject, much more needs to be done by the application of this learning, consecrated by the Christian spirit, to clinical work, and by the collection and comparison of the results of such work. This is the method of medical and industrial psychological research, and it may well be copied by the Church. A number of ministers and others, are indeed working separately along these lines, but their work needs collation and pooling, and its results ought to be available for the training of yet more students of the science. The whole of this book, indeed, is a cumulative proof of the necessity of some such centralisation, of the need of recognition by the Church in some shape or form that it has in psychology a mighty new instrument for the advancement of the Kingdom, which (we have it on the highest authority) is *within* us ; and more will be said later in support of this plea.

We must begin then, by learning something of the power of this great instinct, and thereafter endeavour to see something of its treatment in the New Testament, and of the consequent necessity of readjusting its place in our traditional scheme of moral values : leaving its abnormal manifestations, its repressions, and the methods of their relief, to later chapters.

A word, however, must first be said regarding terminology. It is a very definite help towards the objective attitude so much to be desired in this regard, to get away from certain words which, because of their association with popular taboos, have acquired an unenviable connotation. In addition, too, certain of these words are clumsy hybrids of Greek and Latin together. Instead of the word "Mastur-bation," we shall use the Greek derivative Auto-erotism, using the word for other forms of self-love, as well as the masturbatory ; instead of Homo-sexuality, and Homo-sexual, we shall say Homo-erotism and Homo-erotic ; instead of

Hetero-sexual, we shall say Hetero-erotic ; accomplishing in the last two cases, a change from a hybrid to a homogeneous word, and in the first two, changes from words which have an unpleasant taste about them in the popular mind. By using the Greek " Eros " as the derivative in all three, we also get uniformity in scientific terminology, which is good.

V

It will help to clarify our ideas on the subject, if we separate, to begin with, four salient facts about it.

(1) The instinct does not, as was always believed, manifest first at puberty, but is evident very much earlier, dying down to a period of latency, and reappearing in far greater power at puberty. We do not need to accept all Freud's teachings regarding infantile sex life, and the resultant complexes of the young boy or girl. We recognise that they are but hypotheses at best, and while we respectfully acknowledge the power of the brains which work on these hypotheses, and the apparent validity of much of the evidence they adduce to support them, we can suspend judgment and be " benevolently sceptical " regarding them. His theories regarding the "Œdipus complex" and the "Electra complex," which are the outcome of " incestuous infantile desires," while they are accepted with all the touching faith of neophytes in a new religion, by his followers, must be received with very great reserve, until, by some process as yet unknown, we can penetrate the infant mind, and judge its thoughts and reactions to its parents.

But he has established beyond cavil, that human sex life begins at a far earlier age than we had imagined, and it is only the traditional reaction of slight disgust at the word " sex," that makes us draw back from the idea. Childish auto-erotism, and childish exhibitionism are well known and

marked at an extremely early age ; so are the child's extreme
interest in the processes of birth, its preoccupation with the
body, the openings and differences thereof, as well as its
fantasies upon the manner of our entry into the world ;
while the child's reactions towards the parent of the opposite
sex are now seen to be far more subtle, and interwoven with
its infantile sex ideas, than we had ever dreamed. Child
psychology does not directly concern us here, but it must be
remarked in passing that no truth is more firmly established
by the new psychology, than that the child is father of the
man. Bad training and thwarting of the childish instinct
result disastrously in later complexes and disorders, and in
nothing is this more evident than in the sexual troubles of
adult life. These are frequently found to be the results of
childish sexual ideas and habits, such as fixations on the
Father or Mother, or auto-erotic habits, persisting when they
ought to have been far outgrown.

          After a period of latency, the instinct manifests
itself in the well-known bodily changes, and corresponding
mental stresses of puberty, changes and stresses which are
now seen to affect the personality to a far greater extent than
we previously thought. The bodily changes alone are
sufficiently impressive demonstrations of the strength of the
drive of sex. To push outwards from the Unconscious as it
does, with an energy sufficient to modify and recreate the living
tissue of the body is evidence enough of power, but the bodily
changes are accompanied by mental changes equally great.
The growth of the mind at puberty may be attributable in man
to various causes, but one of the main instruments in the
expansion from child mind to adult mind, is indubitably this
instinct, whose touch stirs man's being to its depth, and gives
the young life new kingdoms of thought, and desire, and
relationship to its kind. The process of adjustment to these
new bodily powers, and of accommodation to the new yearnings

after fuller self-expression, or after the ideal mate, is one which strains the personality to the utmost, and has life-long results, according as it is rightly or wrongly directed. We have long been familiar with, and perhaps slightly contemptuous of, these inchoate yearnings and long dreams of youth, the tuning-in, as it were, of the orchestra of life; let us begin to understand them better, as the early signs of that tremendous drive which is the vehicle of the continuity of the whole life-stream of the world, as well as one of the keys that in the hand of God unlock the doors of full-grown mental life and work. It has been an unworthy fear, a deliberate evasion of the truth, which has made men so long label this as " impure," for to have done so is seen to be a denial that God had purpose in making it so mighty.

Incidentally, we reveal our feelings about the powers of this instinct, in the very efforts we often make to repress its manifestations. The lies which are told to children, for example, leaving them to wander in the darkness of phantasy, and ultimately to find out the truth in sniggering, unclean, and furtive ways, in sly whisperings and smutty innuendo, are inexcusable. The neglect of so many parents in this regard, a neglect prompted entirely by their own inhibited and tainted thoughts of the subject, is the direct cause of the widespread adolescent idea, that sex is something evil, yet fascinating, to be giggled at in corners, and to be pushed out of sight when parents or teachers or elders appear. It is also the cause of the attempt made by so many adolescents, to fall in with the teaching given, such as it is, to regard sex as altogether impure, and so thoroughly to ignore or repress the instinct, as to lead to grave psychological consequences in later life.

The parents who hedge, and hesitate, and then lie, when asked a clean direct question by a child whose un-clouded mind has no *arrière pensée* whatever, do that child a grave injury and show themselves unfit to face one of the great duties and privileges of parenthood, namely, that of passing on to the child for whose being they are responsible, clean and adequate ideas regarding the facts of birth and of sex, when asked for them.

It is perhaps a digression, but it may be said, that when asked such questions, the safe rule is, to be prepared to answer truly and simply without hesitation or evasion, giving just as much information as is asked and *no more*. To hesitate, sows the seed in the child's mind that this is a queer secret, and incites his curiosity ; to give *more* than is asked, burdens and perplexes, and in any case is needless, as, if and when the child wants more, he will know to whom to come ; but to answer gravely, reverently, and with a full knowledge of responsibility in so doing, is a parent's clear duty, and ought to be one of his or her sweetest tasks. If this be done, it is matter of experience that there is neither shock nor surprise, and the child takes the information given, in its stride, unexcited and unashamed, with no extra curiosity whatever, and the foundation of a right and honourable attitude towards the whole matter is laid.

The power which declares itself thus at puberty, remains in evidence throughout the whole of mature life, and the normality or otherwise of the adult, is often determined by his ability to accommodate the circumstances of his life to the demands of this overmastering urge. Frequently those demands are only made evident by analysis, for the individual concerned is conscious solely of symptoms which seem to have no relation with it whatever ; but when divested of secondary motives and excuses, he has to acknowledge how much of his strength has been spent in evading and inhibiting this instinct, and how much happier he would be, if he could in some fashion equate its demands with the setting and the conventions of his outward life. His great danger is, that when the instinct cannot, in his estimation, be rightly used, as in marriage and procreation, he should stop short with repression, and not learn when necessary, to take the further step of sublimating his desires, calling in the higher powers of religion and service, to help him in the task. Conflict and suffering in this respect, are indeed inevitable in the life which is unregulated by the control of higher ideals, so strong is the power with which we are dealing, and so constant its demands to be let out. The whole teaching of psychology is, that it *must* be let out, and that there are only three ways in which it can emerge, namely, normally, abnormally, and through sublimation. It is not there to be repressed or tabooed, for the instinct which at the first shakes the foundations of the house of life, and which remains seated near the centre thereof through the whole of our span, is ignored at our peril, and if we sow repression, we reap disaster.

VI

(2) A second salient fact in this regard is, that, in the light of the knowledge gained on the one hand, from the study of anatomy and cellular physiology, and on the other, from analytical psychology, it has become clear that we have to depart from the idea that in this mind-body entity of ours, there are two rigidly defined and separate sexes, each complete, with its own character and functions. On the bodily side, there is no such thing as an individual completely man, or completely woman, to the exclusion of all the characteristics of the opposite sex ; for every man has in his body rudimentary female organs, and every woman, rudimentary male ones, while, until well on in pregnancy, the child is bi-sexual, and only then proceeds to develop towards the final sex, male or female ; so that from the anatomical point of view, complete sexual differentiation does not exist, a characteristic which is shared by humanity

with the rest of plant and animal creation ; for however uni-
sexually these may develop, there always persist vestiges of
bi-sexual character. Not only so, but the theory has been
advanced, and much research devoted to it, that every tissue,
and each separate cell of the body partakes in this double
character ; that in every part of all of us, characteristics
which anatomical science knows as evidence of masculinity
or feminity are variously blended ; and that therefore our
true sexual proportions are not alone determined by the
organs thereof, but by taking into consideration the evidence
which is furnished by every cell of our multi-cellular organism.
There is an infinite gradation of the two sexes, but at the
extremes, no organism has yet been observed which is wholly
and utterly masculine, to the exclusion of all feminine
characteristics, or vice-versa, the composite being always
perceptible, however much one element may preponderate.

This slight hesitancy, as it were, on the part of
nature, in bodily matters, is parallelled in the mind as well,
for there is no such thing as a personality that is altogether
and completely either male or female. Since the links
between mind and body are so close and interwoven (and in
the case of the instinct under consideration, they are especially
so) we must expect the departure from the idea of the absolute
male or female, and the conception of sexually intermediate
types, to shed considerable light on psychological problems.
This is especially true, when we have to take account of the
extremes of such types, namely, the effeminate man and
the masculine woman, whose deviations from normality are
so marked, and so misunderstood, and to whose peculiar
psychological difficulties, the knowledge that in certain
degrees all of us share at least *some* characteristics of the
opposite sex, should bring sympathy and greater understanding. In addition, this spells enlightenment, when we come to
estimate and to judge certain homo-erotic and other types,

which are definitely abnormal, and which have been in the
past contemptuously segregated, instead of being analysed,
and where possible, remedied.

Much attention is at present being directed to the
puzzling phenomena of the rhythms which are discernible
in all organic life, the mysterious ebbs and flows of the
hormic tide, obedient to no known laws, and apparent
both in bodily and mental activity. Some such rhythm has
been discerned in the part of life which we are considering,
for it has been noted that individuals oscillate as it were,
between the masculine and feminine elements in their
constitution, almost with periodicity. While it is outwith
the purpose of this book to discuss the point, it is relevant
to say that on this basis, and on the basis of the conception
of sexually intermediate forms, a much more accurate and
subtle science of character can be built up than has ever been
attempted. It may become possible to supply graded categories, in order to help our psychological judgments of
individuals, instead of the present hard and fast line merely
between men and women, in which case, we shall be able to
say of any individual character that it is compounded of so
many parts male, and so many parts female, and which
element was in the ascendant at the moment of the thought
or act that is *sub judice*. While this is as yet a science of the
future, it is nevertheless possible, even for those who are not
psychologically expert, to look within, and see in the varied
elements of their own experience, this bi-sexual character
observable, and to look around and discern, on the faces and
in the lives, of normal men and women, something at least of
this fundamental duality.

VII

(3) The great development noted in the instinct
at puberty is, as has been said, not its first manifestation,

though its most sensational. It has, in its course from infant to adult life, certain well-marked stages of development.

In child life, its whole tendency is auto-erotic, and the child is preoccupied with the sensations and pleasures of its own body, as evidenced by the characteristics already noted in (1). The child seeks its satisfactions in this respect, within itself, and without any of that search for partnership which is the universal characteristic of the later development of the instinct. Much has been made by the Freudians of infantile sexual reactions towards the parent of the opposite sex, but let it be said again, that in spite of the detail adduced, and the manner in which later experience is made to dovetail into the hypothesis, we have at present literally no means of direct contemporary knowledge ; all that we *can* say of the early sex life of the child, must be based on observation of its pleasures and habits, and these are definitely centred on self, are auto-erotic.

A well-marked change occurs, when the child makes its first social advances into a wider world, in school life, and at this stage, the instinct is entirely homo-erotic. It is the stage of violent and intense friendships of boy with boy and with older man, of girl with girl and with older woman, of " schwärms," often short, always strong. It is a well-defined stage, and lasts till the dawn of puberty, and often through its beginning.

With puberty, however, the normal instinct becomes hetero-erotic, both by reason of its own inherent urge, and because of the broadening of social contacts into circles where the sexes are not so strictly segregated ; it assumes in the normal individual, its final form, and continues so established through life.

Frequently, from one cause or another, the instinct becomes fixated at one or other of the earlier stages

of development, remaining centred on some childish or infantile object, while the individual grows to adult life. It
stays at this stunted level, carrying on its childish energies
into the full-grown body, and becomes the cause of many,
though not all of the homo-erotic manifestations of later
life, and of the habits of auto-erotism which make so
much unhappiness. Arrested development of the instinct
is a root cause, though by no means the only one, of
later abnormalities, and it is correspondingly dangerous to
interfere at any stage of its growth by means of lies or
taboos, or by keeping a child too long " at the apron strings,"
and refusing to let it seek its normal outlets in the
widening circles of life.

(4) The most menacing and inscrutable aspect of
the power of sex, the root cause of many of the conflicts it
occasions, and of so great a proportion of the distresses
and compromises of adult life, is the fact that in man its
urge is permanent and enduring, uninfluenced by time
rhythms, and that in this respect, man stands alone in animal
creation. In the animal kingdom, it is regulated by periods,
breaking out at its inevitable times, mightily, catastrophic-
ally, yet with natural directness, in a rhythmic urge which
blazes and has its day and disappears until its hour returns.
In man, it is a permanent restlessness, a chronic urge that
knows neither time nor law nor rhythm, and which produces
in the harassed life, results that are far-reaching and sometimes tragic. Man is eternally on the horns of a dilemma,
for if he gives his power full rein, and ignores all that would
atrophy or inhibit, he plunges his life into chaos, and perhaps
becomes outcast (and rightly so, since he will have upset that
balance which makes life liveable among his kind) ; and if he
lays down barriers, and tames the unruly spirit, its rebellious
power can shake the seat of life, in crisis after crisis. Thus
much of his strength is spent in vain search for an elusive

compromise, and it has to be confessed that the average man steers a perilous course between the Scylla of imperious desire, and the Charybdis of hard repression.

VIII

Since then the dilemma is as broad as humanity, its issue ought to be faced on ground equally broad. No *laissez-faire* gospel, or cry of " back to nature " will suffice, and indeed the whole path of the merely intellectual attempt to deal with the instinct, is strewn with tragi-comic wrecks of all ages and sizes, from the structures of the Utopia makers and eugenists, to the writings of Malthus, from the attempts to regularise prostitution, to the companionate marriage, and the sterilisation of the unfit. The issue must be faced on far broader ground, for the reason that all such attempts overlook one great fact which is vital, namely, that the over-repression or the hypertrophy of the instinct, together with the resultant conflicts, are not due to the instinct *per se*, but to that which conscious intellect and will have made of it, and that the clue to dealing with it, is not to be sought on these levels at all. If the human intellect has tangled the matter so hopelessly, the seeker after truth should be careful not to put his trust too closely in that self-same intellect. Reason and logic have had their way with it, philosophies have been built to hedge it in, will power without stint has sought to canalise it, and no one of these has given either law or order to it, but all are the sport of the very instinct they seek to regulate. In nothing is this truer, by the way, than in the popular campaign whose noises sound so loud just now, that in support of Birth Control; which outcry, while birth control can indubitably be granted in certain limited and proper conditions, has very frequently nothing to do with either birth or control, but it is simply an easy means to make indulgence possible and promiscuity safe.

The mind has been presented with what, on the intellectual level, appears to be a bundle of contradictions ; an instinct which must contradict restraint, if it is to be appeased ; only a negligible proportion of humanity capable of self-control on intellectual direction ; a very large percentage driven to a neurotic standstill because of it ; and the vast bulk of civilised men quite without consistent thought on the subject, and driven therefore to taboo it by will power ; all which taboos, the instinct is proving itself triumphantly capable of contradicting. Over against this uneasy constellation of ideas, there is set another, equally vague and uneasy ; the dim desire for a system of moral values that is not founded on man's caprice ; the innate dislike of the tyranny and exploitation, which self-indulgence involves ; and the inchoate hope that somehow science plus ethics will yet unify and state the one great meaning of life, in animal and in man, and give man therein a ruling idea, which will dominate and tame his unruly instincts.

The way, therefore, seems to be clear for an appeal in this regard, to something in us which is at once outside and above both the failures of the intellect, and the weaknesses of the will. Here once more, it is most instructive to observe in how many writings on the subject, while due emphasis is given to the dark power of the instinct, and to the difficulties and failures of the mind in harnessing it, the writers jib at the last, the most obvious and necessary step, and refuse to allow the possibility of spiritual control, outlawing the one faculty which above all others, can interpret human loves and hungers in the language of the Divine, and can establish a centre into which flow all the streams of the area of life, each contributing, none dominating, and all controlled and directed, towards man's optimum development. They will go as near as they dare, and invoke the prophets of the lesser moralities, calling on Nietzsche, or Goethe, or Havelock Ellis, but would seemingly not write at all, rather than name the name of Christ. Churches and priests are mentioned, often to their detriment, and religious systems castigated, for what they have failed to do, and the powers of religion, and of the spiritual life, are left there, as if that were the limit of their strength. It is another impressive demonstration of the futility of diagnosing and prescribing for the ills of the human mind, without a training which has tested its spiritual, as well as its intellectual powers, and without an experience within the writers themselves, of the reality and rationality of a spiritual interpretation of the universe.

Even granted the possibility of a limited control, in a limited number of specially gifted human beings, through the influence of such philosophic moralities, there remains the vast mass of men, without capacity or opportunity to learn its fine-drawn distinctions, and in any case, quite unwilling to allow its power to rule. A system such as only the aristocracy of the mind can understand, and which only the few can practise, is incapable of dealing with an universal instinct ; and what is needed is the one power common to all, though unrealised in many, the power inherent in the very name Religion, which by its derivation speaks of binding and loosening, of curbing and release, and which carries the whole tremendous dilemma up to its own high plane, and submerges the smaller passions in the passionate fires of love to God and our neighbour man.

IX

The spirit of true religion in a man is the one and only thing which can exorcise the evil that lies in sex, and sublimate its fires ; and in reading that categorical statement, let it be remembered that all the other weapons in the armoury of the mind, have been tried and found wanting. There immediately therefore emerges a task, urgent and important, for the Christian psycho-therapist, be he minister or not, for so far, the Churches, with the partial exception of the Roman Church, have not grappled with this problem of the sex instinct, but have acquiesced in archaic standards, and in restrictions imposed on it by those who are far from the spirit of Christianity; nor have they yet seen the need of specialised training to deal with this, as with kindred problems of psychology.

Part of that task has already been accomplished by the researches of the medical psychologists, who have taught men to approach the whole question fearlessly and sincerely, have sought to free it from ignorant taboos, and have estimated its strength and influence on the personality, but who, in this, as in so much else in psychology, have stopped there, and left the question in mid-air. The further task, and it is an urgent one, must be undertaken of relating this instinct (and indeed the whole instinctual life of man) to the religious instinct, of restating its moral aspects in the light of our new knowledge, and of finding afresh the mind of Christ regarding it. When this is done, the Christian psycho-therapist will be the true, indeed the only, mediator of healing and peace to sex-tormented minds.

X

We are thus led straight to the question : What is the right Christian attitude towards the sex instinct, and what is the New Testament view of the matter ? It is an enormous and vital question, but one which, though it be impossible to treat at length, can yet have its authoritative elements briefly stated.

(a) The New Testament view, and especially the view of Christ Himself, are not necessarily the same as those

6

which have been developed and standardised by the Church. For many centuries, and indeed till the recent all-round loosening of rigidities, and consequent growth of understanding, the view of the Church was moulded, not by the New Testament, but by the writings of the early Christian Fathers. The very pressure of the circumstances in which these men wrote, striving as they did against the impact of an impure pagan society, where sex life was utterly unbridled, made the swing of the pendulum a natural thing ; and the echo of their rhodomontades against the whole instinct, making its suppression in celibacy the almost absolute prerequisite of a Christian life, and insisting on a duality between spirit and flesh far deeper than that warranted by the Gospel, has persisted till now in the standards of the Church. The repercussion of the ascetic and eremitic ideal, perpetuated in the monastic systems of the Middle Ages, is felt even yet in the narrow ignorances which do duty for Christian views on the subject in many parts of the Church.

(b) It is fundamental to state that in this, as in all other questions, we turn with reverence, not to the Gospel writings first, nor even to the sayings of Christ, but always and primarily to the Person of Christ Himself. The principal error of all " amateur " writers when they touch the fringe of Theology is, that they persist in regarding Christianity as primarily a creed, or a set of principles, when its core and essence is neither creed, however transcendental, nor even the glory of the Sermon on the Mount, but the Person of Christ ; a fact so clearly and repeatedly stated in the Gospels and the New Testament, that only superficiality can explain ignorance thereof ; and it is this most vital fact alone which differentiates Christianity from all other religious systems of the world. Concerning that Person and His nature, more controversy has raged, than on any other one subject within the range of the human intellect, but every shade of opinion, from the extreme Catholic, through the Unitarian to the Agnostic and the Rationalist, unites in agreeing, that whatever else He was or claimed to be, He was complete in His humanity, a member of the great family of mankind.

In this particular connection therefore, the attention of enquirers ought to be directed to two views of the Person of Christ which are stated in the New Testament, and which have profound relevance, when rightly pondered.

(i) " The Word was made *Flesh*, and dwelt among us " (St. John i. 14). That is to say, the Logos of the Christian system came, not as Spirit alone, or Reason, or Mind, but as that which stated the perpetual unity in man between these, and the tissues in which they are clothed. By accepting these as His vesture, He for ever glorified every part of them.

(ii) " He was in all points tempted like as we are, yet without sin " (Heb. iv. 15). Here again it is our own hands that would draw back the hem of Christ's garment from all contact with this power. While we do not lift our eyes to the sacred inner places of His mind, unless He has lifted the veil for us, we yet dare to know that he faced *all* the passions and temptations of humanity when He accepted it, and that His answer to them is to be sought supremely in His example. It is not for us to read our own limitations into His completeness, but to face the full implications of the fact of the full humanity of Christ, and to realise that here too, by His own experience of what we are, He is able to say to the storm, " Peace, be still."

(*c*) This Christo-centric nature of Christianity is the reason why misunderstanding people seek in vain in it, for detailed rules, and plans to cover every phase of life. They will not find them, because they look too low ; but they *will* find, in a right apperception of the Person and Work of Christ, a final answer to every question that they set. Just as He, for example, never attacked the horrors of slavery, though living in their midst, yet He abolished, and is abolishing it from humanity, by the simple process of making it impossible to be a Christian, and at the same time own a slave; so here, by living a life before men in which every power was sublimated to the one great task, He set a pattern which His bitterest enemies have never been able to impeach, and gave the living proof of the powers of the spirit to deal with, and use, every single instinct of the human make-up, for its own higher purposes.

Without that example before their eyes, the attempt of certain psychologists to create a unity for life which excludes the spiritual, might be excused; but to study the human mind and life, while refusing the study of the greatest mind and life in history, is, to say the least, pusillanimous. In so doing, they are blind to the fact that the essence of Christianity is, that what its Founder did, He empowers His followers in their degree to do; and that whether they (the psychologists in question) like it or no, these followers are testing, and have tested, that power by millions, and have not found it wanting in any single instance. Otherwise He would be a solitary and impossible Ideal, instead of being One whom the common people hear and follow gladly; a fact which still confounds the scribes.

XI

(*d*) Yet He did not, in His teaching, leave us without clues to His mind on the subject. Apart from isolated texts, He touched it very directly in three ways; and if His teaching in regard to these three parts of human life be followed, it becomes impossible to regard the procreative instinct as anything but God-given and holy, and, as such, to be desecrated neither by fear nor lewdness.

(i) His love of children and babes, implies not only His knowledge of the avenue through which they come, but His blessing on the creative urge which calls them into being.

(ii) His voice was the first in history to call Woman to her proper place in the scheme of creation. A member of a race, each man of which daily thanked his God that he was not made a woman, Christ cut right athwart every tradition of that and other races, and gave, and gives, woman her emancipated place. All others who seek to do so, do but follow Him ; and however high their aim, they have not yet attained to what He did two thousand years ago.

(iii) When He sought to put within the feebleness of words the highest concepts of the Creator and His work, and to make the frail mind of finite man see a little of God, and of how he stood to God, He chose, out of all language and experience, the categories of the family, as the highest, and, indeed, the only ones, wherewith to do so. Since He thus made parenthood a foretaste of Heaven, and an echo of the Creator's own nature and purpose, He defined His own and our attitude towards it, and its attendant instincts, with crystal clearness. He gave to it a name so God-like, and a place so sacred, as to put it, with all its passions and its functions, close to the control of God ; and by so doing, He made it possible for ordinary ungifted men and women, to whom rarified intellectual ideals were impossible, to feel that their ordinary powers of sex could be spiritualised and controlled.

We have, however, guidance yet more direct, to the mind of Christ on this subject. After speaking words that are hard and unwelcome to the modern ear, on the subject of marriage and divorce, He says (St. Matthew xix. 12) : " There are some eunuchs, which were so born from their mother's womb; and there are some eunuchs, which were made eunuchs of men ; and there be eunuchs, which have made themselves eunuchs, for the Kingdom of Heaven's sake. He that is able to receive it, let him receive it." This is a " key " text on this point in the Gospels, and amply confirms the evidence of the last three paragraphs. There *is*, He says, a power which can control the sex instinct in men and women, for in the Christian system it has to take its due place with the rest, in subordination to the one great fact of citizenship in the Kingdom of Heaven. Anything less like the mind of Christ than to distort the words into a command for celibacy, as has been attempted, cannot be imagined ; but He *does* say, and He emphasises the saying by His own life-pattern, that the powers of sex are in the grasp of a greater power, when men and women follow Him, and that to deny oneself, and to struggle for the mastery of sex in His service, produces not disaster, but strength. In this respect, as in all others, the Christian life is not, as so many like to picture it, a life circum-scribed by fine-drawn rules, or set to tread an impossibly ascetic path, but is simply the Christ-like life, moulding intellect and instinct alike, to no hard and fast pattern, but freely, with the freedom and the mastery, which come to those who strive to have " that mind in them which was also in Christ Jesus."

This text cannot be taken alone, but as related to that whole scale of moral values, which, as propounded by Christ, is immeasurably more lofty than that contained in any other system, and which, in its scope and power, ruthlessly changes many of the man-made views of the sinfulness of certain sins. On this one subject alone, He reveals a breadth of view unshared till recently by any of His followers, a calm and revolutionary decisiveness, which they have rarely under-stood. Unless this be so, why did He pour out the treasures of His thought on God, before a Samaritan woman doubly outcast to the pious Jew by her race, and by her living in adultery ? Or why, at one time, cast out, in that white anger so rare in Him, the money-changers from the Temple, and at another, allow Mary Magdalene to anoint His feet, and wipe them with the hairs of her head, saying to the ignorance which protested, that her sins were forgiven because she loved much ? Or why that refusal, so strange to men, to condemn the adulteress they brought to Him in order to confound Him, and the adamantine sentence which smote like a sword the parallel and equal sin of the men who brought her ? Why indeed, unless to show that His thoughts are not as our thoughts, and that hypocrisy and impenitence and pride are as leprous as adultery in the eyes of God ? Not that He, whose immaculate purity even the foulest of His enemies could not, and cannot assail, could ever condone the wanton degradation of so high an instinct ; but His even-handed judgment put first sins first, and always gave to love and repentance their compensatory weight.

Let this not be thought an excursus. If there is to be a Christian psychology at all, here as everywhere, we go to the fountain-head for right values and judgments. In this regard, we have seen enough in Christ, to abolish old narrownesses and fears, to approach this instinct with reverence and purity, and to apply to its illnesses, the healing truths of a Physician greater than them all.

XII

(2) THE RELIGIOUS INSTINCT

Those who make religion a mere faculty and not an instinct of the mind, forget the main postulate of religion, which is God ; and those who thus limit religion, and yet write from the religious point of view, are doubly forgetful. The core and essence of religion is, that since God is, He has enabled men to know Him. Man's awareness of God, whatever form that awareness takes, is not a thing mediated wholly from outside and above himself, but is something which is always inner and intuitive, and is the highest manifestation of that instinct of Incompleteness which dominates so much of his life. The instinct which searches, is met by something which reveals; and this is the twofold truth in all forms of religious experience, from the most primitive, up to the Christian. It makes the apperception of God more than a mere faculty, but an inborn necessity, if man is to be man.

It is not so difficult now as it once was, to postulate God in relation to a science, since the crass materialism of the scientific mind has so largely passed. That materialism has been made impossible, partly by the further advances made by the very sciences which created it, and partly by the realisation that the mind which can observe the universe, and rule out the Creator, is not observing it as a mind at all, but only as an intellect. It is this last fact which causes the present distrust of the once lauded "scientific mind," for it is felt that by arbitrarily ruling that logic and reason are the sole avenues to knowledge of creation, the "scientific mind" is guilty of self-mutilation, and amputates itself of powers at least as far-seeing as these.

Unfortunately however, this materialism lingers in the science now under observation, and while Freud has to some extent shaken loose from it, yet he and all his followers, together with the great majority of psychotherapeutists of all schools, have no place whatever for God, and no respect for religion as the mediator between the Creator and His creation. The temptation to write and work as a "cold, detached intellect," used to be common among scientists, and still is, among the scientists of the mind; but it is rather an evidence of undeveloped mentality, than of the true scientific spirit.

It is no part of the purpose of this book to enter

upon apologetic. Apart altogether from the structure of
Theology, and the facts of revelation, the axiomatic basal
fact of God makes necessary an answering instinct in man.
Either such an instinct is native to man, or is implanted
into him at some stage of his development. For the latter,
there is no evidence whatever ; and if the power to know
God be native to man, and appears at its own time in the
growing mind, making its groove there in response to certain
perceptions outside itself, and to certain inner needs, then
it is as much an instinct as Hunger. And if it be said that
many men appear to do without it, let it be answered that
that is because their Incomplete instinct is for the moment
satisfied with union with life as they find it ; and that in
crises, when that union is cracking, these very men, like all
their brothers, feel the desperate need of completion by union
with something more stable and enduring, and call instinctively and urgently upon their Unknown God. Since
one criterion of an instinct is universality and uniformity, it
can safely be stated that every man, whatever cultural level
he may occupy, has at some time or another in response to
observed phenomena said, " A power not myself is working
here ; this is God for me." In its ascent of the scale of
culture, this response has purged itself of the primitive, and
attained the spiritual, but it is an instinct which responds,
and no developed faculty.

From this emerges one fact which is vital for our
present purpose. To thwart the energy of an instinct by
mere repression is disastrous for the mind, as repressed force
always hits back. This holds good as much here as elsewhere, and the sole reason why complexes and neuroses are
invariably traced back to instincts other than the religious,
such as the sexual, the self-assertive, and so on, is that those
who thus trace them, being without experience in religion,
have no other means of diagnosis, and must act according to

their knowledge. "Quis custodiet ipsos custodes?"; which being interpreted means, "If the physician himself need healing, what is the plight of the patient?" In not one analysis in a thousand, is any attention given to the religious history of the patient, his fears and errors in this regard, his fixations and repressions, while of course the minutiæ of all his outer history are dug up and examined. Obviously this happens, because the analyst is unequipped by personal experience, infantile in his reaction to religion, and has thus good reason for the use of every label save the religious, when describing the needs of the patient.

A priori, the thwarting of a mind in its desire for God, even though that thwarting, as so often happens with other instincts, be half or wholly unconscious, must produce serious consequences. Why then is it thought unscientific to say that much of the sickness of humanity is caused by hunger for God, by unsatisfied and thwarted desire for spiritual things? Who is to diagnose such sickness, and judge its causes? Certainly not the psychiatrist who ignores religion, and analyses only the unspiritual components of his patients; but supremely one who has been trained in the school of religion as well as the schools of science, who adds to his faith, knowledge, and who can interpret the sufferer's needs, because he himself has hungered for God.

XIII

This, however, is but half the case for the religious instinct. It is implanted not only to satisfy itself, and fulfil its yearning for completeness, but to receive the intimations of God and the unseen, being not only the urge towards God, but that part of the mind which is sensitive to God, as a photographic plate is sensitive to light. This, too, is the inevitable corollary of the fact of God, and those who, judging religion

from the outside, seek to codify its forms and effects as they
would those of geology or botany, are ignoring its fundamentals, and denying the power of the Creator to speak as well
as create, simply because they do not happen to have heard
Him. Deafness and blindness are not exclusively physical,
and some of the struggles of these men to evade the implications of God and the spiritual are pathetically hard. To say,
as they do, that the spirit in man, and its powers of hearing
and speech, are assumptions incapable of proof, begs the
question ; for who assumes that they are assumptions, if
not a thinking entity whose every act of thought is incapable
of that type of space-time proof, which he desires for religion ?
It is here, as Jung so wisely says, that " Freud shipwrecks on
the question of Nicodemus, ' Can a man be born again ? ' " ;
and on that rock his barque is not alone. And he goes on,
using words that are familiar to Christian ears, though he
does not accept the Christian position :

> For thousands of years, rites of initiation
> have been teaching spiritual rebirth ; yet strangely
> enough, man forgets again and again the meaning of
> Divine procreation. This is surely no evidence of a strong
> life of the spirit ; and yet the penalty of misunderstanding
> is heavy, for it is nothing less than neurotic decay, em-
> bitterment, atrophy, and sterility. It is easy enough to
> drive the spirit out of the door, but when we have done so,
> the salt of life grows flat, it loses its savour. Fortunately
> we have proof that the spirit always renews its strength.
> Ever and again human beings arise who understand what
> is meant by the fact that God is our Father. The equal
> balance of flesh and the spirit is not lost to the world." [1]

Incidentally, it is interesting to notice the reaction of " orthodox " psychologists, to thought such as this. It is, we are told,

[1] Jung : *Humanity in Search of a Soul*, p. 14.

" proof of Jung's desertion from the ranks of science, and his retreat into the obscurantism of a gnostic religion." [1] In other words, they say that even a very great psychologist is childishly wrong, and betrays his science, when his greatness leads him to know God, and to discern His workings in the human mind.

In this life, the religious instinct is neither satisfied entirely, nor complete. At its best, in the best of lives, it is most conscious of its failures, and the obstacles in its way. But it exists, and in proportion as it dominates the rest, not working as an anodyne that dulls the faculties into submission, but as the quickener that fructifies them all, life is made tranquil, normal, and secure. This is the changeless testimony of those who have tested it, and given it its chance. With one voice they say that it is not only the crown of life, but its only crown ; not only an instinct, but *the* instinct ; not only a path along which they travel towards knowledge of God, but an avenue through which God and eternity are perceived and incorporated in time.

[1] *Journal of Medical Psychology*, March 1934.

CHAPTER V

THE FLIGHT FROM REALITY

REPRESSION AND THE COMPLEX

Limitations of our field; the grave dangers of overstepping them; neurotic terror of reality; neurotic isolation; purposive character of all symptoms; consequent Conflict; meaning of Repression; it is not Suppression; nor is it volitional; meaning of the Complex; complexes of instinctual source; complexes of experiential source; autonomous nature of the complex.

I

WE turn for the moment, from the structure and content of the mind, to begin the consideration of some of its disorders. The more extreme of these, we do not touch, since they are too inextricably linked with grave bodily and mental upheavals, for the non-medical man to interfere, and since the operations of what is popularly called spiritual healing, are not here envisaged. Yet there is a vast range of nervous and mental disorders, which our new understanding of the structure of the mind, of the function and strength of its instincts, and of the mechanisms it employs to deal with life, enables us to interpret and alleviate.

Before entering on the consideration of any of these, let the explicit proviso be made, that no case whatever of such disorder should be touched, unless there has first been carried out a physical examination of the case by one qualified to do so, and an assurance obtained that the patient is organically sound, and that such symptoms as he exhibits are not, for example, epileptic, or those of incipient dementia. Much harm has been done, illnesses have been aggravated and lengthened, and life-long consequences incurred, by the careless interference of the unqualified ; and if such interference is to be deprecated in bodily affections, much more must it be deprecated in the case of the neurotic patient, whose mind hinges precariously between balance and unbalance, and whom a touch may precipitate into very deep waters indeed. The cause of psycho-therapy has suffered injury at the hands of those who, without any analysis of their own lives to prepare them, or indeed any first hand experience of psychology, not only misinterpret its terms by uncomprehending use of them, but touch other lives in the name of psychology, and expect to heal them.   To that extent, the somewhat excessive reaction of the medical profession against any interference whatever, is justified ; and it is only a very profound conviction that there *is* here a field in which the properly trained Christian minister can operate, which prompts this entire survey.

II

Before entering on detail, we may begin by defining certain characteristics common to all psychopathic disorders, and discernible under all varieties of outward symptoms. The neurotic shares them with all his fellow-sufferers, whether he be neurasthenic, hysteric, or sensitive.

(1) Broadly speaking, the first and universal characteristic of the neurotic, whatever his trouble, can be defined as his terror of reality.   Life presents itself to him as too hard to be endured, he retreats before its impact, and flees from its reality into the realms of fantasy and perversion. In so retreating, he does violence to his deepest instincts, which bid him seek his completeness, by contact with his

kind and with God ; and the resultant conflict of instinctual desires within himself, plus his refusal to face the truth of life's realities, is one of the root causes of his trouble.

Such recoil is, of course, characteristic in some degree and at some times, of us all, but the normal man vanquishes his fear, and turns once more to grapple with life ; the psychopath not only yields to his fears, and tries to ignore life by shutting his eyes to it, but compensates himself in an imaginary kingdom, self-created, self-centred, and substitutionary for the facts he is unable to endure. The essential fact of his flight from reality is, that while its consequences in the shape of fantasy and perversion are visible and conscious as symptoms, the true motives of the flight have become unconscious, and are often only discoverable after patient analysis. The revelation thus gained of the strength and ramifications of the unconscious motive, is indeed one of the most striking in psychology, and the uncovering of it is one of the chief means whereby nervous disorders previously inaccessible, can be classified and reduced.

Let it be noted, too, that the hard reality from which he flees, is by no means necessarily that material reality which so many psycho-therapists envisage as the only reality, and which excludes the spiritual. One of the commonest refusals of life, is the refusal to face the realities of the God-sent moral laws which govern it, and of the spiritual influences which direct it, and here, too, the same inevitable consequences follow. A world imagined without God, is as much a fantasy as any other, and it is a poor psychology which refuses to see, parallel with the results of shutting out life, the bitter consequences of shutting out God.

Much psychological research has been devoted to the origins of the guilt sense, and the growth of the idea of sin, frequently with the object of reducing them to something in man which discounts the power of God. Such a line of research is outwith our province here ; for the present let us but note, that while the sense of guilt and sin is, and has been, hideously and unnecessarily aggravated in the unbalanced and the neurotic, there remains, even after that has been smoothed away, an unalterable residuum which cannot be evaded, simply because in it there is a direct intimation of the fact that man lives his life in the presence of God ; and many a man has shipwrecked because, though aware of that, he has refused to face it.

(2) This flight from reality compels that tragic loneliness, which is so striking and so pathetic in the neurotic. There is an impalpable barrier between him and the world, and he lives in solitude behind it, torn between the compulsion of his private fantasies, and the natural longings he has for contact and companionship. Conscious of his isolation, he yet maintains it, and thus attains the well-known delusion of the psychopath that all the world is arrayed against him, and that he is entirely misunderstood, even by those who know him best. All the energy which normally should pour out through the channels of his "Incomplete" instinct, is frustrated and introverted, and his every symptom is exacerbated by the fact that he endures it in mental solitude. At the same time, he remains acutely conscious of his environment, and part of his torment is, that he cannot " get in," that his technique of contact is undeveloped, and that he has to remain aloof, though longing to mingle with his kind. He thus suffers the double disability (caused primarily by his own action in closing the gates of life against reality) of a self-imposed loneliness, and a very alert consciousness of his isolation. It is a twofold pain, for which no mere " Adjustment to reality " is an anodyne, but which needs a deeper " religio," a binding again to the world and to God, for its permanent cure.

(3) Without any exception, every symptom pro-

duced by the neurotic in his flight from reality, has a purpose, and expresses a desire on his part. This is a hard saying, but axiomatic in psycho-therapy. To say that he produces his symptoms on purpose is not to say that he wittingly does so, for an illness consciously assumed, is malingering, and he is certainly no malingerer. It is not conscious but unconscious desire which motivates his outward symptoms, and in every case his illness is an instrument used by his unconscious mind, whereby to escape from the intolerable situation caused by his flight from reality, and to gain an imaginary security. The energy which is thwarted of its proper outlet thus spends itself, the conflict is resolved, and the neurotic proves to the onlooker and to himself, by his phobias or his bodily pains, that he is obviously too delicate to face life. He seeks to justify through his illness, his own fantasy that he is truly a special being who needs special consideration, and he works off his unconscious and thwarted sexual or other desires, through the fears of his mind and the pains of his body. In every case, he sets up a defence mechanism, to protect himself from the abhorred reality, and the purposive nature of his unconscious action will be abundantly seen in a later chapter, when we pass those mechanisms in review.

(4) We are led by these considerations into the immediate presence of Conflict, because the first result of such an attempt to evade life and rearrange it, is that desperate and incessant conflict, which is so characteristic of the neurotic personality. Here, too, he shares something common to us all, but in his case, the conflict of which we are all aware in some degree, uses up all that store of energy which is needed for other affairs, and unbalances the whole life. Conflict does not always produce disorder; rightly conducted, it leads from strength to strength, up to victory over the immoral and the unworthy. But it exhausts the neurotic, because its motives are unrecognised, or such as he dare not acknowledge.

The physical weariness, for example, of the neurasthenic, is the outward effect of an inner and unrelenting internecine war, whose campaigns are carried on unknown to him, though he faintly hears the battle-cries. The unequal struggle thus carried on by all psychopathic personalities, is therefore based on repression ; and with the utterance of that word, we come at once to the root cause of most of their troubles.

III

The word "Repression" is a key word in the new psychology, and must be taken in its right and technical sense, for there is much loose thought gathered round it, and it has an easy popular connotation which is far removed from the truth. Its vague and slip-shod use is responsible for the notion that in deprecating repression, psychology advocates unrestrained freedom in self-expression, regardless of social and moral consequences : a grotesque perversion. Two things must be clearly understood regarding it.

(i) It does not mean suppression. Suppression is a right and legitimate part of the good life, and there is no Faith worthy of the name, which does not preach suppression as a necessity. But suppression is always a conscious thing, whereby the personality, in full view of two alternatives, chooses the higher, and consciously forsakes the lower, or *vice versa* ; in either case, knowing full well the consequences. Repression, on the other hand, is a continuous and unconscious process, which, though it may have begun in a moment of conscious recoil, operates and endures below the threshold of consciousness. It is abundantly possible for the repressed experience or desire to be utterly blotted out and forgotten by the conscious mind, and yet for the conflict it causes in the unconscious mind, to be both lasting and exhausting ; while a suppressed experience is never forgotten, and a suppressed

motive or desire round which conflict ensues, is always conscious. This is an important distinction, and our recognition of the unconscious character of all repressed material,
leads us to appreciate the far-reaching achievements of
psycho-therapy, in probing to where it lies, and allowing its
accumulated poisons to drain away.

(ii) Will power has nothing to do with repression.
True, the first moment of refusal to face the fact repressed,
may express the will, as may the desire to be quit of the un-
desirable thing, but once repressed and out of sight, it lives
where the will cannot reach it. Hence the futility of the old-
fashioned prescription to those afflicted with " nerves," to
" forget about it," or " make an effort of will," or find surcease
in tonics and change of scene. Repression is no single isolated
act, but a process always going on, which, once initiated,
functions in the unconscious, and functions whether the
consciousness wants it to or not. Indeed, the more the psychopath wills, the more he hurts himself, for his mental channels
are blocked, his " bearings are seized," and the impact of the
will only adds to the obstruction and the heat. He proves in
his life the Pauline " Law of reversed effort " ; saying, " The
evil which I would not, that I do," and the greater the effort,
the less the result.

The truth behind repression is a singularly impressive one, namely, that a desire or emotion, once called forth,
can never rest till it finds expression. If the personality decrees
that it is impossible to fulfil the desire, or admit the emotion,
the conflict can be, and often is, fought out consciously, so that
the energy in question is expended there and then ; but if not,
and the illicit matter is repressed, its energy is undistributed,
remains potent, and never rests till it finds an outlet, perhaps in
a symptom that appears quite unrelated to its parent emotion.
And when it is remembered that an equal and constant
amount of energy is spent in " sitting on the safety valve "

lest the repellent thing reach consciousness, it will be realised how wearing and how wearying is the lot of the repressor. Indeed, this repressive force is so watchful and so strong, as to have been elevated by Freud and others, into a sort of inner independent personality called the Censor, whose business is said to be to select from the unconscious material what shall, and what shall not, be permitted to reach the conscious; and only in dreams does the Censor nod occasionally, and let a hint of inner trouble pass his guard. There is a certain cogency in the hypothesis, as we shall see when we look at the activities of the complex, and the way it speaks in dreams; but be that as it may, we note for the present, that the energy involved in repression is both incessant and unconscious, and that when it bursts forth in a symptom, emerging like a subterranean river from the earth, that symptom is often far distant from its true source.

Groddeck puts the matter in his own pithy way :

"What is repressed does not vanish, it only loses its place. It is pushed into some corner or other where it has no right to be, where it is squeezed and hurt. Then it always stands on tiptoe, pressing from time to time with all its strength towards where it belongs, and as soon as it sees a gap in the wall in front of it, it tries to squeeze itself through. Perhaps it may succeed in so doing, but when it has got to the front, it has used up all its strength, and the next good push from some masterful force hurls it back again. It is a most disagreeable situation, and you can imagine when anything so repressed, crushed, and battered, at length wins freedom, what leaps and bounds it will be taking; except indeed that its clothes are all soiled by the struggle, torn and crumpled, that the naked skin shows through everywhere, and is not always clean, and that a peculiar smell clings round it of the crowds it has been squeezed among."[1]

IV

The Complex. This repressive force works in two ways. It prevents certain primitive things from ever coming up into the conscious mind at all, and it pushes down certain distasteful experiences of that conscious mind into the unconscious. In either case, that which is so repressed continues, as we have seen, vital and energetic, and it forms in the unconscious, what is known as a Complex. Here, again, it is regrettable that the word has passed too easily into superficial use, becoming a convenient label wherewith to classify and excuse the shortcomings of ourselves and others ; to call a thing an " inferiority complex," for example, is neither to define nor understand it, for though a feeling of inferiority may be its symptom, that feeling may spring from very diverse complexes, and in the end have nothing at all to do with inferiority.

What then is a complex ? Through the working of the laws of association, every idea presented to the mind in the course of its experience, tends to link itself with associated ideas, or with instincts already there. Thus our mental furniture is largely composed of what are called constellations, that is, of large or small groups of ideas or sentiments, all clustered round one subject and its derivatives. These groups are a great part of our equipment for intercourse, for rationalisation, and for creative work. Now that same law holds good for unattractive, as for attractive material, with the difference that the material we dislike is pushed under, and forms in the unconscious the nucleus of a complex, and attracts to itself all allied thoughts and experiences, to form a buried system. A complex is thus

[1] Groddeck : *The Book of the It*, p. 42.

an unconscious constellation, formed first by a nuclear idea repellent to the mind and thrust down, to which has been gathered by accretion similar ideas and emotions, the whole forming an interrelated unity.

Such complexes may be divided into two classes : those caused by the working of instinctual energy, and those caused by the experience of the personality in relation to its environment of society and work.

(i) We have seen enough of the power of an instinct, to realise how formidable may be the disturbance caused by the repression of one or more of them. In such a case, the repressed material magnetically gathers to itself all the ideas and emotions associated with the instinct, and becomes a complex potent for evil.

" The repression may be directed against fear and all manifestations of fear ; or against the sex instinct and all its manifestations. Then every memory of experiences inspired by fear, or coloured by sex emotion, and every anticipation or fantasy similarly inspired, falls under the repression. The soldier who has learned to believe that any sign of fear is disgraceful ; the saint who retires to the wilderness to meditate on spiritual things and avoid all occasions of lust ; these are examples of such general repressions ; in both cases, the repressed tendency is apt to break through and manifest itself in dreams and perhaps in waking fantasies. Or, as in many religious orders, the general repression may be directed against every expression of the self-assertive impulse, against all pride, vanity, ambition, rivalry, all desire for power, authority, leadership, distinction ; and then, as among some of the narrower sects thrown up by the Reformation, the impulse manifests itself in pious railings and biblical cursings against all persons in authority, prelates and popes, and kings and magistrates." [1]

When any of the great instincts—for example, sex—is thwarted and repressed, its energy, therefore, centres in a complex, whose strivings and groanings are the root cause not only of visible sexual or other troubles, but of the intense and nameless anxieties, the hysteric states, the obsessions and the phobias with which psycho-therapy has to deal.

This is also abundantly verifiable in the case of that instinct which reaches towards God. To deny the religious instinct is not to atrophy it, for its hidden strivings shake the very ground beneath us, and are producing to-day that discontent with life, and that vague restlessness, to say nothing of that fevered disregard of the moral code, and that overcompensatory slighting of all faith, for which so many futile remedies are given. The very fact that so much of humanity to-day *knows* itself to be drifting rudderless, is proof that man possesses the Incomplete instinct, and that he will not find haven till that instinct be satisfied and complete, in union with the highest. Repression of the religious instinct has produced the inevitable complex ; and, as with all other complexes, this, too, will not be resolved till it is acknowledged, dragged into the light of consciousness, and released from repression.

(ii) When a shock or other distasteful experience is repressed, it, too, endures in the unconscious, still with its attendant emotions, and, as in the case of the instincts, becomes the nucleus of a complex, which tends to gather to itself the emotion of every experience which bears the least resemblance to that repressed. It may be a feeling of antagonism to a parent which is buried, or a shock sustained in early youth, or a rebuff to ambition ; in each case, the

[1] McDougall : *Abnormal Psychology*, p. 227.

buried emotion gathers to itself " seven others worse than the first," and, finding a new abode, sets up house as a complex, and assumes the right to grumble and to vex.

Here is an illuminating instance :

"One of my patients, a former Sunday-school teacher, had become a convinced atheist. He insisted that he had reached this standpoint after a long and careful study of the literature of the subject, and, as a matter of fact, he really had acquired a remarkably wide knowledge of religious apologetics. He discoursed at length upon the evidence of Genesis, marshalling his arguments with considerable skill, and producing a coherent and well-reasoned case. Subsequent psychological analysis, however, revealed the real complex responsible for his ' atheism ' ; the girl to whom he had been engaged had eloped with the most enthusiastic of his fellow Sunday-school teachers. We see that in this patient the casual complex, resentment against his successful rival, had expressed itself by a repudiation of the beliefs which had formerly constituted the principal bond between them. The arguments, the study, and the quotations were merely an elaborate rationalisation." [1]

It is one of the mysteries of the mind that a complex, formed in either of those two ways, with its associated emotions and ideas, becomes more and more isolated and independent. When it is a powerful one, long established and deep centred, it seems almost like a small independent mind, a miniature principality owning no allegiance to the conscious personality, sending out messages in dream and fantasy at will, obstructing at every turn, and at war with the greater empire in whose midst it finds itself. There is a very obvious analogy between this, and the conception

[1] Bernard Hart : *The Psychology of Insanity.*

of being " possessed by a devil," so familiar to us all, as with the classic examples of " split personality " which have been exhaustively worked out by neurologists and alienists, but it is not for discussion at the moment. It is sufficient to observe that the presence of an almost enemy citadel in the midst, is gravely dangerous to the kingdom of the mind, and that its reduction is the only hope of peace. The siege and reduction of the complex by psycho-therapy, is a great and pioneer achievement ; and when to it is added the allaying and exorcising powers of the Christian Faith, the warring mind sees peace in sight, and can hope for the victory of the best.

CHAPTER VI

THE FLIGHT FROM REALITY (*continued*)

DEFENCE MECHANISMS AGAINST REALITY

Nature, the Mother of invention; her mechanisms of escape used by all; their danger in proportion to the power of the complex; examination of the teaching of Christ on this point; the meaning of Fantasy; its familiarity and dishonesty; religious fantasy; the meaning of Projection; morally and socially wrong; the meaning of Inversion, or Over-compensation; familiar in life and religion; its extremes and dangers; the meaning of Conversion, in the psychological sense; the meanings of mental and of physical conversion; the meaning of Dissociation; its range and dangers; religious dissociations; Rationalisation the lubricant of all these mechanisms.

I

NATURE, always resourceful, has herself evolved means by which the troubled personality can deal with the warfare of the complex. Conflict unresolved is the one thing which the personality cannot endure, and energy once summoned, and unreleased, is an impossibility; and since the inhibition, the watchful Censor, the repressive force, call it what you will, will not allow the conflict to reveal itself in its true light, the warring elements must be disguised if they are to appear and discharge their spleen. Nature thus dictated to is indeed the mother of invention, and when, though the conflict calls urgently for settlement, its armies are not permitted to engage in open field, she finds ingenious means of evading the decree. Here, also, the " new " psychology has been the pioneer, has stripped the disguise from the combatants, and has mapped clearly the devious paths by which they reach the field of battle.

Before considering these defence mechanisms which the mind has evolved in order to protect itself from strangulated warfare, there are three general considerations to be stated.

(i) As we review them, we shall be struck by the fact that they are indulged in, not only by the neurotic, and even the insane, but by us all. There is here no sharp dividing line, as many think, between the normal and the neurotic, the sane and the insane, but a gradation of trouble which shades imperceptibly from the harmless fantasies of childhood, right to the secluded lunatic, or from the petty evasions and byways that we all allow ourselves, up to the world of delusion which encloses the maniac. The man who, in face of the real world, selfishly tries to build up a world of thought and imagination of his own, is very brother to the ruin who " glimmers dimly in the corners of our asylums." They are all revealed as dangerous, these little daily habits of ours, and the voice of psycho-therapy speaks not only to heal the neurotic, but to cleanse the more or less normal, and to declare the laws of ordinary mental hygiene. It tells of a downward path, easy to begin, but which, once begun and followed, leads without pause or turning to the perilous places of the mind ; and in so speaking, it surely echoes another Voice that also speaks of a broad and easy way.

(ii) What makes those tricks and mechanisms so dangerous, then, and produces the symptoms of the psycho-path ? It can be clearly discerned and laid down, that their danger varies in direct proportion to the power of the complex behind. Mental illness or functional nervous disorder vary in gravity, according to the strength and duration of the repressed feelings or instincts of the patient. What may be airy imaginings in a child, may become dangerous fantasies, when driven on the wings of a great complex, and the danger is not in the mechanism itself, be it fantasy or another, but in the impelling power behind it. The deeper the repression, the stronger is that impelling power, along whatever path released ; and the neurotic is simply a man whose complexes have been strong enough to overpower part of his personality, and force him to speak and think and act in ways which are anti-social and abnormal. The danger line is not crossed, moreover, when the symptoms of disorder become manifest to the eyes of others, and call for cure ; it was crossed long ere that, when repression took place, and the power-house of conflict was set up in a complex. And he is wise, who, noting the signs of an incubating symptom, a maturing complex, flies early to the therapist and eases his bosom of the perilous stuff.

(iii) The student of the New Testament, familiar with the system of moral values explicit there, at the fountain-head of the Faith (which differs vitally in emphasis and scope from that which sometimes bears the Founder's name) cannot but be deeply impressed by the fact, that when he reviews these evasions and mechanisms of the mind, and appreciates their danger, he is walking very near to familiar ground. To some, it will be a startling fact that the first to speak uncompromisingly of the gradual nature of the downward path, the evils of repression, and the risk involved in the use of these mechanisms, was Christ Himself. " Judge not, that ye be not judged " has a very familiar sound, when we read of Over-compensation and Projection ; the command regarding the " mote and the beam " was given long before Transference was heard of ; He who said to the paralytic " Thy sins are forgiven thee," and made *that* the condition of his cure, spoke of Conversion (in the psychological sense of that word) long before anyone ; when He spoke the parable of the pharisee and the publican, He made clear how much He knew of Unconscious Motive; and He who knew of the ominous and empty house of life, and of the seven who pounce on it, knew the powers and the limits of Catharsis. His followers have gone to the Old Testament and the Judaic Law for their model, and have endeavoured to make the mind fit the law; whereas Christ, Who " knew what was in man," first read the mind, and then stated its laws; and psychology but follows in His steps. His miracles of healing, of course, used as well, spiritual powers we have as yet hardly touched; but here we *can* understand, and marvel at His prophetic psychology.

II

When men want to evade the unpleasant, and resolve their conflicts, they do one or more of certain well-defined things.

(1) We take first, as the easiest to understand, the method of Fantasy; of all our mechanisms of defence the commonest, and like the rest, two-edged. We all escape to " Castles in the air," but such castles are dangerous only when we live in them all the time.

To realise that this is the commonest escape from life, one has but to recall the immense fictional and imaginative output of the novel, the stage, and the screen. When we see a play or read a novel, we do it to " escape from ourselves," or to " kill time," phrases which unconsciously reveal that we see in those new worlds of adventure and desire, some fantasy of our own lives writ plain. The emotion which catches us as we follow the imaginary, is a transferred emotion, for into those strange desires we read our own longings for freedom and fantasies of greatness. And when it is remembered that the love motive is the burden of nearly all such " escapes," the direction of our favourite fantasy, often unconscious, can be perceived. It

is a natural enough escape, and only becomes dangerous
with those who indulge in " drunk and disorderly " novel
reading, or feed on the cinema till it kills their appetite for
life.

Fantasy is always self-centred, and, on analysis,
reveals its origin in a complex, more or less mild, formed at
that stage of life when first we discovered that we were not
so clever as we imagined, and that the world passes by our
magnificence without a glance. That infantile secret, we all
repress, and in later life it emerges, often harmlessly, and
spends itself in fantasies of power, excitement, and adventure.
In some cases, when the repressed desires have become
extremely strong, owing to the inhibitory circumstances of
the life, which finds itself cribbed, cabined, and confined,
this way of escape can lead straight to the gates of the asylum,
which is populated in part by those unfortunates who have
let go the world, and live in everlasting fantasy. The man
who believes himself Napoleon or even Jesus Christ, has
found peace in his fantasy, but in an asylum, and at the
expense of both his intellect and the world.

The alert ear can detect the beating of the wings
of fantasy under many of the things we say of ourselves,
and the ways in which we deal with each other ; it is an
instructive and amusing occupation. Why do people say,
with a half-deprecatory endeavour to smile, " But of course,
I wasn't asked," if not to make their would-be humble words
conceal a fantasy of their own importance ? Why the hyper-
sensitiveness to the slightest criticism which so many display,
seeing insult and almost seeking it at every turn, if there be
not an underlying and powerful fantasy of their own immaculate perfection ? As we shall see when considering
Projection and Over-compensation, almost every over-exag-
gerated expression, say of humility or superiority or goodness, is upborne by fantasy, and declares its opposite.

Now the danger of fantasy is not that it turns its back on life and reality ; so do creative and legitimate imagination, in the realm of art. But whereas the latter is born of conscious ideals, and tries to express them honestly, the former comes from unconscious repression, and is fundamentally dishonest. It short-circuits effort, side-steps ideals, and denies the very truth the fabricator of it ought to face. It is not difficult to see how exaggerated and consistent fantasy-making leads to serious disorder. The struggle to live up to a fantasy, or the struggle to reconcile more than one, at once heads the maker of it straight for a nervous breakdown ; for even as fantasy refuses to face reality, reality has a perverse knack of refusing to face fantasy, and always overrides it in the end.

And when the neurotic does break down, he does so for one main reason, in order to preserve his fantasy ; his smash is purposive, though he does not consciously acknowledge it. " See what I *might* have done, had I not broken down ! Who knows how high I might have flown, but for my poor nerves ! " There was a half-truth in the old idea that " nerves " were an excuse ; for we now know that the disorder cries aloud, " Since fantasy plus health are not permitted by reality, then let health go ; fantasy or nothing." Clinics and consulting rooms know well the hobbling and the maimed psychopaths, whose maladies are self-induced, though unconsciously, in order to perpetuate their fantasies of power, fear, or sex ; and when the results of analysis are accepted by them, the body heals as by a miracle.

Religious fantasy can be the subtlest of all ministrants to an inflated self-assertion. The two girls who justified their leap to death from an aeroplane, because " An exception had been made " (by God) " in their case " ; the shrill critics of the Faith who prophesy in the columns of the

Letters to the Editor ; those who take it on themselves to issue rhodomontades of judgment in the name of the Church or of religion, without either the authority of that Church, or the experience of loving Faith ; one and all declare the commonest, the most insidious of all religious fantasies, namely, " I am an exceptional person ; God has made special concessions to me ; wisdom will die with me." They create the most foolish of all the paradises of the fool, by the self-administered flattery of their special favour in the eyes of God ; and it requires no great extension of that line of defence against the stern realities of God and the Christian Code, to lead the religious fantasiast very near religious mania, or the crazy solitude of the man who thinks that he alone in all the world knows and can interpret God.

III

(2) Projection is another, and a familiar mechanism, which is simply fantasy in more tangible form. It is the tendency present in us all, by which the unpleasant facts and faults in ourselves are fathered on to other people whom we meet ; by which repressed material in ourselves, is discharged by being " let out " on somebody else ; by which we project our own complexes onto the world around us, viewing it through complex-coloured spectacles.

" It is literally true that in judging others we trumpet abroad our secret faults. We personalise our unrecognised failings, and hate in others the very faults to which we are secretly addicted. We say their conduct is incredible, monstrous ! We are annoyed with the incompetence of others, only because we refuse to admit our own real incompetence. We are intolerant of the lazy, slovenly, footling ways of others, because this

tendency is a constant temptation to us. We condemn
the bigotry, meanness, or cynicism in others, because we
are potential bigots, misers, and cynics. We cannot bear
conceited people, because we are conceited without
knowing it. Saul breathed out threatenings and slaughter
against the Christians, probably because he was already
three parts a Christian. And on the other hand, we forgive
in others, what we desire to forgive in ourselves, for by
so doing, we temper the sting of self-condemnation.
Allow any man to give free vent to his feelings about
others, and you may with perfect safety turn and say,
" Thou art the man ! " [1]

The relief gained is instantaneous, for the projector admits
his own conflict, and passes judgment on his own faults, only
he does so in the person of somebody else, and thus obtains
the double benefit of the relief of repression, and the joy of
sitting in the seat of judgment, an act which always elevates
us in our own estimation.

This is a mechanism which impinges directly on the
sphere of morals and religion, as being one of the most
dishonest of them all. Fantasy is comparatively harmless
beside it, for fantasy harms only the mind that creates it ;
but this is twice cursed, harming both him that gives and
him that takes. It not only usurps the prerogative of God
in passing judgment, but assumes the rôle of God in assessing
the penalty also, and seeing that it is well and truly enforced.
The only refuge is that ruthless self-analysis, and that
tolerance which is just, because founded on the love of God
and our neighbour, which are the central postulates of the
gospel of Christ. Unfortunately however, self-analysis is
made very difficult in this regard, because one of the first
results of the habit, is the rapid numbing of the critical

[1] Hadfield : *Psychology and Morals*, p. 35.

faculty.   Self-righteousness is a very flattering medium through which to view the world and oneself, and its presence cancels out self-criticism.

In some respects, the habit constitutes a grave social danger. In extreme cases, the projector is deluded into accepting the repressed desire as a real fact of experience : and among the results of that are, for example, the false accusations made by unbalanced women of assault and rape, of paternity, or promise of marriage, and so on. To this danger, the doctor, the clergyman, and the social worker are alike exposed, and there are tragic histories on record, in which some frantic man or woman whose mind this mechanism has perverted, has objectified an obsession, and made ruin of a valuable life, by accusing it of that very thing their own complex unconsciously desired ; and it is found that most of such complexes are sexual ones. While, to go farther down the mental scale, the delusions of the insane, their voices heard and visions seen, are but projections of their own inner voices and images of their own disorder.

It may easily be seen, therefore, that one of the means by which the analyst diagnoses the nature of his patient's complex, is the study of this mechanism at work in his life. A man's hates and loves in the world around him are the echoes of his own repressed motives and desires, and point infallibly back to the inmost faults of the man himself ; and here, too, psychology has shown not only to the psychopath, but to the normal man, what a mirage of life this fateful habit projects, and what pitfalls there are at the feet of all of us.

(3) Inversion, or Over-compensation.   This is a mechanism akin to Projection, and is really a form of one of the oldest arts known to man, that of making a virtue of necessity. In order to keep down the things of which we are ashamed, and assure ourselves that they are properly

buried, our frequent tendency is to exaggerate their opposites in ourselves, to over-compensate our pendulum, so that it swings to the very extreme of its beat, to try to blot out that which we do not like, by standing on our heads to look at it.

It is a most familiar mechanism. Who does not know the loud and blustering type, whose motto is " I like to speak my mind ; no nonsense about *me* " ? Observe him well, and you see behind the sound and fury, a very timid and uncertain little soul indeed. The cock-sure man, for ever laying down the law, always dead certain he is right, compensates, by being dogmatic, for a very strong inferiority complex. Behind the flamboyant national motto " Wha daur meddle wi' me ? " is the most romantic and sensitive Celtic race. The haughty " I keep myself to myself " is not strength, but weakness hiding behind a mask. The man who stands firmly on his dignity has usually very little to stand on. The undersized man makes up for his lack of inches, by the size of his manners, and the bigness of his voice. The under-sexed and impotent, revel in smutty stories and imaginary exploits of passion. The woman of a certain type, hunts down like a vindictive tigress that other woman who has crashed morally. In religion, none are so bigoted as the converts from another sect ; the pharisee who prays " with himself," in the bitter word of Christ, and over-compensates in tithes of mint and anise and cummin, is not yet extinct. The list could be greatly extended by us all, and from our own experience ; but broadly speaking, whenever we hear, with the well-known emphasis, " I should never *dream* of doing it," or " I can't *imagine* what made her——," we may be well assured that the speaker both dreams and imagines the thing he scourges, and we can read the emotion of his emphasis like an open book. They do not see, these over-compensators, how thin is the defence they throw up to conceal reality ; like murder, reality *will* out, and make their deeds betray them.

It is a dangerous mechanism, though often a humorous one to observe. The phobias and obsessions, the ritual actions and perversions, which we shall review in the next chapter, are all tinctured by it, and are over-compensatory for some compelling fear, or anger, or sex drive. That which is so laughable and harmless in the old maid or the stout little man, becomes graver, when we see a neurotic convulsed and torn by exaggerated guilt, or wasting his days in performing some meaningless ritual, designed to keep his devil in subjection. It may be one of the great instincts which compels him to do and be these things, but the mechanism he selects is this one, so ordinary and so dangerous.

IV

(4) Conversion is the term chosen to represent a mechanism of great importance to the psycho-therapist, one which is fundamental to the understanding of nervous disorders, and which has nothing whatever to do with conversion in the religious sense of the word. It expresses itself in two ways, mental and physical.

(i) In the *mental* form, it consists simply in the transference of the emotion from a constellation of ideas which has been repressed as unacceptable, to another constellation, which we permit ourselves, and in this form, it is excessively common. The man who is intensely worried about his business, and takes it out on his unoffending wife and family at home, is an example ; so is the man who has been " done down " by a lawyer, and who transfers his hatred of that one firm, to the law in general, and all its works ; so is the man we all know, whose self-love has been injured by a fellow church member, who vows never to darken a church door again, and transforms his secreted instinct of self-assertion, into hatred of religion. The sexually starved woman, who becomes meticulously house-proud, or lavishes her heart out on a cat or a parrot ; or the cantankerous politician who is for ever " agin the government," simply because some boyhood slight has warped his self-esteem, are further examples, though perhaps extremer ones, of a habit to which nearly all are prone. These all convert the emotion they do not want into one they do, by opening up another channel for it than the blocked one, and so they achieve a certain peace and relief, at the price of truth.

It becomes clear, therefore, that this mechanism is at the root of the well-known neurasthenic symptom of extreme irritation at trifles, and of exaggerated importance attached to trivial details. The sufferer is working off his repressed conflicts and simply *has* to explode at a touch, because he will not allow his anger or his fear their proper outlets. On the Godward side of life, we have much to learn by observing it, for it is at the back of many a travesty of religion. The pharisee to whom reference has been made, was a type of religious neurotic, working off his secret inferiority and his fears, by excessive rituals and purifications, and his successors, whose religion begins and ends in vestments and genuflections, are with us yet. How many of the cruder ideas of expiation, old and new, seeing God as a judge Who might be bought off by various external posturings, were conceived at the bidding of this mechanism ! The root of the power and hold over men of the propitiatory idea, and of much of the old sacrificial system (which ideas still survive, disguised, in many a princely donor to charity, as in many a humbler man who " never misses a service ") can be found in the desire to work off the pricks and goads of sin, and silence the conscience, not by inner repentance and humility, but through the satisfaction gained in spectacular acts, or orgies of religion. Such men convert the emotions which ought to cleanse their hearts, into easier channels, and work them off, in order to go on as before ; it is a fraudulent conversion, an escape mechanism from the realities of God and sin.

(ii) *Physical.* In other cases, the mind seeks relief from an intolerable situation, by producing bodily symptoms, which are, as it were, symbols of the inner emotional conflict. While it is impossible in the present state of knowledge to say exactly along what paths the emotion is converted into physical disorder, and how far exactly it is satisfied thereby, there is no doubt of the connection between the underlying conflict, and the totally dissimilar symptom produced by it. The writer, for example, in the early part of a long analysis, suffered from a severe and well-defined sciatica, for which no possible physical reason could be found, but which was clearly the outward declaration of an inner emotional conflict, and which faded as the analysis progressed.

This part of our subject opens up too broad a field to be considered here, for it includes most forms of so-called hysterical manifestations, as well as those cases in which a definite trauma or nervous shock has immediate physical results. The group of symptoms called " hysterical " has grown far too large ; the word has become a convenience rather than a definition, having long outgrown its older and narrower limits, and tending to include almost every functional nervous disorder. But within the knowledge of all of us are simple examples of the partial riddance of distress effected by physical means, and the immediate symptom produced in the body by emotion. Blushing is a very well known example, as are mouth-watering and tears ; so are the frequent disturbances of heart or breath, skin or digestion, caused by emotional storms. It is only a difference in intensity and duration of emotion which produces more marked symptoms, say of bodily sensation, such as anæsthetic regions which may be cut or burned without any feeling of pain, or any bleeding ; or motor affections, such as contractures, local paralyses, and the like ; or affections of the senses, such as mutism, or blindness, like, for example, that of Paul at Damascus. All these have been observed and diagnosed in countless cases, but they will not, as a rule, come within the sphere of the minister or social worker. Yet he ought to know of their existence, their background, and their place in the general scheme, as well as the fact that psycho-therapy alone, without other and physical treatment, can effect most remarkable cures in just such cases, by the mere discovery of the emotion or instinct at fault, and its re-education along normal lines.

V

(5) Dissociation. From our study of the nature of the unconscious mind, and our observation of the isolated character of some complexes, the idea of an independent part of the personality, functioning, perhaps, in opposition to the conscious part, has become familiar. Extreme cases have been encountered and studied in minute detail, in which several distinct personalities have existed at the same time in one body, each occupying the stage at various times, and each contrasted with its neighbours in character, knowledge, and memories. These cases of split personality are, no doubt, quite abnormal, and result from severe shocks which have so deeply disintegrated the personality as that parts are completely splintered off, and manage to set up a separate existence within the psyche.

Lesser dissociations of the personality, however, are by no means uncommon in nervous disorders, and they frequently occur in ordinary life without attracting notice.

We all know, for example, the "religious" man, who on Sundays, can join with fervour and apparent sincerity his fellow-worshippers, and who, at home and in business, is hard, and mean, and unloving. The well-known ease with which we view as excessively sinful the sins of our neighbours, while passing no such strictures on our own, is a daily example of this tendency ; while, in the criminal, the opposing characteristics of extreme gentleness as a father and home-lover, and of cruel and vicious criminality are frequently observed. The psychopath, who finds no difficulty in separating his errors from his conscience, and who, despite his sensitiveness, will perpetrate the most amazing sins without a tremor, shows clearly that a large part of his personality is rigorously excluded from a share in his more normal activities, and that his particular complex not only lives apart, but is a law unto itself.

It is characteristic of those who thus live in pigeon-holes, not allowing religion to interfere with business, or family love with an immoral life, that they see no inconsistencies in so doing. They have succeeded in so separating the activities of their life, that for each water-tight compartment they seem to have a differing set of motives, morals, and emotions. Their conscience does not trouble them, and they are conscious of no inner conflict either of desire or instinct ; which is indeed an ominous symptom, betraying a deep dissociation within, such as has led to crises in many lives. Such a crisis often comes as surprisingly to the sufferer himself, as to his friends, for he has had no qualms, and they have seen no warnings. It must be emphasised that to live in dissociated ways of this kind has very grave results, and to feel no conflict regarding it is a mental anæsthesia of a very dangerous kind. When we come to the study of nervous disorders, we shall observe that dissociated or disintegrated personality is a prime characteristic of some of the worst among them, and that there is no part of the mind which is immune from it.

VI

Such are the chief mechanisms of the mind that desires to avoid too close contact with the reality of things. Before we pass from them, to consider the nervous disorders themselves, there is one thing to be said regarding them all. Those who use them, are obviously only too anxious to keep them in good running-order, or rather, in good running away order, and one of the main things which they use to lubricate the bearings, is the old and well-tried habit of excuse making. In psychology, this is called Rationalisation, and consists really in the art of being wise after the event, of producing what seems to be a perfectly good reason, but which is only an excuse for continuing to run away. It is a popular lubricant, and even the mildest Projector or Compensator will furnish you with excellent excuses for his hatred of so-and-so, or his dealings with himself, excuses which are far more excellent to the makers than to anyone else, rationalisings which make the conscience slippery, and reduce the wear and tear of the machine. The flaw in them is that they are not truth, but only rationalisings, that is to say, quite logical, only founded on bad premises, like the logic of children and of lunatics. The difference is only one of degree between these ordinary excuse makers, and your neurasthenic, who is full of plausible reasons for the cause or continuance of his illness, or your paranoiac, who lives in a perfectly rational system, and is completely logical, and yet has to be shut up, because it is all unreal.

CHAPTER VII

THE MALADJUSTED MIND

PSYCHOSES, NEUROSES, AND PSYCHO-NEUROSES

Classification of mental disorders ; the three major psychoses, Schizophrenia, Paranoia, and Manic-Depressive states ; all these need the physician ; the meaning of Neurosis ; Psycho-neuroses ; their two main characteristics ; their classification ; Neurasthenia ; its source in repression ; its religious aspect ; Anxiety states ; their prevalence ; their instinctual root.

I

ENOUGH has already been said to demonstrate the essential sanity with which psychology approaches the problems of the mind, and the clarity with which it defines, for example, the powers and scope of the Unconscious, and of the instincts, as well as the ways in which the flight from reality is conducted. That clarity and sanity are inducing an entirely new attitude towards mental disorders of every kind, and the long horror with which the thought of mental illness has for ages been enclouded, is being dispelled. Though there are certain accurately delimited and extreme states from which there is no recovery, yet these are few in comparison to the far larger number of disorders, for which new hope has been ministered by psycho-therapy ; and that awful border-line between sanity and insanity, which having crossed, a man was marked and doomed, has largely disappeared. On the other hand, certain mysterious and abnormal manifestations for which no adequate reason had ever been found, and yet which occurred with a distressing

frequency in valuable lives, are now explicable, and their
diagnosis and healing, in very many cases, have been made
sure. Right understanding is ever a solvent of intolerance,
and here, as elsewhere, the average and traditional code of
morality finds its values subtly, but decisively changed ; not
that sin can ever be aught but sinful, but the emphasis is
altered, and where we now see a clear illness, we have learned
to restrain the word of judgment, and are thus approximating
more closely to the mind of Christ.

          In proceeding to explore and understand the more
clearly defined mental disorders, the need for such understanding on the part of the minister or social worker, must be again
affirmed. Let no one think that such explorations are the
exclusive right of the doctor, or that their terms are too
technical for the non-medical man, for they are not. The
Christian psycho-therapist ought to have a working knowledge of at least the extent of the field, before he can go on
to apply Christian methods in it. At the outset, then, there
are three terms to be explained, each of which covers a
certain part of the field, namely, Psychosis, Neurosis, and
Psycho-Neurosis.

          (1) *Psychosis.*—The word is used to cover three
very severe types of mental illness, which are far more
than disorders, and with which only the skilled physician can
deal. If they are mentioned here at all, it is in order that,
perceiving their symptoms, the minister or other person
consulted, can at once direct the patient and his family to the
proper place.

          (*a*) It has been said that if one were to visit any
of the great asylums, and ask the doctors in charge what type
of mental disease brought most of its inmates, he would use
the word Schizophrenia, and say that the disease was irre-
coverable. It is a Greek derivative, and signifies " broken or
split personality " ; it replaces an older term, Dementia

Præcox (which means loss of mind, especially characteristic of early youth) being introduced by Bleuler in 1911 as more accurate, since youth is no criterion of the illness. Schizophrenia is a condition of the mind, in which the unity of the personality is broken into several complete self-governing entities, disintegrated into subsidiary personalities, each speaking and acting on its own, so that all normality is lost. It takes many forms, and has many degrees, but through them all one central symptom is manifested, by which it can always be recognised; the sufferer gives evidence that all the holds on life and reality of which we are normally aware, are being slowly and surely loosened, and that he is being more and more ruled by the shadowy personalities he has himself created. The other symptoms of the schizophrenic state—such as incoherence, emotional instability, attention to bizarre hallucinations and delusions—are of enormous variety, cannot be detailed here, and are, in any case, not usually met with outside the walls of an asylum. The essential thing to remember is, if there be any suspicion that this state lies behind any observed symptom, the doctor must at once be called in. Two observations may be added, that it is very slow and gradual in its onset, and that there are in it strong hereditary elements.

(b) Paranoia is the name of the second type of illness, and means, literally, a mind " beside itself." It is an illness which does not affect the patient's mind, except at one or two points, leaving him, in all other respects, capable of the activities of life ; and even those insane points, he is able to co-ordinate quite logically with the rest of his experience. Most of us have met the patient who is able to converse and act normally for long periods, till ONE subject is broached, which, like the releasing of a spring, reveals a hopeless aberration. Paranoiac thinking is curiously common, even among the sane ; the harping on a grievance, the building up of a system of deluded gossip on imperceptible grounds, or the milder fantasies of persecution, are all ordinary enough examples of paranoiac thinking. Between these and the true paranoid, whose life is dominated and enclosed by a fixed idea or a delusion, there is a very wide range of disorder. This delusion, unlike that of the schizophrenic, is fixed, elaborated, and logically systematised ; it is of slow growth, and to minister to that growth every circumstance of life is bent and warped. Here, too, when met with, however persuasive, logical or plausible the patient may seem when supporting his idea, only a doctor can deal with the case, and his verdict on it will not be a hopeful one.

(c) A distinction used formerly to be made, between states of mind which were known as maniac, characterised by wild racing of the machinery, and those which were melancholic, where all was black in the outlook. It is now recognised that these are opposite and alternative manifestations of the same trouble, now called the Manic-Depressive state. Its characteristic is that the pendulum swings from one extreme to the other, with an intervening period, more or less brief, of normality, and that this swing recurs with predictable regularity. Single states of mania or depression occur in other diseases, but this one is marked by the alternating periods of elation and depression being complementary to each other. Wherever, therefore, in consultation, even mild states of either are observed, wisdom dictates investigation of the past history of the case, and if complementary symptoms have at any time been marked, it should be assumed to be a Manic-Depressive condition, and the doctor called in. Here, too, there is a strong element of hereditary predisposition which may help in diagnosis, and unlike the other two, this state is recoverable under wise treatment, though there is, of course, a marked tendency for the symptoms to recur.

These are the three main Psychoses ; and while

advising that should suspicion of any of them present itself in investigation, a doctor be at once called in, a word may be said regarding the third, and the help which a tranquillising and sane religion may give. That word is said here and not in the later chapters which deal with treatment, because we do not return to the subject of the Manic-Depressive states. Experience has shown that in these states, nothing can alleviate uncomprehended depression, or put the brake on elation, or hasten and prolong the period of normality, like the quiet and steady observances of religion, even though the clouded mind cannot at the moment fully understand them. Should the sufferer have to be secluded for a time, he ought to carry into that seclusion the certainty that he will recover, and that he must, at all costs, maintain the ordinary practices of the religious life. Give him that twofold counsel, and urge him, even though all is dark and Faith seems useless, to continue to pray, to attend his church, to make his Communion, in trust and patience. If he puts his darkened mind in the constant presence of God, the promise will not fail.

II

(2) *Neurosis.* A certain amount of confusion has been caused by the use of this word, to cover illness which is psychogenetic (*i.e.* of purely mental origin), as well as that caused by disorder of the physical nervous system. The latter is the true Neurosis, and it seems simpler to reserve the use of the word for it alone. A neurosis is thus an ailment of the actual nerve itself, inflammatory or other, and the word ought not to be used, as it sometimes is, as equivalent to the popular word "nerves." This latter word, indeed, is often used as a species of vague label, with which to cover all manner of uncomprehended mental symptoms, and, so used, has no accuracy whatever ; because, though psycho-somatic

unity is a fact, and though the nervous system may be, and often is, affected by a mental disorder, the primary cause is that mental disorder, and the actual " nerves " have nothing to do with the symptoms. The true Neurosis, therefore, is obviously an illness with which only the neurologist can deal, and our strict limitation of the use of the word to cover such illnesses clarifies the issue, and leaves us free to turn to that great field which is the primary concern of this book.

III

(3) *Psycho-Neurosis.* The word is used to define those many disorders of the mind whose root cause is acquired, whose symptoms may be both mental and physical, and in which each symptom points to some instinct, motive, or idea. In contradistinction to the Psychoses, which imply in nearly every case a congenital or hereditary mental defect, they are acquired in the course of life, and while, like the Neuroses, they have neural symptoms, these are secondary, and the root of the disorder is usually instinctual, and always psychogenetically determined.

Two broad preliminary characteristics of them all may be stated :

(a) With proper treatment, all the psycho-neuroses are recoverable ; and this definite statement is the direct outcome of the research and experience of the " new " psychology. For the first time, the psycho-neuroses are not only classified and understood, but, whatever their duration or severity, a course of treatment can be indicated, which will extirpate them, and re-establish the mind on normal lines. Relapses there may be, but these are caused by the non-co-operation of the patient, not by the errors of psychology ; and it is of course obvious, that without a whole-hearted desire to recover, and a sincere rapport between patient and therapist, no lasting results can be won. Given those, relief occurs with a certainty and promptitude, which are unparalleled in any other treatment whatever.

(*b*) Psycho-neuroses are always distinguishable from other mental illnesses, by the fact that the patient is aware of his illness. Unlike the psychotic, who is content in his delusions, and never able to see how far astray he is, the psycho-neurotic is self-conscious, and has a certain amount of insight into his own disorder. From every interview one carries away the clear impression, that behind all the mysterious symptoms he loves to detail, there is an awareness of, and almost a pride in, his own defects. It is this very awareness of his own condition, which not only makes co-operation possible, but gives a valuable diagnostic clue when one tries to determine whether the illness is psychotic, or psycho-neurotic.

The chief psycho-neurotic states can be defined as Neurasthenias; Anxiety states; Dissociated states; states in which the complex is symbolised in Phobias, Obsessions, Inhibitions, or Compulsions; and though the surface symptoms differ so widely, that each case seems almost a law unto itself, yet, when we probe under the apparent variety, we find broadly similar currents of disorder. This tracking down of isolated and highly individualised symptoms to a common root, is one of the first tasks of the psycho-therapist, and he finds that (unlike physical illnesses, which can be clearly classified as to their causes, symptoms, and course, with small variability) in the psycho-neuroses, the most diverse and puzzling symptoms may, in different cases, point to one and the same thing.

IV

(A) *Neurasthenia :* a psycho-neurosis of frequent occurrence and widely varying intensity. The primary symptom of the neurasthenic is fatigue, chronic weariness

of body and mind, which, whatever he attempts, cripples his
every effort. Unlike ordinary fatigue, no obvious reason can
be assigned for it, and it takes the form of a perpetual dragging
depression, a pervasive weight, which makes the whole of
life one long pull up a steep hill. Constant headache, pain,
especially in the back, weak eyes, inability to concentrate,
irritability—these are ever with him.

> " He begins each day with a sense of mental
> and physical exhaustion, which is accentuated by every
> effort he makes. Mental work produces headache or a
> sense of pressure on the head, reading produces tired eyes
> or a sensation of spots in front of them, standing makes his
> back ache, walking makes his legs and feet ache, sitting
> gives him cramp, food gives him dyspepsia, and excite-
> ment prostrates him completely. Every form of activity
> has its appropriate Nemesis for him, except the discussion
> of his illness. In this case, the signs of exhaustion are
> apt to appear first in the physician." [1]

And the very absence of positive symptoms such as fever,
or acute pain, is an added distress ; so he becomes vale-
tudinarian, and magnifies trifles into cancer or consumption.

The true causes of all this, are for the first time
understood, and neurasthenia seen as a very definite illness,
to be explained in terms of conflict and repression. Whatever
the symptoms, the illness has a twofold cause : strong and
unconscious repression of some instinctual desire, and the
resultant struggle of its energy to express itself. The net
result is, that the energy which ought to be used in the
conduct of daily life is not available, being spent elsewhere,
and life becomes one long unenergised drag. An echo of this
unseen battle is to be heard in the very obvious anxiety of

[1] H. Yellowlees : *Manual of Psycho-Therapy*, p. 163.

9

the neurasthenic, which in turn, magnifies all other symptoms, and forms a vicious circle of exaggeration.

To take but one example : clinical experience shows that a great deal of neurasthenia is caused by the misuse or repression of the sex instinct. According to Freud, it is all so caused, but Freud's use of the word sexual is, as we have seen, unwarrantably broad. Where the sex instinct is misused, as in habits of auto-erotism, a double drain on energy is caused ; on the one hand, acute feelings of remorse and guilt have to be bottled up, and on the other, the auto-erotist has to work up that excitation for himself, which normally comes from outside. It is, however, idle to say, as so many popular pamphlets do, that auto-erotism alone produces neurasthenia, for auto-erotism is itself a symptom and not a cause ; and while it undoubtedly has physical effects, if practised to excess, these in most cases are negligible beside the mental results. Where again, the sex instinct is repressed in whole or in part, and no efferent whatever is provided for its energy, neurasthenic signs immediately occur, as do others much more positive, since, as we have seen, instinctual repressed energy tends to burrow, and must reappear.

This factor of repression becomes very evident in the interviews with the neurasthenic, for though his conflict be unconscious, he gives always the strong impression of hiding something; and in case after case, behind his volubility, part of him is ever on guard, and his censor is awake. The more he talks, the more clear it is, that there is something he does not wish to talk about, and until his resistance is broken down, and the hidden " something " dragged out, no release will come. This " emotional preoccupation," as it has been called, is an almost universal symptom of the neurasthenic, and, when elucidated, it is the first key to his repression and his conflict.

What has been said above regarding the sex instinct, can be extended to the rest of instinctual life. Resentment against the parent, or fear of life, or thwarted self-love, can issue in the like symptoms of distress ; and, let it be very clearly stated, so can repression of the Fear of God and of the spiritual desires of the mind. Neurasthenia can be caused by bad faith with God, as well as by bad faith with life. Nothing is commoner in religious experience, than for a man to throttle down the clear demands of his conscience, or to deny what is an obvious intimation of the unseen. It is perfectly possible, and very usual, to try to de-sensitise the mind of its God-perceptive instinct, but it cannot be done without results ; and why, if the psychologist's " reality " refuses thus to be mocked, and inevitably asserts itself, do we deny the same power to God ? While it is undoubtedly true to say that much neurasthenia is sexual in its origins, it is equally true to say that those who have so looked for its origins, have not had either the experience or the technique with which to inquire into the abuses of the religious instinct, and have therefore labelled the unsatisfied " Incomplete instinct " as sexual or gregarious, nor have they so much as asked the man how he stands with God. The energy men spend in keeping out God, and denying that His is the moral law, is known only to those who are themselves equipped to see the spiritual. Why, therefore, should it be said that there is no connection between the increase of neurasthenia and of overstrain in modern times, and the very obvious repression of the religious instinct which exists ?

V

(B) *Anxiety states*. These form a large and well-defined group, fundamentally akin to the neurasthenic states, though their symptoms are very different. Both are

caused by repressions, but in the Anxiety state, some of the
energy which is repressed, gets out, and instead of being given
its channel, is directed like a kind of spray over the whole of
life, and the sufferer presents a picture of anxious, restless,
and wrongly directed energy. It is thus unlike Neurasthenia,
in that it is the result, not of a total, but of a partial and
incomplete inhibition, which finds its outlet in the mental
symptoms of anxious fear, and in bodily symptoms of tremor,
palpitation, or disturbance.

Incipient and temporary anxiety states are
common to us all, and we can, therefore, the more sym-
pathise with the man, to whom life, in all its phases, is one
long "stage fright," who rises with it, lives with it, and
passes broken nights with fear beside him on his pillow.
It is a state which manifests itself in widely varying
symptoms, only now beginning to be understood. It is
sometimes expressed in acute but occasional paroxysms of
nameless fear, but more usually, in a day-long vague anxiety,
referred to everything with which the sufferer lives. The
slightest circumstance of life is fearfully surveyed and long
debated, from getting up, through eating and working, to
retiring again, and the lightest decision is an agony, and the
smallest responsibility a millstone. It is a tragic sight,
often superficially labelled " overstrain," to see such a man,
whose staring eyes and tense body, startled movements and
hammering pulse, betray the fear with which he lives ; and
the more tragic, because he can put no name to it, or give a
reason for what he still can know as unreasonable. His
anxieties and fears are, therefore, attached to any circumstance of his life which would seem to allow it, and he
magnifies the danger of sickness or death or disaster out of
all proportion, till " the grasshopper is a burden," and all
desire fades out from life.

This is a much more common state than is

supposed, and every case, when examined, reveals disorder in one or more of the instincts, as for example, and very frequently, extreme sexual tension, and deficiency of opportunity for its outlet; that is to say, repression (not suppression) of the instinct, and the blocking of all its normal channels of release. A twofold type of reaction can be noted, according to whether that block is caused by some circumstance of the patient's present life, or by some wrong development in his remote past; and, in either case, some of the energy so repressed, is transformed directly by some inscrutable alchemy of the mind, into morbid fears and anxiety.

It is deeply impressive, to find in case after case that comes for consultation, this root sexual cause appearing on investigation, as the unconscious source of all the trouble; and to see, when it has been possible to rearrange the life, the fears automatically subside, and the anxieties become those of the normal man.

" The essential factors of undue excitation and inadequate relief of tension, are found in such cases as that of certain men in late middle age, when there is disproportion between desire and potency; they are also to be found in young persons during some such stage of tension as a prolonged engagement; and they are most frequently and typically found in cases where harmful methods for the prevention of conception have been resorted to, in particular, incomplete coitus, which is said to be by far the most frequent single cause of the psycho-neurosis. Various accessory factors, such as grief, worry, and mental strain of any kind, of course, play a part in the production of the psycho-neurosis, and may, in many cases, be the factors which lower the patient's resistance and permit of its establishment;

but the essential factor of disproportion between sexual excitation and sexual discharge is invariably present." [1]

In another type of case, the repression is that of the instinct of flight, the desire to escape from some dangerous fact of life, met by the impossibility of doing so. The act of " screwing up one's courage to the sticking point " which we know so well, implies the suppression of the instinct to run away ; but if there be repression and not suppression, the issue is a morbid state of anxiety about everything, and not only the particular thing feared.

When, therefore, the urge towards completeness is consistently denied and refused its outlet or its sublimation, this state of fear is found to be among the consequences. The alchemy which changes repressed desire into fear, is partly caused by the abnormal guilt feelings which accompany the repression of sexual or other desire, and partly by the repressed resentment with life which is always to be observed in these anxiety states. If, therefore, the " Incomplete instinct " when denied expression, pours itself out through channels of guilt and anger, into outward fears and anxieties, it becomes at once obvious what an advantage the Christian psycho-therapist has in this regard. As we shall see, his is the only method which can truly sublimate impossible sexual desires, by taking the Incomplete instinct there manifested, and guiding it towards its highest manifestation in the Religious instinct ; in so doing, casting out all fear.

[1] H. Yellowlees : *Manual of Psycho-Therapy*, p. 187.

CHAPTER VIII

THE MALADJUSTED MIND (*continued*)

The second great group, the Dissociated states ; their nature ; three broad characteristics of them all ; Dissociated states in which bodily symptoms predominate, *e.g.*, Automatisms, Tics, Sleep-walking, etc. ; hysterical distortions of the senses ; Dissociated states in which mental symptoms predominate, *e.g.* Phobias, Obsessions, and Compulsions ; Kleptomania, and Alcoholic addiction ; a spiritual root in all these maladjustments.

I

THE second great group of mental maladjustments may be called the Dissociated States ; that is, states in which the unity of the personality is more or less seriously interfered with, by the energy of repressed complexes, so that part or parts of the personality are dissociated from the main stream, work independently, and produce by unconscious operation, bodily and mental symptoms of the most diverse kind. This type of abnormality is very frequent, and almost infinitely varied, so much so, as to present great difficulties in classification. These states are sometimes called Hysterical, but the use of that word is to be deprecated, for three reasons ; because it has become firmly embedded in popular vocabulary, and means there a very limited, though a neurotic manifestation ; because it conveys no such single characteristic of all the types included in this class, as the word we have chosen ; and because it has come, in the use of various writers, to include practically every mental maladjustment, short of the psychoses. It seems clearer, therefore, to use the word Dissociated for those states, because, under all their variations, in them all, the integration of the personality is more or less interfered with.

It is, however, of interest to recall that the phenomena of ordinary, or popularly so-called Hysteria, were the first to attract the attention of Janet and Freud, the pioneers of modern psychological research, and that its symptoms were the pointers which led to the revelation of the powers of the unconscious ; the attempt to evaluate the characteristics of an illness which had puzzled medical science for centuries, was itself the beginning of a great new science. There was also an interesting foreshadowing of the truth, in the choice by the doctors of old, of the very word Hysteria, for it was their idea that in it, the womb, or " hystera " was displaced, and appeared in other parts of the body ; and it is now known that much Dissociation of the personality is caused by repression or displacement of the sex instinct, and the reappearance of its energies elsewhere.

In these states, then, we are presented with the spectacle of an auxiliary stream of mental activity, more or less dissociated from, and in opposition to, the main current of the personality. How does it achieve expression ? Obviously, along the two avenues of body and mind ; and this division may supply us with a convenient basis for classification, though it ought to be remembered that symptoms rarely occur singly, and that they may be grouped in all possible permutations and combinations.

II

Here, again, three broad preliminary characteristics may first be noted.

(i) The isolation of symptoms from the main body

of conscious activity is very marked. They are frequently manifested in direct opposition to the conscious desire of the patient, and carry an emotional content out of all proportion to the ordinary emotional life. Obsessive and revolting thoughts ; meaningless storms of so-called hysterical emotion ; sudden contractures or paralyses of the motor system ; twitches, tics, or automatisms ; we say on seeing them, that they are " unlike " the sufferer, meaning thereby that they are not only outside his volition, but apart from his normal life of thought and emotion. Widely though they may differ on the surface, they may easily have a common root in one great complex, and their intractability, their very unlikeness to anything else in the known man, proves the independence and the strength of that complex.

(ii) One curious proof of that strength is the pervasive power possessed by a complex. It seems to have infective characteristics, and to be able not only to work within its own domain, but also to colour the main stream of personality. Though he is well aware that he is ill, and has a seemingly sincere desire for recovery, the patient often makes irritatingly slow progress, and, when one symptom is ameliorated, he will substitute a new, and perhaps totally dissimilar one, and appear to be back at the beginning again. The true parasitic nature of a complex is nowhere better seen : it proves its life, and expresses its unwillingness to be " squeezed out," by twining its roots with those of the main stem, and interpenetrating every branch.

(iii) In the dissociated states, we have passed beyond mere Repression, with whose effects we were concerned in the last chapter. The immediate effect of simple repression is conflict and distress for the patient, consciously manifested ; but when dissociation takes place, and the repressed energy is let out in a symptom, mental uneasiness and distress are curiously absent from the normal

life of the patient. It is as if the complex repressed, has
sunk to a deeper level in the unconscious, and become utterly
blotted out from memory, so producing no direct symptoms
of distress ; it expresses itself, not through the anxieties of
neurasthenia, but by intruding upon the normal personality,
and taking control of part of its activities, or even by abolishing it altogether from time to time. This factor of relief
from mental distress in the patient is very marked, and has
been called " unnatural indifference," or, by the French,
" une belle complaisance," and it is proof that the strength
of the complex has passed beyond merely mental affects, and is
able to express itself outwardly. It explains, too, the cheerful
callousness of so many patients to the graver consequences
of their symptoms on others in their surroundings ; they
have, in this respect. literally passed beyond distress, and
there is no moral stigma to be attached to their hard-
heartedness.

The following are, in brief, some of the more
obvious manifestations of the Dissociated State. It must be
clearly understood that they *are* briefly indicated, and are
only the more common ; to do anything more detailed, would
need a whole text-book. And while the differentiation is
made between bodily and mental symptoms, it must be
remembered that in every case, bodily symptoms are the
direct expression of mental disorder, and must be regarded,
both in diagnosis and treatment, from the mental, and not
the bodily end.

III

(A) Dissociated States in which BODILY symptoms
predominate.

(a) Automatisms. These are uncontrolled and
uncontrollable symptoms occurring, some during normal
consciousness, some when consciousness is abrogated (as in

somnambulism), and are widely varied, ranging from simple
bodily affects like tics and paralyses, to sleep-walking, fugues,
and automatisms of speech and writing.

A " Tic " is a recurrent twitch of some group of
muscles, often facial, sometimes of larger muscles, such as
those of a limb, and is always a resultant of mental disorder
and shock. Analogous to tics, are the cases where involuntary
or stereotyped movements are made, or where paralysis of
one or more groups of muscles is maintained ; as are also the
" hysterical fits " commonly observed, and which vary
from overwhelming emotional outbursts, to convulsions akin
to those of epilepsy. In each and all of such cases, an attempt
is being made by the underlying and unconscious force to
express itself, sometimes very indirectly, as in a facial tic ;
sometimes more directly in a forced involuntary movement,
which reproduces exactly, a movement that occurred at a
moment of forgotten trauma (*i.e.* shock) ; or sometimes in a
hysterical fit, which reveals itself on analysis as a more or
less successful attempt to reproduce the emotions of some
traumatic experience lying at the root of the dissociation.

These are obviously cases in which a comparatively
small part of the personality is dissociated ; only enough to
cause those very partial, though very disturbing symptoms.
A far graver dissociation is indicated, when the operating
complex is so large as to force the sufferer into what is called
a "Fugue." A fugue occurs, when a man suddenly disappears
from his normal haunts, and is found, often much later,
living in a totally dissimilar place, with no recollection
whatever of his ordinary life ; or else comes suddenly " to
himself," amazed, and with no consciousness of how or when
he left his home. Here, so grave a split has taken place, that
the dissociated part can present to the onlooker the appearance
of normality, and can function for long periods without
arousing suspicion of disorder. Some very profound shock

has caused it, and it is usually found that the secondary personality expresses a regression, more or less infantile, and is realising a long repressed fantasy. The fact that each such personality is amnesic of the other, that their characteristics are widely dissimilar, and that the secondary one can so impose itself as to blot out the older and normal one for long periods, is indicative of the independence, as well as of the strength, of a complex " adrift and roving " within the mind.

A precisely similar state of affairs occurs in sleep-walking, only there, the dissociation is not so grave. Normality retains control during waking hours, and only when consciousness is in abeyance, is the secondary personality strong enough to force the body into action, and produce the phenomena of sleep-walking. " Automatic writing " is akin to the somnambulistic state, only, in this case, the subject is awake, but totally unconscious of the movement of the hand. Without trespassing at all on the domain of the spiritualists, it can clearly be said that the unconsciousness is genuine, and the hand truly anæsthetic, but that on analysis, and especially under hypnotism, the writing can frequently be shown to have been the expression of repressed and unconscious experience.

Abundant clinical evidence of all these automatisms is available in any text-book of medical psychology, and the most interesting generalisation to be made from them all, especially those of the last two paragraphs, is, that each gives its own proof of the activity of the dissociated part, an activity often elaborate, which thinks, plans, and acts, and has in it intelligence and purpose. There is, of course, unconscious motive and purpose, even in a Tic ; but a true Fugue is an impressive mental phenomenon, and one whose study opens up the whole implications of personality and consciousness. Research into such " multiple personality " is one of the most fascinating parts of the new psychology

and it has important repercussions in the moral sphere.
It furnishes one more proof of those deep powers of the
unconscious, in that it can, when called on, furnish forth
a complete secondary personality, with thoughts, desires,
and purposes of its own, independent of, and outside the
control of, those of the conscious personality. Treatment
which can synthesise the complex-personality and the normal
one, and cause both to flow together in common emotion and
desire, is logically bound to deepen and enrich the psyche.

(b) Closely akin to the Automatisms, and arising
from precisely similar causes, is a vast group of symptoms
which are known to affect nearly every part and organ of
the body ; and here, again, the vital consideration is, that
under all their outward variety, each and every affect,
no matter where, is a visible token of an inward dissociation. Each sense can be affected ; we have blindness
and deafness, total or partial, as well as mutism or stuttering ;
very commonly, there is anæsthesia of large tracts of the skin
(noted, in the old days, as the sign of a witch), or, on the
contrary, hyper-æsthesia and irritability. Every form of
digestive disturbance, as well as disorders of the heart and
lungs, have been observed in this connection ; and in brief,
not to catalogue what is, after all, varied only on the surface,
but identical in origin, a psycho-genetic symptom can be
projected on to any part of the organism which the
unconscious may choose for its own purposes. Such
symptoms are relieved, not by treatment directed towards
the merely bodily affect, as was attempted for centuries,
but only by treatment which begins at the mental end, and
seeks the complex there. When that can be done, and the
complex released, the symptom instantaneously loosens,
and finally disappears. True Faith Healing is another, and
a very deep matter, which enshrines a mighty spiritual
reality ; but there is no doubt that this instantaneous

phenomenon lies at the root of the so-called miracles of healing, that happen where no real Faith is, and where a blundering hand has hit on the secret of release.

IV

(B) Dissociated states in which MENTAL symptoms predominate.

In the previous chapter, something has been seen of the mental effects of repression, and we have now to see how the dissociated complex can produce its mental, as well as its bodily repercussions. In this case, however, the repressed energy manifests mentally, not as a diffused and general anxiety or weakness, but as a phobia, a compulsion, or an obsession which is more or less directly associated with the idea repressed, and which is a symbol of its power. Such rituals of fear and compulsion, act as escape mechanisms, to prevent the sufferer from getting too near the intolerable complex, and they always reveal themselves, on analysis, as symbols of that complex. He symbolises the psychological material which he dare not face, in a compulsive act or thought. There is, therefore, opened up an entirely new approach to a vast group of very perplexing cases, such as drink or drug addicts, kleptomaniacs, and the like ; and while it is true that in the first two of those types, other, and physical causes may co-operate in producing and prolonging the craving, it is a new and blessed experience to see in how many cases, the mental causes of repression and escape reveal themselves on analysis, and respond to treatment in a manner which, on the surface, looks miraculous.

(a) Phobias are exceedingly common forms of this mental compensation, this compromise mechanism, by which one thing or class of things, is singled out by the patient, and made the object of intense and uncontrollable

fear. Any approach to, or thought of, those things is a
terror to him, and he will elaborately and painfully rearrange
his whole life in order to avoid them. A number of Greek
derivatives have been used to define some of the more usual
of these phobias. Claustrophobia is the terror of enclosed
surroundings, and makes narrow spaces or rooms, and
especially railway carriages or lifts an unspeakable torture ;
Agoraphobia is its opposite, and is the terror of open spaces
or of crowds of any kind ; and both are frequent. There
are, again, the terror of height, Aerophobia, and the fear of
lightning, Astraphobia. Any such Phobia has usually a twin
root ; it is begun by some incident of terror, often, but not
always, in childhood, and while the incident itself is totally
repressed, blotted from memory, and recoverable only on
analysis, the fear remains, dissociated from its source, and
attached to the symbolic objects of the Phobia. There are
thus both trauma and fear associated with its beginning,
and when these are reassociated and restored to conscious
memory, the Phobia vanishes.

(b) Obsessions and Compulsions ; a Compulsion
being simply an Obsession translated into action. These
vary enormously in degree, from the very mild obsessions
most people have, as to what is lucky or unlucky for them
to do, up through the complicated rituals the psychopath
imposes on himself in order to " square " life, to the extreme
compulsions of alcohol and other drugs. Many of them are
nearly Phobias, with the difference that in this group, the
fear is symbolised, not in an object, but in a compulsive act,
or acts. Obsessions, again, may be purely mental, taking
the form of the fixed idea, or of morbid scrupulosity, and
they may be regarded as the direct complements of Inhibition. When we inhibit anything, it tends to return as an
obsession ; we may take as an example, the obsessive results
in modern writing and life of the Victorian inhibition of sex.

The root idea beneath all their varied forms, is the idea of escaping from something terrifying and intolerable, or of effecting some compromise with life, which will allow the performer to slip by, without facing the abhorred reality, or of expiating by some ritual, the half-personified antagonisms around him. In each case, that root idea is not consciously expressed, and the compulsive act or thought is quite outside volition. It is the direct outcome of unconscious repression, it expresses unconscious motive, and it is driven outwards by unconscious energies ; and only when those forgotten traumas, desires, and forces are recovered through analysis, will the obsession slacken and disappear.

V

Kleptomania, for example, one of the commonest forms of the compulsive act, has been found in very many cases, to have its origin in some sexual trauma of childhood, and in general, to be intimately associated with sexual repression ; even the superficial observer can note how many of the reported cases are those of women at, or near, the profound disturbances of the menopause. An allied " mania " (though the word is really quite out of place in this connection) is what the French call *manie de toucher*. It may take the form of a morbid dread of infection, expressed in incessant hand-washings, and terror of touching people and things ; or of the fear of *not* touching, and express itself in ritual compulsions of being forced to touch certain objects, before doing anything at all. In both these examples, the " mania " is the expression of some thing unconsciously dreaded ; but in other cases, it may be the expression of some thing unconsciously still desired, which was desired and forbidden in childhood, by one or other parent. Mild examples of this are the tendency to use " bad " language,

or to rebel against authority, and do the exact opposite of
what is suggested, while graver examples may be noted in
certain forms of sex perversion. It is only a step from such
tendencies to the tyranny of the " fixed idea," and the
torture of the " obsessive idea." The former often takes
the form of the persecution mania in one or other of its
many forms, and may, unless dislodged, lead directly into
paranoia, while the latter often appears as an intrusive
obscene or sacrilegious idea or word, and imposes an almost
intolerable anguish of effort to keep it under. Both are
capable of disorganising the whole of life, and draining it
of its strength, and here also, only analysis can get at, and
dislodge the roots from the mind.

     No affliction to which frail man is liable is more
distressing to society, more complicated in its origins and
more difficult to unravel and eradicate than the habits of
alcoholic excess, or of drug taking. It has been an age-long
puzzle, and one to which no complete solution has even yet
been found. Physical means have been tried, but have
succeeded only where the causes of the habit are demon-
strably physical and organic ; indeed, the only known cure is
a genuine and lasting religious conversion. But in the new
knowledge we have gained here, lies not only a valuable
clue as to the origins of the habit, but a curative agency
of immense possibility, and one whose results are daily
multiplying.

     No part of its symptoms is more difficult to under-
stand than the overmastering power of desire inherent in the
habit, a desire which often cuts across all knowledge, all
volition, and all Faith, and pulls its victim down again and
again ; and it is this repetitive strength of temptation which
is the despair of the reformer in all such cases. But when
we grasp that the man does not act so because he is a devil
incarnate, and desires to poison himself and ruin his life for

10

evil's sake, but because his drink or his drug gives him something which he feels he needs, and which he can get in no other way known to him, we see a ray of light. It is most frequently an " escape " that he needs, an escape from some intolerable fact óf his life, a fact which need not necessarily be a conscious one, but which may lie deep hidden and repressed. This alone goes far to explain the compulsive power and the duration of such habits, and when we regard them from this angle, and begin to apply to them the logic of psychology, our ray of light broadens, and new hope is given for a most intractable situation. It may be escape from a life which has gone wrong socially or domestically, or from a dead monotony of work, or from a periodic depression, or from an inhibitory shyness which yields only to the fictitious release of alcohol, or it may simply arise from a craving for " happiness " ; but from whatever cause it arises, we have taken a long step towards cure, when we trace the reason of the mysterious search for release to its source in forgotten trauma or unrealised desire. The laws which govern the freed complex act at once, the strength is sapped from desire, and we can begin to look for less dangerous escapes, and try to satisfy the hunger for happiness in non-alcoholic ways. And above all, as we shall see, we can put the craving in direct touch with a means of satisfying all the hunger of the soul, and teach the sufferer what He meant Who spoke so often of " My joy."

VI

From this brief survey of the maladjusted mind, and of its dissociations from unwelcome truth, we turn now to learn something of the manner of its relief. That it is possible to do so at all, is, for those who approach psycho-therapy from the Christian angle, a very significant fact, because the psychology which teaches us the way is itself the answer to a profound spiritual need.   The outline sketch of physical symptoms which has been made in this, and the preceding chapter is therefore not irrelevant to a therapy which is predominatingly spiritual ; for, rightly understood, the whole of the two-fold work of the " new " psychology, which, on the one hand, has mapped out such symptoms, and on the other, has found out a therapy for their cure, is evidence of a deep disturbance in the spiritual life of man. So long as man is at one with his environment, however incomplete his knowledge of it may be, he needs no psychological adjustments ; but when, as in the nineteenth century, his environment of possession and of thought shifts and expands, while he himself does not expand in spirit to meet the new conditions, profound uneasiness and even disruption, are the natural consequences.·

The insistent need thus produced by the new consciousness of dark strivings within, and of blind forces without, has made us aware of the psyche, whether we will or no, and our study of this need is crystallising into a science. Viewed thus, the psychological *preparatio evangelica* becomes luminously clear.   We had lost the certainties in which, however deluded, our brethren of former days put their trust ; we had set up, to meet the stresses of new knowledge, ideals of material security, philanthropy, and automatic progress ; and the discovery of the utter inadequacy of these, together with the impact of the yet greater forces of the twentieth century, are the direct causes of our psychological troubles, in nations as in men.   Its roots, therefore, are not in the mind, but in the spirit, and the very myopia that keeps medical psychology from perceiving this, makes all the more clamant the need for scientific work by " spiritual men who discern spiritual things."

This is the true explanation of the fascination that psychic life and its problems have for the modern man, a fascination expressed in many strange cults and experiments. In a psychology which allies itself with the Person and work of Christ, he is, however, on safe ground, because that alone can fully answer the restless strivings of his psyche, and heal the disorders which result therefrom. It alone can explain man to himself by explaining God to him, and tell him anew that in the Father's House are many rooms, and a place prepared for him.

CHAPTER IX

THE LIFE-CURVE

Psycho-somatic unity; the true meaning of health; the infinite variability of man; the three forces which mould him; of these, the spiritual the greatest; in this variability, there are landmarks to guide us; the four danger points in the life curve.—(i) Puberty; a double task faces the individual; signal opportunity for Christian pyscho-therapy; universal rites of initiation; need of a parallel in the Church. (ii) Vocation; an unrealised strain; our tragic system; the task of a Christian psycho-therapy. (iii) Marriage; limits and complications of this discussion; marriage more than reproductive; marriage a spiritual bond; disaster follows the ignoring of psychological facts; approach of the religious and the mating instincts. (iv) Second half of life; failures here of materialist psychology; psychology of this half of life; its crises due to three fears: fear of pain and failure; fear of losing youth; fear of death; each of these, only to be met by religion.

I

SUCH, then, is the wreckage of the battlefield, a casualty list which to-day is piling up to sinister proportions. When we survey it as we have been doing, and turn the pages of the history of that immense and baffling warfare of the Psyche with the forces of an evolutionary world around it, and with the dark powers within itself, the fact is very clearly brought home to us, that body and mind are not two, but one. It is a conclusion strengthened by our growing knowledge of the manner in which, even in normal, healthy life, the body is affected for good or evil by the instincts and acquired habits of the Psyche. Psycho-somatic unity is more than a mere hypothesis; every evidence points clearly to the fact that " the spirit is the living body seen from within, and the body, the outer manifestation of the living spirit." The Psyche has other voices than those of speech and thought, other avenues through which to declare its desires, for it can articulate through the machinery of the body, and cry aloud its needs ; it can use the whole physical frame as the vehicle of its development. The more we know, for example, of instinct, the more we see that the brain alone is not its home. The more we study " suggestion," the more we realise that the psychical can dominate creatively any part of the physical at will. Indeed, the psychic web is woven in and around every organ of the body, and can speak through it in a language whose rudiments we begin to understand. Health, therefore, becomes a word whose centre of gravity tends more and more towards the psychical, and psycho-therapy is growingly perceived to be the ruling factor in all curative process.

For us, however, that is but part of the truth ; for our whole thesis is that man is a developing entity, poised between the natural and the supernatural. And since, in that entity, the spirit is to rule, man fulfils his destiny when the spiritual takes increased possession of him, and he reacts more and more sensitively to the intimations of God and the unseen. His true health, therefore, has other elements in it than the worldly, and there is a strange foreshadowing in the old usage which makes " Health " and " Salvation " synonymous words. It is a clear instance of the subconscious mind of man working in his language, here, as in so many other places. When Tyndale, for example, makes Christ say to Zacchæus, " This day is health come to thy house " (where the Authorised Version says " salvation "), his translation spoke deeper than he knew, and made luminous the deep intent of Christ ; for true health is impossible, apart from God.

Till now, three separate groups of healers have sought that health. The doctor has proclaimed it to consist in the best possible functioning of the bodily economy in

relation to its environment, " the free equilibrium of all
functions proper to the species." The psychologist has
probed the mind, and released its poisons, and thereby
restored its balance and its health. The minister has, as his
name suggests, endeavoured to mediate the cleansing powers
of the Spirit of God to the soul of man. Yet so far, in spite
of solid achievement, each of these has missed the mark
because he has worked on but a part of an indivisible whole,
and has ignored that psycho-somatic unity, which is the very
essence of human nature. Once again, therefore, the way
seems to be clearing for the advance of a Christian psycho-
therapy which will envisage spirit as well as body and mind,
and will seek to enfold their earthly trinity in a unity of
saving health.

II

A further consideration emerges from our survey
of the battlefield. Each child of God who struggles in its
arena, does so as a clear-cut individuality, differing in vital
essence, in environment, and in reaction, to every other
combatant. This fact alone immensely complicates the task
of stating a characterology, and of reducing to any defined
system his immeasurably varied responses to the demands of
life. Our difficulty in ascertaining the truth is added to by
the fact, that he can tell us of himself only through the
avenues of two or three of his senses, and that he inhabits
a different incommunicable universe from that of even his
nearest and dearest.

In addition, too, to its individual constellations of
gifts, and its specialised reactions to life, the psyche bears
within itself clear evidence of racial and family heredities
which must also vary indefinably with each separate personality. No explorer of the subconscious mind can possibly
doubt these things ; and (in passing) it is all the more

strange to see a whole school of psychology, led by Adler, which denies both inborn gifts and the facts of heredity. It is Adler, for example, who says :

> " The traits of character are by no means, as many believe, inborn endowments of nature. They correspond to no inborn powers or substrata, but they are—very early though it may be—acquired, so that he may be able to maintain a definite behaviour. The importance of inheritance with regard to all psychic phenomena, and in particular to the origination of character traits, must be denied *in toto*."

Now it is simply impossible at this time of day to regard the psyche, at the beginning of life, as a *tabula rasa*, and the individual, as a colourless creature who acquires his idio-syncrasies at the behest of life's educators. While the graving tools of life are sharp enough in all conscience, they cannot work in a vacuum, or on a formless mass of jelly. The mere fact that they can and do grave, implies resistance ; and the fact that such resistances vary indefinitely proves the infinitely varied nature of the substance on which they work. We can say with truth, that each of us brings to his life an immense endowment, not only of potential and unfolded individuality, but of racial and other inherited instincts and predispositions, and that each of these strata in a man's make-up varies indefinitely in depth and strength. And so, when to this infinity of differences, there is added that other infinity of the different impacts of life on each separate man and woman, the resultant permutations and combinations are beyond thought itself.

It is, therefore, no longer possible to answer confidently the Psalmist's question, " What is man ? " Biology, of course, can give us, on its own level, answers more or less clear ; and a psychology which recognises the subconscious, the interlocking of body and mind, and the opposing tensions of instinct and will, can also fill in part of the outline. But no answer can be complete which does not go on to envisage " Thou visitest him. . . . Thou are mindful of him," and as we see, it is just here that non-Christian science refuses to define the full stature of humanity. The three forces which mould a man are—God, and the world, and his own psycho-somatic imperatives. Each of these forces operates in infinitely variable ways ; and since the subject himself is, as we have seen, highly variable, his characterology becomes extraordinarily difficult to define. What we can, however, do—and the psycho-therapist, of all men, must see that he does it—is to take cognisance of all the facts and not of some alone. We can but say that this complexity we call man, enters time as an individual bundle of individual capacities, weighted also with inheritance and predisposition, uneasily poised between the subconscious and the outer world, and receptive, if he will, of the intimations of Divinity ; and that his life is explicable only as the ante-chamber of Eternity The one thing we can posit with certainty is his development. The hormic urge is ineradic-able. There is no such thing as a static personality, and the individual is inexorably driven along a path which leads from the instinctual and primitive towards the clear-cut, isolated, and developed man. Our survey should by now have taught us that the major part of the troubles of the mind are caused by attempts to thwart this universal destiny, and to flee from the basic necessity of becoming a defined and independent human being.

III

Yet in this uncharted wilderness of character, landmarks can be clearly seen, and one of the more obvious is, that this variable subject, in his variable progress, enters several clearly definable danger-zones, and that his " life-curve " has certain vulnerable points, where crisis inevitably meets him. Something straddles his path, not an Apollyon, but some power from his own inner depths, or a command from God, and he may not evade the issue without grave consequence to himself. As he emerges towards maturity, and still more (as we shall see), as he enters the second half of life and feels the shadow of its end, there are certain battles which he must fight, certain adaptations which he must achieve, before he wins the password to the next stretch, and can embark upon the new phase of his journey.

Though his circumstances and reactions are almost infinitely variable, his life-curve is not ; and, broadly speaking, the life-curve encounters crisis at four great points in its progress. First, at puberty ; next, when choosing a vocation, a niche in life ; next, when selecting a mate ; and lastly when, after the climacteric, man faces the narrowing of life's powers and the road downhill. The normal life makes encounter at fairly well-defined periods, though crisis may be delayed or accelerated in the cases of the early-gifted, the late-gifted, the degenerate, or the weak-minded. Each endeavour to meet such crises may be described as an effort to grapple with, and master, oncoming reality ; and while the issue of the struggle differs widely in individual lives, battle in some shape or form *must* be joined, for cowardice and evasion at these moments mark the person-ality most gravely, arrest its development, and lead directly to the maladjusted life.

(A) Puberty, biologically and psychologically, marks a crisis in the life-curve, so radical as to deserve the description of a new birth. Profound disturbances and alterations take place in the structure and rhythms of the body, while the birth of new emotions and desires is accomplished in mental upheaval and expansion. Fresh and untried relationships to family and society begin to beckon ; and, if it has not previously been warped or inhibited, the religious instinct rises to consciousness as naturally as the sun.

At puberty, the individual is faced with a double task. Standing as he does before the doorway which leads from the shelter of the family, out into independent and separate life, he has not only to overcome the infantile within himself, but to achieve freedom from the parent, before he can begin to see himself as a coming adult. To the imperfect accomplishment of this task can be traced all the psychological disturbances of puberty and a very large proportion of those of later life ; for it is obvious that he who has not outfaced this first great crisis, enters the subsequent battles of life halt and maimed. At no period of life, too, is the problem of guidance more delicate and manifold. On the one hand, the over-anxious or over-authoritative parent can, and does, cause repression and " psychic cramp " ; and the adolescent who is " tied to his mother's apron-strings," or " under his father's thumb," is in a prison (albeit built in love), whose chain-scars remain to the end of life. He suffers from a mental rickets ; he cannot support his own weight, and even though he develop well in later life, his framework always shows the mal-formation. This is especially true when he faces marriage. On the other hand, the growing pains of life may so daunt him that he turns back to the well-remembered comforts of earlier childhood, and remains emotionally infantile, though perhaps intellectually maturing ; and to this first flight from reality can be directly traced those habitual flights in later life which we have already observed.

When trouble does rise, and guidance is urgently needed, there is here an unparalleled opportunity for the wise and Christian psycho-therapist, who can release or restrain alike, with a judgment and proportion impossible apart from the knowledge of Christ. This opportunity is the more signal when it is remembered that it is during the latter part of puberty, and in the immediately post-pubertal period, that a really notable flowering of the religious instinct takes place. Mere statistics in the things of the Faith are specially unreliable, but Starbuck, in his *Psychology of Religion*, found that in all the cases he investigated, both boys and girls, there was a definite religious awakening about the age of sixteen, preceded and followed by lesser moments of awareness. What is more natural than that the budding mind on the threshold of its career, pliant and hyper-sensitive, receptive and inquiring, apperceptive also for the first time of the greater mysteries of life around and within it, should not also feel a deeper throb, and receive for the first time the intimations of its own immortality ?

There is a deep if unconscious wisdom in the universal intuition of humanity, that this is the age at which to initiate into the mysteries of life and of religion ; and in this respect, the mind of a large part of the Church has been in line with those world-wide pubertal rites, in making Confirmation take place just about this age. But Confirmation is too often inadequately and too easily pre-pared for, and it has been divorced from its wider meanings, for there is more in it than the Sacramental. It should be allied with Christian initiation into life in general, and into the deeper implications of the New Testament, and the dawning religious instinct should have its hungers far more fully satisfied. The nameless unrests and blind longings of puberty are in large measure due to the hunger on the part of the created for the Creator ; they have so far, in western civilisation, been left for the secular society to satisfy in a casual, altogether worldly, and half-smiling manner ;

the youthful Psyche has been left to face the crisis of puberty without its most potent weapon, and enters on its next stage unstabilised and permanently weakened.

We lament to-day that the Church seems unable to " get hold of the young," and that her Gospel, make it as broad-minded and tolerant as we like, seems demagnetised. Have we perhaps made the gate too wide ? Would there not be more reverence for, and response to, a " strait and narrow " initiation to her mysteries, an austere and even painful preliminary to an adult fellowship which seeks to make the Divine life real on earth ? There is an unapprehended message to youth in the command of Christ, " Enter ye in at the strait gate," and the life of which He speaks is not alone the spiritual life ; life in its fulness is only to be found after struggle and even—as He said—violence. Since, therefore, we have seen puberty forcing an entrance into fuller life with strain and crisis, and since also we have this word of Christ, backed as it is by the universal intuition of the race, the watchmen at the gates of the Christian life cannot be at ease. Christian psychology has much to study and much to gain in evolving a true theory of initiation, and in aligning it with that flowering of the religious instinct which we have already noted. In so doing, Christian psychology will be the first to define completely the crises and the tensions of puberty, and to declare the way of their release.

IV

(B) Vocation. Very shortly after his first great period of conscious crisis, man is called on to determine his relation to the wider society which now begins to impinge upon his life, and to find that place in it which will enable him fully to develop his capacities and powers. The selection of a vocation, a groove into which to fit those powers, and one which will normally have to accommodate them to the end of life, is accompanied by psychological strain, not sometimes recognised at the time, but which often becomes evident later in life, when the results of a faulty choice have led to disaster. It is for this moment that society has, with a certain measure of success, tried to " educate " him by means of its schools and colleges, to " lead out " his powers to meet the crisis of decision ; but so far, society has not really faced the corollary task of providing vocations fitted for the powers it has evoked, and a vast amount of educational misfits result.

In the ideal society, no doubt, each individual will find exactly that vocation to which his particular constellation of gifts entitles him. There is an obvious connection between the manifold gifts of man and the manifold purpose of God, and the Designer of a man must also have designed the place in which that man will attain his optimum development. As society is constituted to-day, it is a place which not one man in a hundred succeeds in attaining ; and there is no worker among the young who has not stood many a time beside the grave of ambition and character, and seen good gifts aborted, and the youth crushed into a grotesque misfit of a calling, because it was the only one available. Not only so, but the very conditions of that calling are all too often such as to strangle the nascent powers of the mind, and to force the youth out into life with the delusion that work is of itself a drudgery, and leisure the only thing to be desired.

Such factors of choice undoubtedly accentuate the psychological crisis which occurs in this post-pubertal period, when the youth leaves for the first time the shelter of the home, and tries, for the first time, to pit his powers against the world. Unlike that of puberty, this crisis is not self-induced, but is forced on the individual by society ; and while the strong and greatly gifted characters do succeed in carving out their own especial niche, the average man awakes too late to his defeat, and finds himself secured for life to a calling which is no calling, but literally a self-denial. As things are, little can yet be done to assuage the critical consequences. In some quarters far greater care is now taken in sizing up and advising the youth on leaving school ; but this care is often set at naught by the stern facts of the labour market. Industrial psychology also is seeking to minimise the dulling and thwarting effects of monotony and unsuitable conditions. But these are only partial remedies, and much more radical cures, economic and educational, must be tried if the widespread psycho-neuroses caused by occupational misfits are to be abolished.

In the meantime, however, three things may be indicated, of which the Christian psychologist must never lose sight. First, that a vocation or calling is the inherent right of every child of God ; it is part of the purpose of his being here at all. The word vocation, too, must not be limited to the " professions," but ought to be applied to all. Second, that the first verses of the fourteenth chapter of the Gospel according to St. John refer not alone to a world which sets this one right, but to the coming Kingdom which shall be " on earth, as it is in heaven," where there shall be a room for each in the many mansions, and a place prepared. And third, that only by the alchemy of a religious Faith can the drudgery imposed by man on man be so sublimated, as to yield fruits of character and strength ; here, as everywhere, it is the function of religion to turn liabilities into assets.

V

(C) Marriage. When we touch the manifold problem of marriage, we enter disputed ground, and it is no part of the purpose of this book to discuss the questions of its regulation by society, or of its dissolution. For the present, we shall regard marriage as but one outcome of that crisis which every normal life has to face, when the deep and urgent instinct of Incompleteness bids it seek a mate among its fellows. Round the period of the maturing of that instinct, cluster a number of major psychological problems, of which marriage is but one. When, for example, it has to be suppressed for economic reasons, and marriage is denied till long after the age when mating is desired, or denied *in toto*, the strain upon the personality is obviously as great as any imposed by an unsuitable or thwarted marriage. Indeed, the struggle between this insistent and constant instinct, and the social and economic factors which beset it, is protracted, and far-reaching in its results on the Psyche ; and when, to these factors, we add the intellectual and the spiritual, which may also inhibit and deny, we begin to see how broad is the battle front, and how complicated its strategy.

Not only so, but when the great step has been taken, and the mate selected and the joint life initiated, new and delicate stresses test the whole personality, and it is early evident that marriage is no mere satisfaction of a physical instinct for reproduction, but a fusion of two entire personalities which affects every part of each, and calls for endless experiment, and can lead to endless disaster. It is indeed not too much to say that most of these disasters are due to forgetfulness of the simple fact that marriage is, in more senses than one, a twofold state, being psychic as well as physical. Physical attraction, however insistent, is no foundation for a lasting marriage, nor is Platonic affection, so-called ; true marriage is wedlock of body, mind, and spirit.

If, then, we delimit the scope of our survey to marriage as a psychological state, several outstanding facts at once emerge.

(1) It is a fundamental mistake to approach the problems of marriage (as indeed the problems of sex in general) from the angle, " Man is a mating animal." The reproductive instinct is but one part of that more comprehensive instinct, called here, the Incomplete ; and only when that fact is kept well in view, can marriage be set in its right perspective, and the whole question of sex, its limits and its sublimation, be approached. That instinct of Incompleteness matures very definitely after adolescence, and since the sexual is but part of it, it follows that satisfaction can only come to it in a marriage which is a spiritual, as well as a fleshly bond— satisfaction, that is, on the human plane ; because when that mighty instinct calls imperiously, it calls for a God as well as for a human communion, and that is precisely why religious yearning and youthful conversion appear, as we have seen, just at that age when the search for the mate begins. In this simultaneous longing of flesh and spirit, there is no incongruity, for both are congruous, and proceed from the same mighty urge. Since, then, sex and religion thus approach each other at a danger spot in the life-curve, the fact that the " Word was made flesh " unfolds yet another of its infinite number of meanings ; and, incidentally, we are presented with a new insight into the age-long problem of how to " attract the young."

(2) Matrimonial shipwreck is pathetically common, but the way to avoid a repetition of it is not to set out on the same course in another ship as flimsy as the first, or to return to the haven of single blessedness, but so to strengthen the vessel that it will ride the storm. To offer easier divorce, or companionate marriage, or temporary unions, as remedies for disaster, are as wide of the mark as to expect a pill to cure a sprained ankle ; such medicines will ease the tension and purge the body politic, but the true strength of marriage, as of the body, must come from within itself. When we

understand the psychology of marriage better, such expedients will seem as primitive and barbaric as the almost blasphemous contemporary custom of giving Christian marriage to men and women who are not Christian, and expecting them to keep the Christian vows in their fullness until death.

Broadly speaking, disaster comes when psychological law is ignored. Either the marriage is founded on such false psychological assumptions as that desire is the whole of life, or that the mind alone counts, without the flesh, or without the spiritual, or that a normal personality can mate with an abnormal, without injury to itself; or else the man is ignorant of the fact that the psychological make-up of the woman is widely different from his own,—or *vice versa*. Harmony can only be restored when the whole psychological truth of each partner is envisaged, when body, mind, and spirit are alike recognised and allowed to develop together in the interwoven life of the man and the woman, and when each of the two personalities is given its fullest rights. Here, as always, that harmony can only be initiated or regained, when the spirit is allowed to rule both the mind and the flesh, and here, as always, only a psychology which can address itself to the whole of life will succeed. No really Christian marriage has ever failed.

(3) It thus becomes evident that the approach of the religious to the mating instinct is one which is not confined to adolescence, but that it ought to be continuous through life. The solution of the whole problem of marriage lies in the recognition of the indivisibility of the Incomplete instinct. Force it to seek its outlet in the flesh alone, and you will fail; or shut off and abort its yearnings after completeness in God and in the spiritual, and it will refuse to be at rest in any lesser satisfaction; but allow it its legitimate outlet, and its highest desires will dominate all the others and bring them into harmony. On this presupposition alone

can a true marriage be consummated, for it is the only
presupposition which sets both man and woman in the sight
of God, and makes their whole united life a journey back
to Him.

VI

(D) The Second Half of Life. While psychology
has given us a conspectus of the structure of the mind which
applies, irrespective of age, to all minds, it is nevertheless a
curious fact that the failures of psycho-therapy are mostly
with men and women in the second half of life. The
medical analyst, as has already been pointed out, is an
excellent investigator but a poor constructor, and it looks
as if he were powerless, unless aided by the full tide of
youthful vital force. When life begins to draw inwards,
and vital force contracts, and the experiences of pain
and loss, together with the prospect of death, have to be
faced, problems arise, to which those of turbulent youth can
never compare, and stresses have to be met, such as adolescence never knew, and met with a lower ratio of strength.
The problems and psycho-neuroses of earlier life are caused by
flight from the realities of sex, or the regression to a childish
status in some shape or form; if, without prejudice, you
probe the psycho-neuroses of middle life, they reveal that
they are caused by refusal to face the spiritual, and by
starvation of the religious instinct, and that is why medical
psychology has no effective remedy for them.

All the psychology of youth and early maturity
is outward-looking, and the problems of that period are
caused, as we have seen, on the one hand, by a man's too
great obsession with himself, and on the other, by the first
impacts of the world and of society on the plastic structure
of the psyche. His vital need is to learn to live in company,
the company of God as well as of men, and so to grow that

he shall leave the childish and the infantile behind him. Medical psychology finds its greatest success in the directing of such minds, for their system is a literal education, a " leading out," towards fullness of earthly life, and towards such a loosening of parental and other fixations as will allow the growing powers to root and develop naturally.   But as life turns towards its afternoon, other horizons than those of youth open up, other calls have to be answered, and the orientation of life changes.   A totally new set of problems emerges, having little or nothing in common with those of youth and early manhood, and not nearly enough attention has been given either to their emergence, or their solution. The whole energy of psychology so far, seems to have been spent in the service of the young, and the typical psycho-neuroses of later life have not been explored.   Failure to understand or cure them has been accounted for, quite inadequately, by the hardening process of life, and the supposition that a psycho-neurosis of very long standing proves too deeply entrenched to be moved ; but the real reason of failure is error both in diagnosis and in method.

Such failure is once more symptomatic of the readiness, on the part of most psychologists, to evade all spiritual issues, wherever found, because the problems of the middle-aged psychopath are three, and every one, in the last resort, spiritual.

(1) He is afraid to face the experience of pain, or to acknowledge to himself that he has been a failure ; so afraid, that often all his energies are given to the work of deception—of making and upholding a façade before the world, behind which he lives in constant fear of being found out for the man he is. It is profoundly significant that clinical experience has proved the great complaint of this period to be the feeling of uselessness, of having come to a dead end.   Patients say that life has halted them ; it is no

use pretending any longer ; they are surrounded by a circle of closed doors ; and that therefore both desire and hope are gone. But when probed, there is usually revealed the fact that they themselves have halted, and not been halted ; and that, if doors be shut, they have shut them on some failure or grief too unpleasant to be faced. That " dead end " feeling, being translated, is found to be simply the compensatory device of self-pity, well disguised, and a flight from the reality of discipline through pain or failure ; and only the therapist who can teach the sufferer to think *through* failure and personal grief, and brace him to face the discipline of life, will succeed. To do that, needs, of course, another armoury than that of medicine.

(2) He is afraid of losing his youth ; that is, he fears to make the change of outlook rendered necessary by his years, and rather than look forward, attempts to carry on, without modification, the psychology of youth. It is the commonest psycho-neurosis of middle life, manifesting in very varied forms, and is frequently unconscious. The neurotic " loneliness " of this period, for example, is often traceable to desire to cling to the ways and appearance of youth, and reluctance to advance, with one's contemporaries, into the necessary changes of the years. These Peter Pans of middle life, these " grizzly kittens " of society, need a more tender handling than they frequently receive, for they are true psychopaths. So also are the ultra-conservatives of the 'fifties, the fanatical praisers of the bygone, who carry their obsolescent slogans into a generation that knows them not. Unless the true and spiritual glories of maturity can be shown to survivals such as these, and their narrow way made to widen towards a more perfect path, there is no cure for them ; and patient analysis under Christian hands is the only hope.

(3) He is afraid of death. At this stage in life, " world-security " begins to fail. The laborious and

acquisitive "digging-in" of earlier life is accomplished, and the subsoil begins to be seen as shifting sand; every self-protective and self-assertive instinct rises in revolt; and there dawns that terror of the end, which psychiatrists know so well. This is an anxiety situation which drives the personality into illegitimate extensions of its powers, and many of the breakdowns of middle life are traceable on analysis to such morbid fear. This fear, frequently unconscious, can show itself upon the surface in many guises. Exaggerated conscience is one—the middle-aged pharisee or fanatic can find his explanation here; exaggerated generosity is another—a policy of "fire insurance"; so are extreme valetudinarianism, and hypochondria. And when these strains approach the breaking-point, it need not surely be reiterated that the sole restorer and deepener of the personality affected, is, and must be, the therapist who can, for death, read Life.

CHAPTER X

AIMS OF A CHRISTIAN PSYCHO-THERAPY

Every psycho-neurosis a failure; re-adaptation can never be wholly defined; open-minded attitude of the therapist; Christian hope for the neurotic; the fundamental discovery of analytical pyschology; the release of the complex; its results; its dangers; here, a Christian psycho-therapy unique; its postulates; its necessity; its links with discovered aims and methods; alliance of science and religion.

I

THE next stage of our inquiry is now immediately obvious. Having observed the symptoms of the psychopath, we have now to inquire as to the aims and methods of his healing. And though, as we have seen, his ailments and his character are almost infinitely variable, yet broadly speaking, every psycho-neurosis surveyed in the preceding chapters may be described as a *failure* in some shape or form, on the part of the psychopath. It may be a failure of adaptation to the demands of society, or a failure to face the fact of God, or a failure so to adjust the inner forces of the personality that they shall function in harmony, yet in every case the resultant psycho-neurosis is no accidental visitant from without, but a consequence directly necessitated by the preceding refusal, a nemesis self-imposed and inevitable. The task of psycho-therapy, therefore, presents itself as a twofold one, of re-education, and of readaptation. There must not only be a readjustment and re-education of the forces of the psyche itself, both spiritual and intellectual, but also a rearrangement of life, a readaptation to the social forces which impinge upon the personality.

It is clear that the problem thus raised is one which can never be wholly defined, nor universally, but that it must be stated and faced anew with each separate case. The goal and the methods of psycho-therapy, therefore, must necessarily vary with each individual psychopath, and there is nowhere a hard and fast rule, an invariable system producing invariable results. The realisation of this fact is of supreme importance at the outset, for while there are many well-tried and successful methods of psycho-therapy, they must be regarded as infinitely flexible and variable, as variable as the problems with which they deal. In this connection it is worth while noting, that the existence of the many schools of psycho-therapy is evidence, not of confusion in the science, but of the fact that they are attacking these problems on a very wide front, and finding results all along the line ; there is room for all so long as they do not attack each other.

Only after a comprehensive study of the whole personality, history, and environment of his patient, will the therapist envisage at once the result for which he hopes, and the methods which he will use. Such a study clearly demands two things. It needs a trained and sanctified mind for its conduct, and it vitally needs co-operation and desire on the part of the patient. Without these latter, the therapist's work is vain, and it is frequently a matter of extreme difficulty and delicacy to secure them ; for a neurotic may, and often does, profess the utmost eagerness to be healed, and present at the same time the utmost resistance to the hand which would root up the complex his unconscious loves so well. Indeed, the detection and overcoming of unconscious resistances are often the hardest tasks of the therapist, and he has to steer a very tortuous course between such obstacles, and the emotions which the disturbed unconscious lets loose upon his unfortunate head.

This necessary attitude of the psycho-therapist to his elusive problems has been very wisely stated by Jung, when he says :

" The human psyche is highly equivocal. In every single case we must consider the question whether an attitude, or a so-called " habitus," exists in its own right, or is perhaps only a compensation for the opposite. I must confess that I have so often been mistaken in this matter, that in any concrete case I am at pains to avoid all theoretical presuppositions as to the structure of the neurosis, and as to what the patient can or ought to do. As far as possible, I let pure experience decide the therapeutic aims. This may perhaps seem strange, because it is usually assumed that the therapist should have an aim. But it seems to me that in psycho-therapy especially, it is advisable for the physician not to have too fixed a goal. He can scarcely know what is wanted better than do nature and the will-to-live of the sick person. The great decisions of human life have as a rule far more to do with the instincts and other mysterious unconscious factors than with conscious will and well-meaning reasonableness." [1]

The point needs emphasis, if only to make it clear that in psycho-therapy we are presented with no " cure-all," no rite of superhuman efficacy which will make straight all paths in the desert, and create on earth the heaven of perfect health in body, mind, and spirit.

That will come when the Kingdom of God in its

[1] Jung : *Humanity in Search of a Soul*, p. 69.

fullness comes, and when it so comes, many other powers than those of psycho-therapy will have prepared its way. The primary aim of psycho-therapy is not to effect a species of miraculous graft, and superimpose at once, new and better characteristics upon those already there; but when faced with the maladjusted personality, its aim is, by release and restraint, to effect the optimum adaptation of that personality to the threefold demands of God, of its own forces, and of society, and the attainment of such efficiency and joy in life as shall best express and employ its own particular powers and energies.

And when it is remembered that the "great refusal" of the psychopath is often the result of an innate weakness, an inherent lack in the psyche itself, the need for this qualification in the aims of his therapy is obvious. The very fact that such protective symptoms as we have seen in previous chapters are thrown up by the neurotic in self-defence is itself a declaration of an inborn lack in some particular; and this fundamental must never be lost sight of in psycho-therapy. Early shock, and bad habit, and wrong environment all play their parts in the evocation of a psycho-neurosis, but the wound on the personality was first inflicted through a chink in the armour of life. We who believe in Christ can, of course, never subscribe to the dictum, " once a psychopath, always a psychopath," but all psycho-therapy, whether Christian or not, cannot ignore the truth that there is in all of us a primary structure of endowment, perfect in none, and in some, alas, much more partial than in others; and it is the " man with one talent " who is most prone to lose his way.

That having been said, it can, however, be added with great emphasis, that it is exactly in this regard that a Christian psycho-therapy is supreme. When others despair of the man with the one talent, and of the limited adaptation he seems able under their hands to achieve to a world that appears to need many talents, the Christian system, and the Christian system alone, teaches hope even for him, and the possibility in *this* life of a goal as high, and a development as useful, as any the ten-talented man can have. A system of Christian psycho-therapy will produce results out of hopelessness, which, to such as deny the validity of its powers, are literal miracles.

II

The mental and spiritual health at which we aim is, therefore, seen to be a highly individualised and variable goal ; yet in reaching it, the therapist, Christian or otherwise, uses certain well-defined and invariable methods which must now be examined. It is the discovery and practise of these methods which constitute the special achievement of the new psychology.

The whole examination in which we have engaged, of the structure of the mind and of mental maladjustments, has made it abundantly clear that in these disorders the unconscious mind plays a mighty part. In almost every case, as we have seen, the surface symptom, when probed, reveals deep-seated mischief in the dark regions of the unconscious. It therefore follows, that for the relief of the symptom, we have somehow to " get at " the unconscious mind, make it declare its motives and desires, and, by probing to the seat of repression in the unconscious, reveal the complex and release its energies. And the entire system of psycho-therapy is based on the truth, that when we so do, relief is instantaneous and lasting.

When once the unconscious memory which is the *fons et origo* of the particular disorder is restored to consciousness, it obviously ceases to be repressed, takes its place along with the rest of experience, and, however abnormal, becomes thus normalised. Such a process may be either brief or exacting, according to the depth of the repression, but when completed and successful, the result is invariably the draining of the power to hurt, and the end of mental schism. The complex is as an abscess of the mind, which, when lanced, releases its poison, and the *vis medicatrix naturæ* can then have its chance.

The importance of this discovery for psychic health can hardly be overestimated. It is a threefold discovery. The revelation of the power of the complex, semi-autonomous and energetic, to overturn the balance of mind and body and destroy their peace, is but the first part of the achievement. There remained still the problem of how to reach it, deep buried as it always is among the roots of life, and of how to restore it to conscious memory ; and it is the discovery and use of analysis, of free association, of dream analysis, of suggestion and hypnosis, as pointers to, and probes for, the subconscious regions, which make it possible to speak of psycho-therapy at all. And when it was found that the buried complex, if brought to the surface by these means, at once discharged its pent-up energies, and ceased its rebellious power, the threefold discovery was complete. How to diagnose a complex ; how to get at it ; and how to restore its diverted energies to their proper channels ; that is at once the revelation and the method of analytical psychology.

Many other problems, of course, remain even after that is accomplished. The still invalid mind has to be tended and shepherded, re-educated till it can walk alone, taught to effect sublimation, and directed so as to see the hidden hand of God. It enters on a long convalescence, spiritual as well as emotional and intellectual, but the crisis is passed, and given patience and Christian wisdom, the re-edifying of the broken structure is sure.

III

Now, such a disturbance of the contents of the
psyche is not to be entered on lightly or unadvisedly, and is
obviously fraught with extreme dangers to the balance of
the whole. The bringing of unconscious content into
consciousness is analogous, as has been said, to a surgical
operation, necessitating precaution, delicacy, and a thorough
training on the part of the operator, and is not to be
undertaken by the unskilled hand. It gives us to think,
when we learn that "the vast majority of mental
diseases, in so far as they are not of a definitely
organic nature, are due to a disintegration of consciousness, caused by an irresistible inundation of unconscious
contents." [1]

Indeed, the path of psycho-therapy is strewn with
the wrecks created by the heedless amateur, who has picked
up the jargon and rushed in where angels should fear to tread.
But be it noted, it is also marked by the mutilated failures of
those who, with no equipment save that of material science,
have, in their analyses, come on bitter spiritual need, the
agonies of a search for an unknown God, and the deep
yearnings for a Rock of certainty underfoot, who have pronounced these to be but illegitimate projections of a disordered psyche, and have wounded instead of healing.
Medical psycho-therapy has as many failures as successes,
especially with men and women in the second half of life ;
and it would be instructive to find how many of these failures
split on the sunken rock of religion.

It is precisely here that Christian psycho-therapy
has its opportunity. A therapy which starts from the fact
that it has behind it the healing power of Christ, which en-
visages every psychopath as a potential Christian, and which,

[1] Jung : *Contributions to Analytical Psychology*, p. 388.

over and above its processes of reconciling conscious and unconscious, never loses sight of its purpose of leading a man's soul nearer God, can never fall into either of the two errors already named. It has far too much reverence for the dignity and integrity of man, ever to descend to the level of the bungling amateur ; and it has far too much sensitiveness to the voices of God, ever to let its science be earth-bound.

And further, when the complex is resolved, its subterranean energy released, and the mind eased of the perilous stuff, only half of the battle of therapy is won. There remains the whole task of the re-orientation of the personality under the guidance of some dominating force which shall not only prevent the re-energising of the complex, but use harmoniously powers previously at war with each other, and enable the man to reach his optimum. It is noteworthy, that towards victory in this second half of the battle, analytical psychology, as commonly practised, offers curiously little. It has coined the " blessed word " Sub-limation ; but sublimation cannot be given to a sufferer like a dose, and must be backed by imperative inner desire on the part of the patient. Without this, sublimation becomes but a refined form of repression, and is a bandage, not a cure, for the wounds of the mind. Since instinct, feeling, and emotion, twisted and retarded, have produced the complex, only a therapy which can re-educate instinct, feeling, and emotion will complete its cure ; and the average practitioner is an excellent digger but a bad builder, because his foundations are on the sand. To reawaken the psychopath to beauty, charity, and holiness, and to show him those incarnate in a Person ; to touch his maladjusted life to the finer issues of loving his neighbour and loving his God, are the unique prerogatives of a Christian psycho-therapy, and it is high time that they were exercised.

IV

It is clear, therefore, that the whole approach of a Christian psycho-therapy to its cures, is, and must be, vitally different from that of any other school. The doctor, however high his ideals, is not equipped for spiritual surgery; nor, as we have noticed, does he frequently desire to be. He is ill at ease in that whole region of his patients' experience where the search for God goes on, and where spiritual hunger is felt; indeed, his whole presuppositions deny him the right of entrance there. But the presuppositions, on the other hand, of the Christian psycho-therapist, place first things first, and among all the schools of psychology he is unique in that he possesses a rationale of man and of the universe, which is, if not complete, far more so than any other, and in that he possesses a wholesome awareness of his own unimportance.

His fundamental is, that man is the creature of God, and will again meet his Creator; and that, in this creature, not only have intellect and a personality been implanted, but also a capacity to perceive the Creator. From that fundamental, all else grows. When that creature suffers, *i.e.* separates himself from God by his own act or weakness, there is that in God which speaks at once; and the response of the Creator to his separated creature is the reconciling Word of God, Jesus Christ. More, too—in that reconciling, at-one-ing Word, are revealed certain other things without which the world must perish; release from guilt and fresh impetus of life, together with a love, that is the bond of peace of mind.

These things will receive neither elaboration or argument here; they are the axioms of the Faith, and their apologetic must be sought elsewhere. And in all that has been written here regarding the wanderings and pathetic deceptions of the mind, they are implicit.   We see them, not *qua* illnesses, interesting, and sometimes curable ; we see them always in the light of these presuppositions of the Christian Faith.

But the point has been raised in certain quarters : Why a Christian psycho-therapy at all, when the whole fabric of the Gospel is instinct with the promise of fresh power and forgiveness, and when the healing power and companionship of Christ are already there, offered for all ?   Such a point sounds reasonable, but is specious.   There *is* need of a Christian psycho-therapy, precisely as there is need of a Church visible ; the reason being, that the Gospel, though self-evident, needs declaration and unfolding for the needs of men.   When the Kingdom of God is come, for example, " on earth as it is in heaven," there will be no more sickness, as also, there will be no Temple there ; but, till it comes, in this imperfect world, we shall use and thank God for the skill of physician and surgeon, as for the upbuilding ministries of the Church.   It is precisely so with Christian psycho-therapy.   When the mind is blocked and warped, all its perceptions blunted, and its powers alienated and misused, we shall best make straight the way for the Gospel, if we first remove, by the new powers committed to our hand, the obstructions which thus hinder it.   *We* do not heal, any more than does the physician heal the body ; it is the in-scrutable *vis medicatrix Christi* for which we do but open up the way.   And if we have been given new knowledge of the structure and functions of the human mind, in health and in sickness, we do right to make our new knowledge serve the highest purpose of that mind, and open it towards God. No Christian psycho-therapy can ever usurp the prerogative of the Gospel, or be, in itself, a means of salvation.   It can only point to the one universal Means ; and if, to do so, it clears the mist from the maladjusted mind with reiterated

and emphatic success, and enables that mind better to see
its God, its need is clear, and its blessing is assured.

V

The immediate question, therefore, is : How, and
where, is this specifically Christian outlook to find its alliance
with the methods of psycho-therapy. It has become evident
in the course of our survey, that the latter science is a true
præparatio Evangelica, and that there is no fundamental
dissimilarity between its healing purpose and that of religion ; on the problems of the psyche, at least, science and
religion are no antagonists, but, having a similar purpose,
can work hand in hand. Yet, unlike other systems, a
Christian psycho-therapy has a twofold aim. In the first
place, it shares with materialist psychology the technique of
" tidying up " the mind. It, too, uses every discovered probe
and pointer to the subconscious—analysis, dream-analysis,
association, suggestion, and the like—but it uses them with
a greater purpose in view, and its special function only
begins where other psychologies stop. Even while fulfilling
this first purpose, it never loses sight of its greater purpose,
which is, to make health and salvation synonymous ; any
lesser aim leaves the sufferer uncured and endangered, for
to stop short of the healing of body, mind, and spirit alike,
is to stop short of full health and safety. Through all its
use of the technique of the analyst, this essential aim can
never be forgotten. A " patient " to the doctor, is a child
of God to the Christian therapist, and his need is viewed
not only in the light of science, but in the light of Eternity
also. At every stage of analysis, whatever the means used
in its course to lay bare the seat of disorder, both therapist
and psychopath will have to " practise the presence of God " ;
a very difficult and delicate thing, often, for the latter, but

12

one to which, however strange he be to it, he must at once be introduced, even though it be " as a little child." From the start he ought to know that the whole purpose of his treatment is not only to sweep and garnish his mind, but also to make room in it for an expected Guest.

To effect such an alliance between science and religion in this regard, much research has yet to be done, and it is perfectly obvious that it must be done clinically. Meantime, there are two reasons which prevent progress. While there is an enormous volume of results, clinically obtained, and published, these results are but partial, in that they are largely got by methods which ignore or evade the spiritual. In addition, as we have seen, while the actual methods used on most cases are fairly constant, their application is a matter of infinite flexibility and variability, and a true technique can only be learnt through much clinical experience ; and clinics under skilled and experienced Christian therapists are all too few, and their results, as yet, sporadic. For these reasons, therefore, at present the alliance merely consists in the adaptation and use, by Christian hands, of methods which materialist psychology has proved to be successful ; but in the future, we shall be able to advance that alliance along at least two lines. We shall, in the first place, be able, after the clinical experience of which I speak, to present such a case to the materialist man of science for religious psychiatry, as will be unanswerable and will command not only his sympathy, but his co-operation ; doctor and minister will work together freely, passing cases to and fro. And we shall also be able to present such a record of spiritual healing to the Church, that she will be forced to draw nearer than hitherto, in order to see this great thing which has come to pass ; and thus, from either side, science and religion will move nearer to each other.

In the succeeding chapters, then, we shall review,

one by one, those methods, always from the Christian angle ;
and if, as a result, a growing number of Christian ministers
and others are moved, anxiously yet prayerfully, to attempt
some of them, that clinical experience, whose lack we de-
siderate, will begin to grow, and the foundation of a practical
school of Christian psycho-therapy will have been laid.

CHAPTER XI

ANALYSIS

Its nature; threefold parallel with Christian method; its initial stage; superficial resemblance to Confession; meaning of Rapport; a covenantal relationship; sincerity and faith in the therapist; meaning of Resistance; surface and unconscious resistances; difficulties of the labour, meaning of Abreaction: not to be confused with religious Conversion; its limits; meaning of Transference; a form of Projection; second stage of analysis; explaining the patient to himself; the spiritual essential here; concluding stage that of reinforcement; readjustment not enough; materialist psychology insufficient here; the Christian dynamic; religion the great sublimating power.

I

THE process used in investigating and adjusting a maladjusted mind is called Analysis, and consists in inducing the mind, by various means, to reveal its conscious, remembered content, and also to bring up to memory level those forgotten and subconscious emotional energies which have caused its complexes. Schools of analysis are various, but various only in the manner in which they label and distribute the material thus given out; the methods they use in analysis are the same, and they share one common aim, namely, the restoration to conscious memory of the repressed memory whose energy is warping the mind, and the assimilation of that energy to normal personality. It is frequently a long and exacting process, but once the resistances are overcome, and the subconscious discerned, relief is invariable; and then, on the heels of analysis, comes the constructive effort to re-establish the mind in unity once more. And at the outset, it is well to understand that it is a process hard to comprehend by those who have had no living experience of its rigours and releases in themselves, or in others whom they have watched. In this, of all subjects, reading and experience are very widely different. While the background of theoretical knowledge is essential, no real therapy is possible without that living experience ; it is good to be able to say to the sufferer " I have seen others, and I can help you " ; but far better to be able to say " I, too, have been there, and I know." Yet, however hard it be to define on paper a method so variable and empiric, an outline of the stages of analysis is necessary, in order to understand its theory, at least, and in order to see how such methods as free association, dream analysis, or suggestion, fit into the scheme.

There is one parallel, and that an important one, between the task of the scientific psychologist and the work of the Christian Church, in that both are seeking to redeem, though with very different premises, and for very different ends. In this common task there is also a similarity of method which is most striking. Let anyone, be he pastor or psychologist, approach his erring fellow-man and seek to do him good, and at once he perceives a threefold endeavour to be necessary. His approach must, of course, be met half-way, by willingness on the part of the subject to acknowledge his errors, by desire to be free, and by trust in the healer-to-be : no faith, no healing. These given, the first endeavour will be to locate the errors, and their accompanying symptoms in the life ; the second, to provide a rationale for the life thus begun to be liberated, an explanation to it, of itself, its errors, and its world ; and the third, so to strengthen that life and so to prune away its errors, that the man will find it more and more difficult to err. In the end, whatever his premises, the therapist's aim is to leave a transformed human being, developed, balanced, and fully conscious.

Such a process is, of course, the time-honoured method of the Christian Church, viewed from the merely human end ; but it has been a method partially studied and loosely followed. Analytical psychology is a recent science, and till its advent the Roman was the only branch of the Church to practise in any fullness this threefold technique of liberation. It is, however, noteworthy that the methods evolved by analytical psychologists of all schools, present a precisely similar threofold division ; man's reaction to the problems of the psyche seems to be invariable, whether the psyche be regarded from the religious or the materialist angle.

The Christian minister, engaged in pastoral and parochial work, can but rarely, if ever, have opportunity for prolonged analytical investigation, though, of course, the time may perhaps come when certain trained and chosen men and women will be set apart by the Church to that end. Yet the student of Christian psycho-therapy should know, at least in theory, the stages passed through in analysis, and should note that whatever his efforts at the cure of souls, they, too, must manifest the same three stages ; and even a slight knowledge of the phenomena of analysis will be of the utmost service to him there.

II

Analysis naturally commences at the surface, and with that part of the surface which lies nearest the psycho-neuroses of the patient. Its initial stage is the emptying by the patient of the content of his conscious mind, in the presence of the therapist, in order to give the latter a conspectus of the life, of the setting, and of the hereditary background of his patient. About this stage there is nothing very new; but two things regarding it should be noticed. The first is, that this emptying process takes place regardless of all moral inhibitions. The moral scruples and guilt sensations which normally " bottle up " so much of the mind, as well as the reticences of ordinary social life, are utterly disregarded ; *all* must be declared at this customs barrier before the new country can be entered and explored. It is here, of course, that the more obvious and conscious resistances are encountered ; but these must be overcome at the outset, and the patient made to realise that what matters is the truth regarding his mind, and the whole truth, oblivious of its nastiness or otherwise. The therapist is neither judge nor critic, save of symptoms and their consequences, but simply, for the time being, a receiver—the patient ought to be made to feel that he is speaking *in vacuo*, a difficult but necessary preliminary to analysis. The second is, that the therapist begins to sift out from the mass, not the things which seem to matter, but those which are pointers to the unconscious, where the root of the matter lies. The very first sitting will, of course, reveal to him where the surface symptoms of the psycho-neuroses are; experience alone can guide him in this sifting process, but at this point he also begins the more direct probing of the subconscious by analysing with the patient his dreams, by using hypnosis, or by discerning, through " word association," where the hitches in his mind occur.

The ancient practice of Confession is therefore seen to be the mother of analytical psychology, but compared with its offspring, the parent is primitive and undeveloped. Audible confession, in the presence of a sympathetic and a strong mind, is a practice hallowed by long usage, of immense value, and productive of immediate, if temporary, psychological relief. Analysis is sometimes popularly supposed to be but confession writ large, but mere confession plays a very subordinate part indeed therein. Confession of remembered fault or abnormality is only the statement of the results of mental disorder, and it gets us no nearer to its cause. A much longer, deeper process than that is needed, if the latter is to be explicated, a process too, which, contrary to all surface probabilities, often regards conscious memory and experience as obstacles rather than as guides to the truth, and which assesses the values of these, not according to their surface content, nor according to any accepted moral code, but simply according to the manner in which they indicate the depths underneath. It is abundantly true that the mind confesses only so much as the unconscious wishes it to confess, and it needs a trained ear to detect, behind the outer walls of defence, the noise and bustle of traffic in the citadel of the mind.

All confession presupposes two things, a sin and a secret. Remembered sin is only a conscious secret which man tries guiltily to hide from God and his neighbour, till forced to confess it to God or his neighbour. But where there is secrecy, there may be also that supremely dangerous thing, repression ; and it is the secret, rammed down into the subconscious, which is, as we have seen, a prime cause of mental ills. The neurotic, shut off from reality, within prison walls of his own making, and seeing the world through a glass darkly, is ruled by his secrets, and all his strength goes in keeping them. But it is the deep law of mental as of spiritual health, that to attain it a man must give up his secrets, unconscious as well as conscious, for his secrets wall him off, not only from his fellow-men, but from his true self. We are only now beginning to see another depth in the profound saying of Christ, " He that saveth his life shall lose it ; but he that loseth it for My sake and the Gospel's, the same shall save it."

This cleansing process, this rescue of the life accomplished by willing surrender of its secrets, is, of course, the aim of all religious education. It was adumbrated in the old mystery cults and the faiths of the East, where certain purificatory rites were designed to merge the individual's secrets in a greater secret ; and it is part of the strength of the hold of the sacrificial systems over the mind of man, the sacrifice being in one respect an inarticulate confession bearing the secret sins of the offerer. A further step was taken when the practice, peculiar to the Christian system, of confession was instituted ; but, as was said above, its effect is but to touch the surface of the mind, and leave its real secrets, secret still. Catharsis can only be complete when the unconscious, too, is purged of its repressions and secret poisons ; and psycho-therapy, with its attendant instruments of analysis and the rest, is the only means yet discovered by man of doing so.

By man ; for let it never for an instant be forgotten that the whole good news of Christianity rests on the promise of purification through forgiveness. Yet towards the fulfilment of that tremendous promise, psycho-therapy can do two things. It alone can restore to memory the unconscious and forgotten burden which cries out to be lifted. Acceptance of forgiveness implies that what is forgiven is remembered; and in this, psycho-therapy is the handmaid of the Gospel. Not only so, but, for the student of the purposes of God, it can and does give new proportions to guilt and sin; for, to take but one example, a sin, which is on the surface exceeding sinful, becomes less so, when found to be driven on the wings of an unconscious and compelling complex, in whose origin, the guilt is on other shoulders than those of the sinner ; the iniquity of the fathers, visited, perhaps, unto the third and fourth generation.

III

In succeeding chapters we shall examine some of the means by which this "emptying" process is carried out; but meantime we have to observe certain important psychological phenomena by which it is accompanied, phenomena whose definition and classification we owe to analytical psychology.

(1) The first and simplest of these is called Rapport, the psychological relationship established between the therapist and his patient, a subtle, variable, but definite prerequisite to effective analysis. The influence of one personality on another is always difficult to define, but it is a fact; and such an influence is the more pronounced when one mind, of set purpose, is groping in the recesses of the other, and when that other opens all its doors of memory and association to the inquiry. In addition, as we shall see, it is greatly increased by the presence, in that other mind, of unreleased emotions, which the therapist's touch lets loose. The building up of effective Rapport is the first, as it is often one of the most delicate, of the tasks of the analyst, but the acquirement of such a psychic "bedside manner" is, to him, essential, and is, of course, a technique which can only be gained by innate gift, plus experience.

Broadly speaking, Rapport is a covenantal relationship; the meeting of a willingness to help with a willingness to be helped. The larger part of the task of its creation lies with the therapist, for the patient is, by the very nature of his trouble, often debarred from so obvious a relationship. Where the former is met by a willing patient, or one so desperate that he withholds nothing, the work is halved; but where, as often happens, especially with the ministry, he is met by deep-seated suspicion, or even hostility, his first task, before any effective analysis can begin, is to break that

down by patience, by explaining just enough and no more—
for tremendous harm can be done by explaining too much—
and by simple friendliness. Certain medical analysts adopt
the rôle, in their interviews, of disembodied intelligences,
de-personalised entities, silent and watchful receptacles, and
no more ; it is an attitude which creates fear and not rapport,
and one which is really due to reluctance to face the full
problem of relationship with their patient. Another type of
analyst analyses and explains every fibre of every interview,
and drowns rapport in a flux of talk , which is self-assertion
and not analysis. It is easier, perhaps, for the Christian
analyst than for any other to adopt the golden mean, the
attitude of reverent, ready, and affectionate co-operation,
which alone is infectious enough to kindle a like attitude in
his patient.

The nature and equipment of the therapist himself
will come up for later consideration ; but here, it is sufficient
to stress two factors which, from the very first meeting with
his patient, affect his whole relationship with him. In
seeking to help, be it in analysis or in any other way, he faces
a task which needs not only theoretical knowledge, but
character. No charlatan or theorist can ever be a psychiatrist,
for only character can produce character. The re-established
patient is, in a very evident manner, the child, the creature
of his therapist, however much the latter tries to detach
himself and let the patient develop alone. To delve in a man's
subconscious, establishes a bond not easily broken, and the
mark of the analyst, whether he will or no, is for ever im-
printed on his patient. The fact that both have together
tried to face ultimate truth and ultimate reality in the
patient's life, sets up a *milieu* in which imitation simply will
not do ; only honesty and sincerity can work there, as the
amateur will find to his cost.

Not only so, but the therapist needs firm and

unshakeable belief in the truth of what he practises, whether it be religious truth or something lesser ; some such faith is the necessary premise of all forms of mental healing, and it must be absolute, whatever gods it serves. No sceptic can ever be a psychiatrist, for doubt breeds doubt, and the fantasiast, of all men, needs security. Only faith can kindle hope in a sufferer ; even though it be but complete faith in an incomplete system, it will work its miracle, break down resistances, and impel that sufferer to put his hand in his healer's.

These two things are found to be essential in building up Rapport by therapists of every school ; and in this respect the latter are obviously not very far from the Kingdom. If even they begin thus to emphasise the self-preparation of the therapist, it can well be seen how Christian faith and Christian character will equip a man in this semi-paternal, semi-pastoral relationship which we are considering. That whole relationship is primarily based upon a real and living Rapport, built on the foundations indicated ; without it, analysis will founder—as indeed will every form of mutual help.

IV

(2) Resistance. Reference has already been made to those half-instinctive resistances of decency, secretiveness, and so on, which block the emptying process and hinder analysis. It is difficult for a patient to overcome the ordinary conventions of society, and also the silences imposed by his psychopathic isolation, and to realise that his analyst is not there to judge, but to obtain the truth. From the start, therefore, utter frankness must be insisted upon as the standard of all interviews, and where a good rapport has been begun, such frankness becomes gradually easier to the patient. These surface resistances are generally easy

to detect, for very little experience shows when the patient is selecting his material so as to skirt thin ice, or shying like a frightened colt when he approaches certain memories ; and, once detected, common tact will usually overcome them.

But there is another type of resistance, much more subtle and much harder to overcome, namely, what is known as unconscious resistance. This resistance is a defensive reaction of the repressive forces in the patient's subconscious, it acts perfectly independently of his conscious intentions, and stands, like a censor, at the threshold, to prevent the passage towards the conscious level of any material which it wishes to keep secret. It is nearly always true that repression produces unconscious resistance, and unconscious resistance is often very hard indeed to trace to its source. It can be suspected, and its surface symptoms noted ; but it is one thing to suspect, and quite another to dislodge it. For example, when a patient shows (not consciously or intentionally) that he loves his complex and hates to have it dug up ; or when he produces a seemingly endless train of quite genuine symptoms, and the therapist cures one, to find the next produced and waiting ; or when the analysis sticks, and no apparent reason can be given for the deadlock ; in such cases it becomes clear that an opposing force is arrayed to defeat the analyst, deep down, where the repressions live.

Almost every analysis encounters this type of resistance, and it needs great skill, experience, and patience to overcome. The victory is usually won, not by frontal attack, but by gradual undermining of the defence, and by that desertion of the rebels to the analyst, which happens, as we shall see, in Transference. Analysis has been rightly likened to the drainage of a farm with many fields. Each interview drains off a little of the stagnant waste, imperceptibly perhaps, changing here and there from field to field, till the time comes when even the deep marshes are gradually drained, one can hardly tell how or when, and the subsoil freed and purified for use. No one interview can be pointed to as accomplishing that ; but, with watchfulness, the time surely comes when the analyst sees the last unconscious resistance melt, and the future of the analysis clear before him.

Here, again, analytical psychology advances far beyond mere confession, and beyond any systems of self-suggestion or self-analysis. Nobody can analyse his own unconscious ; it is a contradiction in terms to attempt it, and a man may suggest health, or even spiritual well-being, to himself till doomsday and get no further, if his suggestion be invariably censored within, and disarmed in the gates. The way has to be cleared before suggestion can act ; and while self-suggestion and self-analysis have certain limited possibilities, it is supremely true that in analysis the out-sider—the analyst—sees most of the game. Even the explosive and dynamic " suggestions " of the Gospel need a door that opens only from within before they can enter, and if the lock be jammed, or the hand upon the handle impotent and bound, even He will knock in vain. It is abundantly evident, therefore, how vitally important it is to understand and estimate the nature and root of Resistance, variable and elusive though they be ; all analysis depends for success on a clear field and no favour.

(3) Abreaction ; which is a perfectly defined, though by no means universal phenomenon in analysis, and frequently produces complete cures in a surprisingly short space of time. It consists in the bringing back to memory, through hypnosis, dream analysis, or other method, of the unconscious and repressed emotions which vitalise a complex, and the living over again of the experience or trauma which originally caused that emotion. It is an intensive form of

that which we sometimes experience in conscious life, namely, the impulse to tell over and over again some shock we have had, till the very repetition seems to have eased the emotion, and we " feel better for having got it off our chest." Abreaction, however, depends upon the release of unconscious emotion, frequently of tremendous force, and is therefore a much more dynamic phenomenon. We have observed that in certain hysterical symptoms there is an attempt on the part of the psyche to live over again some moment of profound shock which has dissociated it ; and that this unconscious memory is, as it were, battering at the door with its symptom, in the attempt to discharge its emotion and heal its dissociation ; though without success, or the hysterical symptom would abate and vanish. Abreaction differs, in that it consists in recalling the exact trauma itself to conscious memory ; and, when that is done, the original emotions surrounding it are re-experienced in all their fullness, and in this re-experiencing the " complex-abscess " is drained of its poison.

The dissociative power of a self-governing complex is its chief danger to the mind, and when abreaction takes place, the complex is robbed of its armoury of attack ; if, therefore, the force which cleaves the mind in twain is abated, re-integration follows as a matter of course. When abreaction takes place thoroughly, the result, in immediacy and in vehemence, is like a miracle. The storm of emotion induced is often literally heart-rending, but when it is spent the psyche is cleared, unconsciously as well as consciously, and the obsession, phobia, or other psycho-neurosis simply vanishes. To see dipsomania, or stammering, or tic evaporate like mist, and stay evaporated, is a memorable experience whose only parallel is in the phenomena of instantaneous Conversion, using that word in its religious sense.

Indeed, the emotional storm of abreaction and the

subsequent easing of tension are very like the surface phenomena attendant on Conversion, and are sometimes confused therewith. But while their initial results are apparently similar, in the newness of life which they both afford, their causes are widely different. Pure abreaction always occurs on the human level, and is explicable thereon; it is caused by man to man. The whole rationale of Conversion, however, is the working within of a ferment caused independently of memory, by the Divine, a ferment whose explosive energy is explicable on no human grounds.

True Conversion, in the religious sense, is a psychical phenomenon, far too well documented to be discounted by any school, however materialist. It can be explained only by its self-evidence, and, whether it be gradual or instantaneous, is a process in a category quite by itself. Psychologically expressed, it is the flowering of the religious instinct, sudden or otherwise, often after long subterranean struggles towards the light; and that again is the highest maturing of the "incomplete" instinct, finding at last its completion and its rest. That opening of the whole psyche towards God is, however, only one side of the phenomenon, the completion of which is the possessive Power which enters and rules the mind thus opened. Quite naturally, only a therapist who profoundly believes in Conversion can include it among the possibilities of his therapy; and equally naturally, in all his analytical or other work, his one all-embracing aim is, as we shall see, some such turning of the stunted soul towards God. For the present it is sufficient to say, that should he witness, soon or late, a true conversion, his analysis is done. He may shepherd, but he need dig no more, for dissociation and complex are ended; the superconscious has begun, and an altogether new heaven and new earth perceived.

The use of abreaction is severely limited, and it

definitely applies only to such psycho-neuroses as can be directly traced to some momentary emotional shock or trauma. The great mistake was made, when abreaction was first noted and exploited by Breuer and Freud, of seeking abreaction for all neuroses, whether originating in shock or not, and of elevating abreaction into a panacea. Its therapeutic power is undoubted, and its discovery and use are immensely important, but it has a double shortcoming. In the first place, it can only apply when the psycho-neurosis can be precisely dated, in a traumatic moment, more or less intense. It is useless where the neurosis, as so often happens, has its beginnings, not in any one incident or shock, but in an imperceptible and unperceived warping of early life, continued and aggravated for years, and impossible to date. Not only so, but mere abreaction is in itself empty of healing, and is only a means to an end, and not an end in itself, being but the beginning of cure. It leaves the seat of the complex empty and drained, but does not bind up the wound. Much more is needed if the complex is not to fill again with the powers of those " seven others, worse than the first," of whom we know.

That " much more " is supplied by the immediate presence of the therapist, without whose presence no abreaction can take place, who shepherds his patient's new-born unity till it can stand alone. His relationship to the patient is doubly vital after abreaction is accomplished, not only because of the affect of " transference " (see p. 194), which he now accepts, but because of the positive suggestions he is competent to make. Indeed, if the therapist does not perform this supplementary function, abreaction is quite useless. In such a twofold duty, naturally the man of the highest character achieves most success ; and the Christian guide, philosopher, and friend must, in the nature of things, be *facile princeps*.

13

V

(4) Transference is the name given to one of the most important phenomena of analysis, and one of the most difficult and delicate to handle. On its proper understanding and adjustment, indeed, the entire analysis depends, and it differs from all the other psychopathic symptoms we have reviewed, in that it is an effect produced for the first time during, and not before, analysis. It arises directly out of the unique relationship between analyst and patient, a relationship whose only analogy is that subsisting between Father-confessor and penitent, but one which is infinitely more far-reaching and searching. Such a relationship is nowhere more delicate than at that moment, early in the analysis, when unconscious emotion is being stirred in its complex lair, preparatory to release ; for it is then that what is known as Transference takes place, and the therapist becomes the channel through which the neurotic discharges part of that emotion, the object at which he directs it; and on the former's personal skill and devotion in handling and loosening this fresh neurotic affect, the analysis depends for its success.

It is a new phenomenon in the behaviour of the mind. Attachment to some stronger personality on the part of a weaker, is, of course, familiar ; but this magnetic attachment, developed in the early course of analysis, whereby the unlocked emotion from the unconscious flies, as it were, at the first and nearest object presented, and fastens on the therapist, making him the focus of it all, is quite abnormal, often obstinate, and unknown outside the consulting-room. It is not necessarily a transference of affection ; frequently quite the reverse. Nor is it the natural gratitude of the abreacted to the analyst who has " done the trick." It is a purely neurotic affect, often amazingly powerful, and it has to be accepted, temporarily at least, by the therapist, as a lever for further analysis, as well as a relief for repression. Its presence is proof that deeper mental levels are being reached, and that thwarted and repressed instinctual emotions are being tapped. The energy which maintains the complex is being loosened and redirected, and it forsakes its former channel in a symptom, and fastens on the therapist instead. Its importance lies in the fact that, unconsciously of course, the patient has chosen between his symptom and his therapist, and has chosen the latter, and that the latter is obviously in a uniquely advantageous position with regard to the explanation and control of the said symptom.

Transference is thus a projection of part of the patient's unconscious on to the analyst, as a result of the disturbance caused in that unconscious by the analysis, and it is usually the case that such disturbance is caused in that part of the unconscious which encloses the early life and family setting of the patient. His analysis has led him back to the very beginnings, where, in early life, his flight from reality began, and his transference represents his first perception of his mistake, and his first unconscious effort to grapple with reality, the reality nearest him being the analyst, to whom he turns as a " Father-substitute." He is being loosened from whatever moorings he had, and until he finds his true anchorage, he clings intently to the substitute offered in the transient psychological relationship with his analyst.

An interruption in transference is in the highest degree dangerous, and suicide has been known, where it has been broken or mishandled. It is obvious, therefore, that transference presents a situation which must be treated with extreme care, and the delicate and immediate task of the therapist is the analysis of the transference itself, and the endeavour to show to the patient the meaning of his projection. With this task, the second part of his analysis begins, and , in the process, the deeper levels of his unconscious are reached.

<h1 style="text-align:center">VI</h1>

It is a conversion of the transference, a species of sublimation, which now takes place, and the second stage of analysis sees the childish dependence of transference beginning to be replaced by a normal human relationship to the therapist; and it cannot be too strongly insisted upon that this normal relationship is the beginning of cure, for it is the type on which all the ordinary contacts of a healthy mind with society are formed. To create that equal companionship, in the place of the mirage of transference, is obviously a task which demands heart and soul and strength and mind from the therapist, and only he who is as sincere with himself as with his patient, will succeed.

When the transference itself begins to be analysed, and the projection traced to its roots in parent, or in lover, or in mate, then the forgotten and repressed material begins to be exposed, the struggle between the repressed and the repressive force begins to end, and, with the diminution of his symptoms, the patient begins for the first time to see his life and his relationships in a real perspective. In such a process, the utmost interpretative skill in the therapist is imperative, and it is not too much to say that only he who has himself undergone a profound analysis should attempt so perilous an adventure as the disturbance of the repressions of a fellow-man. It is precisely here that the bungler and the amateur, learned in books though they be, wreck the patient upon the shoals of their own personality ; and equally, it is precisely here, that the purely Freudian analysis, which reduces everything *intra fœces et urinas*, finds its full stop, for the simple reason that life can only be so reduced by truncating it.

To guide the second stage of analysis, there are no hard and fast rules. Only experience, plus character, can wield the psychological surgeon's probe. Yet, in the process it may be noted that of all the methods used, dream analysis is here the most fruitful. The dream is the expression of unconscious fantasy, as well as of unconscious desire, and by seizing on every fibre of the dream, and working out with the patient its meaning, the analyst can gradually trace the unconscious roots of transference in the complex, and can plan the means of its conversion. The dream, as we shall see, is the mystic script of the unconscious, and though it cannot as yet be fully deciphered, it is our guide to the secrets of the unconscious, our map of the battlefield.

The whole aim of this part of analysis is to explain the patient to himself, as far as possible in his own words. It is not enough that he should experience catharsis, or feel release; he must have the meaning of his release, and the aim of his purification made clear. He must be made aware of the instability of his own position, not only in regard to transference, but to the whole of life. His parental or other fixations, his traumatic experiences, his sexual aberrations, his spiritual yearnings, all these must be mapped out, as the analyst and he walk hand in hand into the unknown and unexplored country of the unconscious. They are far beyond the territory of surface symptoms and of confessions, and are out to subdue the region where the rebellion was first fomented. In other words, the pilgrim is now in the Interpreter's house, where that wise old analyst of the psychology of the Christian soul, John Bunyan, makes him to arrive, after his catharsis, and before his education; and the pictures which he sees there, mirrored in his own dreams, explained in his unconscious desires, give him new insight into his errors, his powers, and his place in the world of men.

This second stage of analysis, therefore, can be

rightly called the stage of Enlightenment. His symptoms
are, for the first time, interpreted to the patient, and his
rational consciousness is enlisted to accept and act upon that
explanation of his past. Without such acceptance, no more
progress is possible ; and it is rather strange that so many
writers on analysis are content to elaborate the first and
last stages thereof—*i.e.* the exploratory and the educative
—and to take for granted the acceptance of enlightenment.
In practice it is often by no means easy to convince the
patient that this new rationale of his life and his mistakes
is the true one. He has, if all has gone well, already experienced the relief of his symptoms in some measure of
catharsis, and he is all too ready to let the matter rest there.
There is a curious and very strong experience of finality at
the end of each stage of analysis, of which both therapist
and patient have to beware, and which is nowhere stronger
than after the relief of repression ; and there is often
extreme reluctance to accept the need of the next step
forward.

This difficulty of acceptance may be grasped if
we realise that what the therapist is now doing is the
proffering of an entirely new life-structure, to be substituted
for that fixed one hitherto accepted and used by his patient.
Out of the latter's symptoms, his confessions, his revelations
of the unconscious, and his whole life-curve, the therapist
constructs and now presents to the neurotic something
bran-new, which he is asked to incorporate and blend with
the older picture. It is, and must always be, a traumatic
experience of some violence, and it has not always received
the attention which it ought.

The task of therapy at this point is therefore seen
to be a threefold one. Its first and easiest is the explanation
of symptoms, the interpreting of repressions, and the consequent almost automatic inducement of some measure of

control. But there remain the far greater undertakings of
synthesising all available material into a new and coherent
life-picture ; and of inducing the patient to accept that
enlightenment by the surrender of the faulty rationale of
life which has served him till then, for one which is untried,
unfamiliar, and especially difficult to weakened powers.
Here, surely, is a most vital situation, and one which is a
direct incentive to the Christian therapist. It is axiomatic
to such an one that no enlightenment is complete which
leaves out God and Christ ; and if a new picture-construction
of life and the universe and himself is to be presented at
this point to a sufferer, none can approach in completeness
and convincingness that which shows God at the end of the
perspective, and Christ as the Way, the Truth, and the
Life.

The reason why enlightenment is often refused
at this stage and the patient left unconvinced is simply that
the new rationale presented leaves unsatisfied his deepest
instinct, namely, his longing for completeness. The Freudian
enlightenment, which shows him his neuroses as sexual
dissatisfactions, makes him, if he accept it, less than a man,
shrunken and inglorious within ; so, too, the Adlerian, which
bids him but adapt himself to society and be for ever free,
but free in a world where there is no God. Only an enlightenment which convinces spirit, as well as mind and body, will
satisfy, and an Interpreter's House, with no pictures of
spiritual things on its walls, is only half furnished.

How, then, is conviction to be induced, or enlightenment enforced ? To that there is no one answer, any more
than to the question, Why does every reader of the Gospel
not become at once a Christian ? Yet the way of conviction
can be made straight, first and foremost, by conviction in
the therapist himself, by the absence of resistances in his
patient, by the careful use of suggestion, and by taking

thought to make the picture-substitute so complete as to appeal to the whole man, and not only a part. The onus of all such preparation, therefore, is with the therapist ; and here, of all places, there must be none of that neutrality so beloved in some consulting-rooms ; he must whole-heartedly embody Plato's " Eros Paidagogos," that sensitive and affectionate shepherding, for which the supreme example is that of Christ. If the whole analysis be conducted as in the presence of Another, conviction is sure and enlightenment becomes the prelude to illumination.

VII

The way is thus opened up for the concluding stage, that of education and consolidation. Method and progress at this stage naturally vary with each personality analysed, and with each analyst ; but, broadly speaking, under an infinite number of permutations and combinations, one general principle may be said to work in every case. The central aim of this stage of the process is to re-establish the personality, cleansed and enlightened, under the domination of some one all-controlling idea, of such force as to prevent future rebellion in the instincts, and strong enough to redirect their energy, where necessary, in higher ways ; this last, being called sublimation. Such an idea will supply the controlling motive for the new life, suffusing all experience and enclosing all desire, unifying the past, and giving dynamic for the future. Since all dissociation in the personality and all maladjustment of life are due to dual control, obviously, if the personality is to be reintegrated, one ruler must occupy the throne.

This stage is sometimes spoken of as that of readjustment, but more than mere readjustment is imperatively necessary, and that for two reasons. First, because though freedom has been achieved, and the power of the enemy has been broken, habit and tendency have strange powers ; and unless they be rigidly and continuously dominated, even after catharsis, they will swing the personality back towards the familiar ways. The grooves along which instinct asserts itself in habit are worn deep and smooth, and mere readjustment carries with it no guarantee that the old tendency will not repeat, and use the old channels. And second, because, after analysis, the man has still the same problems to face. Except in rare cases, it is not possible to change his environment, or his vocation ; analysis usually comes to his life too late for that. The same world, the same setting in it, wait for him outside the consulting-room, and the problems which have broken him, though robbed of their insistence, and faced from other angles, are still problems. It is therefore not merely a readjusted personality which is needed, but a reinforced one.

Every personality has to adjust itself through life to three things ; to its own demands, to society, and to God. The truly " normal " personality ought to be capable of continuous self-adjustment to the needs of the first and the impact of the other two ; and, in order to do so, it must, of course, be adequately motivated by its own inner, regnant desires. But an " abnormal " personality, such as we have been considering, needs to be remotivated as well as readjusted, needs not only to have the normal presented to it as desirable, but to be itself kindled with desire therefor. And it is precisely here that psycho-therapy has so far failed, encyclopedic though its knowledge be of the nature of desire, and the power of instinct, and varied as are its theories of personality. Whether, with us, it regards personality as in essence one and indivisible, or else as a congeries of selves, a human " herd-mind," akin to the termite intelligence of the ant-heap, medical psychology has produced no prescription for recreating desire therein, or for providing new and unifying motive.

Its attempts to do so are pathetically inadequate, and reveal in every phrase their own fundamental ignorance of the most dynamic motive in the world. Freud, indeed, cuts the gordian knot, by presenting the perfectly analysed man as emptied of religion and imagination, unarmed against grief and death, drained, and colourless, and content. But most other schools proffer some ideal, however lowly, to be the guiding motive of the new life, some harness, however stringy, to hitch the patient's waggon to a star. Appeals, such as they advise, to the patient's self-interest, his patriotism, his philanthropy, his family love, are good in theory, but operative in practise only when there is a compelling and lasting motive to reinforce them. It is at the crux of the whole matter, that their elaborate system stops short with a jolt, and their careful ignoring of the spiritual brings its own nemesis ; their books literally come to a dead end at this point, and if you ask for the vital thing, a ruling motive strong enough to sway the hierarchies of the mind, you ask in vain.

It is here, if ever, that the Christian voice speaks with weight of authority. There is only one such motive known to man, and that is the desire to seek after, and find, closer union with God ; and there is only one voice which promises that in the exercise of that desire, a man will find life, and more abundant life. A Christian therapist who has led his patient thus far, has therefore here, his supreme opportunity, and he will exercise it in the three time-honoured ways of persuasion, suggestion, and example. These are the three levers which any man, Christian or not, will use when he seeks to influence another, and they are the universal method of evangelism. But here, they will be used with a peculiar intensity and understanding, because a Christian

analyst has seen far deeper into the mind and heart of man
than any other; and man's needs, his experiences, and his
possibilities, come home to such an analyst with unspeakable
poignancy.

Yet these three are only the human means, and
there are others, more powerful by far, and equally time-
honoured in the service of the Faith. Prayer is one; that
prayer which does not demand, but simply lays a man's life
alongside the Life of God. Knowledge of the Person and
work of Christ is another; that knowledge which lifts Him
up, and lets Him fulfil the promise that He will draw men
to Him. And let it be reiterated, that never in the whole
experience of man can these be used with greater possibilities of triumph, than when a mind has thus been eased,
and cleansed, and enlightened, when resistance has melted
away, and the old life is sloughed like a cast-off garment, and
new horizons beckon. It is then, when the heart is tender,
and the mind once more softened and plastic, "like a little
child's," that the mighty instinct of incompleteness can
break the final barriers, and rush to its fulfilment in the Life
of God.

This is a language, so far alien to psychology, but
a language which is reinforced by ages of experience, as
accurate as that of any science, and verified by every higher
power we possess. Not only so, but it is the only possible
language in which to express the necessary crown and completion of the healing we envisage. It is the blending of
earthly speech, with the known Word of God, and it is the
one speech which the superconscious can understand; and
while we can well be content with the vocabulary of medical
psychology in the earlier stages of investigation, it has no
words that fit the necessary finish of the work. When dealing with the highest needs of man, his yearnings for God,
and his destiny in life, there is but one tongue which can

interpret him to himself, and it is the speech neither of philosophy nor materialist psychology.

VIII

We shall have to examine later, in greater detail, some of those educative means, of suggestion and the like, to which allusion has been made, when we consider the methods used in analysis, and the character of the analyst himself ; but something must be said here regarding their effect. That effect has been conveniently summed up in one word, Sublimation. Sublimation is, as we have seen, a universal human mechanism, and is, indeed, the mechanism of normal human life in its expansion and education. " We rise on stepping-stones of our dead selves to higher things," is only a half-truth, for the " selves " are by no means dead ; it is better to say that we transmute the energies of outworn habits into better and higher ways of living, and so advance. Sublimation is the normal means of resolving tension between the infantile and the childish, between the adolescent and the adult, between the maturing and the mature, and the balanced life, is the life which has effected its sublimations, sweetly and easily. Sublimation is also that " second-best " by which a nature, starved of its legitimate outlet, say, in offspring or in love, finds a channel for its repressions in philanthropic and beneficent activities.

Broadly speaking, it is discoverable during analysis that nearly every human achievement, however high, in letters, speech, or art, as well as in religion, has its beginnings in, and owes its dynamic to, successful sublimation of some primitive instinctual tendency. Similarly, in the final stages of analysis, sublimation is needed whereby the hitherto warped instinctual tendencies that have produced the neurotic, are guided into fresh channels, adequate to receive them completely, and leave none over for future repressions. And the one question remains : what is to be the alchemy which thus transmutes the power, which thus cleaves new channels through the mind ? Which question is best answered by another ; has any other yet been found than that which we profess ? There is but one sublimating power, and it is the touch of the Spirit of God upon the soul of man ; in its presence all the makeshifts of the materialist sciences are seen to be the ephemeral things they are, sublimations of a season that cannot last because they carry no inherent power, and answer no deep need. At that touch the superconscious stirs and assumes its right to rule the rest ; the two great fundamental instincts which cry " I am of value," and " I am incomplete," find at once their entire fulfilment in being of value to God and complete at last in Him ; and there can be no repression or warping where every power is operating freely and naturally at its highest because it is in touch with the Power which created it. Sublimation, therefore, to the Christian therapist presents no terrors, since he does not work alone on his patient. Christian analysis is true evangelism ; and this, its educative stage, is the climax of a long process, designed in every part to lead the patient to the presence-chamber of Jesus of Nazareth.

Such, then, is the outline of analysis, a process detailed, fascinating, and unique. It can be long or short, but whatever its duration, it follows the stages we have observed. Some psycho-neuroses yield at once, others after long resistance ; but if analysis be faithfully practised— especially Christian analysis—in full co-operation of patient and therapist, all will yield at last and renewal is sure. In that practice there are certain curative methods of universal use in all the schools, and, after this theoretical survey, we have now to examine these in more detail.

CHAPTER XII

FREE ASSOCIATION AND SUGGESTION

Analytic methods; preliminary physical examination; nature of the interviews; Free Association; its power to reveal the complex; word association; Christian technique of analysis; Suggestion; its nature; its power; faith an essential to suggestion.

I

THE process of analysis outlined in the previous chapter is carried out by certain well-defined methods. These methods vary in application and in scope, but they have one essential factor in common, in that each of them is primarily to be regarded as giving direct indication of the state of the unconscious mind, its motives, its desires, and its disorders. Some of them are not new, having long been used in blundering and hesitant fashion to ease mental tension—such as associative Confession; or to explain the vagaries of life—such as dream-interpretation; or to adjust without reference to the subconscious—such as suggestion or hypnosis. But analytical psychology has brought a revolution both in their use and their scope, has added others, and has clarified all of them. Conscious motive and conscious disorder have long been easy of access and definition; but here is an armoury, given to man for the first time, whereby he may probe deep beneath the surface of consciousness and accomplish the paradox of making conscious the unconscious.

How, then, is the psychic process of analysis

initiated ? Strangely enough, by a thorough physical examination carried out by a competent and fully qualified medical man. The necessity of this cannot be too strongly emphasised ; and that for two reasons. In the first place, mental disorder can not only cause, but be caused by organic disorder, and when the latter is the case, only physical examination can reveal the fact, and physical treatment must be a necessary prerequisite of, and accompaniment to, analysis. In the second place, assurance must be had at the outset, that the major psychoses are absent, and that we are facing only psychic disorder, and not mental disease. In the latter case, analysis will only exacerbate the trouble, and lessen or abolish the chance of ultimate cure. For want of such preliminary examination, analysis may easily shipwreck ; and no analyst should begin even the briefest of analyses till he is assured that his patient is organically sound enough to stand the rigours of investigation.

Analysis is carried out in a series of interviews, usually of an hour's duration, preferably not more than three times per week ; although in urgent cases, or at crises of analysis these rules can be set aside. While, in certain types of analysis, as we shall see, hypnotic and other methods achieve results in a comparatively short space of time, yet, generally speaking, the deeper levels are reached, and the most lasting results in the end achieved, only when the mind is not hurried, and when time is allowed between interviews for the muddied waters to clear. Emotional material given out in an interview must be given time to discharge fully and subside ; time must also be given for dream material to be thrown up and recorded ; and far-back recollection is frequently stimulated by pondering the content of an interview at leisure.

It is necessary, at the outset, to stress the time factor in analysis. True analysis is essentially a somewhat prolonged process, not only because the multitudinous content of the mind takes time to codify and assess, but also because in order to build well, one has to dig deep and drain as one goes. The analyst must be very careful indeed lest he confuse relief with cure. The feeling of relief, and even of finality, which is often experienced by the patient at the close of either of the first or second stages of analysis is a snare and a hindrance, rather than a help. Confession is a sure relief, and so is acceptance of a new way of life, but neither of these, as we have seen, goes to the root of the matter, and their sensation of freedom is but transient. The amateur analyst who achieves dazzling results with a little confession and a little hypnotism, is but scraping the surface of the mind, and he usually leaves confusion worse confounded; for his " cure " evaporates like mist in the heat of the untapped complex, and the last state of his patient is worse than the first. He is directly responsible for a good many of those who pass from mere neuroticism into the darker shadows of lunacy.

In the interview the patient is asked to relax completely, preferably flat out on a sofa, with the room sufficiently darkened to prevent distraction of the eye ; and, in the beginning at any rate, the analyst should be out of range of his eyes. Physical relaxation is a wonderful mental aperient, and the watching analyst should not be over-evident till the habit of free association is formed, and self-criticism, together with the reticences of convention, over-come. The essential prerequisite of all the interviews is, of course, the promise of complete co-operation, and the beginning at least of a good rapport ; these given, analysis can commence.

The first care of the analyst should be, to ascertain unobtrusively and in informal conversation, without any detail as yet, the surface symptoms which prompted and

precipitated the analysis, as well as, in brief, the family
setting and family history of his patient. That having been
done, the method which has been rightly called the sheet-
anchor of analysis can begin to be used.

II

"Free Association" is the name given to this
method, and it consists simply in the patient's saying, and
continuing to say, whatever comes into his mind ; which
sounds simple, but is not quite so easy or superficial as it
sounds. Let anyone, for the sake of experiment, attempt
to express in words, without selection or reservation, every
thought that enters his mind, and let him go on doing so
for, say, twenty minutes, and he will be abundantly aware
of the difficulty of really free association, of letting his mind
run on without the brake ; for he is soon conscious of tiny
hitches, of the resistances of convention or of personal
preference, of the almost instinctive selection of his ideas,
all indicative of the fact that his association is anything but
free. The patient must be told to abrogate entirely his
critical or selective faculties, together with his conventional
inhibitions, and practise, for the first time, not only complete frankness, but complete fluency.

The value of "free association" lies in the fact,
that when the patient so begins, the pull of his complexes
will be felt almost at once, and his flow of ideas will gravitate
inevitably towards them. If but little resistance is present,
he will "give himself away" almost at once ; and even his
resistances will, to the experienced analyst, be pointers in
the same direction. All roads lead to his Rome, and within
a very short time, the analyst will be in possession of the
strength and the location of the forces which he has to
overcome. A complex is, as we have seen, surrounded by a

14

constellation of associated ideas, and wears for itself deep grooves of habit or of symptom in the personality ; and its presence inevitably acts as a magnet to all other ideas. Such grooves are not only outgoing, but incoming, and a complex expresses itself, not only in the habits which it forms, but in the power which it exercises of attracting more and more ideas to its associated galaxy, till, in extreme cases, the whole mentality revolves round its self-created complex.

Not only is free association an invaluable guide to the analyst, but, what is far more important, the patient, in the course of the interviews, begins to be conscious also of the facts which it reveals. Free association, in the first place, has a surprising power of breaking down resistance, of wearing it thin. When every successive train of thought, started no matter where or how, leads in time to the point of the resistance, that resistance, even if, in the first instance, unconscious, begins to be revealed to the patient himself, *i.e.* it begins to be conscious ; and when that is so, its end is in sight, for the goodwill of the patient, and the pressure of the analyst, can deal with any resistance, when once it has become conscious. Not only so, but free association performs the important function of making the patient dawningly aware of his particular complexes ; and to raise the unconscious and repressed emotions of the complex to the level of consciousness, is to discharge them, and is the essential purpose of analysis. It may be, that in his associative trains of thought, memory reaches further and further back, attaining, in time, levels long buried and forgotten ; or simply that every such chain links so directly with the buried complex, that in time these chains become cumulatively strong enough to loosen it from its place, and drag it towards the surface of the mind ; in either case, it is free association which is the revealer of the seat of disorder to patient and analyst alike, and which has power to uproot it, and bring it nearer to the surface of the mind. And when, concurrently, dream-analysis and suggestion are also in constant use, the raising to conscious level of submerged material is greatly hastened.

It may, at first sight, seem strange that so simple-sounding a method should accomplish so much, but, when faithfully and exactly used, it invariably succeeds. It must, however, be accompanied by ceaseless watchfulness and great patience on the part of the analyst, for only he can see where and how a patient, with the best of goodwill, persistently balks at certain points, or how the unseen complex makes him distort all his personal history. Its use is a matter of experience and acquired technique, but, directed by a skilled analyst, it will work wonders.

Along with free association, there is frequently used an allied method devised by Jung, and called " word association." The patient is presented with a catalogue of ordinary words, of all kinds, to the number of a hundred and fifty or so ; and the best results are obtained if the analyst makes up his own list for each patient, on the basis of his knowledge of that patient's background. This catalogue is read out to the patient, word by word, and he is asked to give, in the shortest possible space of time, the word called up in his mind by that which the analyst has read out to him. Thereafter, the catalogue is gone over a second time, in order to see where the second replies may differ from the first. Obviously, in such a list there will be certain words which have so special a meaning for the patient that he will be unable to react to them as promptly as he would to one which was colourless to him ; it links up at once with his inner resistances, it acts as a probe which he resents, and his delayed reaction thus becomes at once a pointer to his complex. Instead of delaying, he may give an obviously impossible and foolish association to the suggested word, or, on the second reading, forget that associated word, or give it incorrectly. In all these instances he throws up a hasty defence mechanism exactly at the danger spot, and the very flimsiness of the defence is its betrayal ; while his own behaviour—embarrassed or blushing—shows that his self-possession is temporarily overthrown by the intrusion of the complex. When the list has been gone through twice, the stumbling-blocks are themselves listed, and put again at leisure to the patient, who is asked to associate freely upon them ; and the result of the whole is a very fair indication of the patient's state of mind.

It is a method of great use in the earlier stages of analysis, when the surface of the mind has to be quickly explored, or when the habit of free association has proved difficult to acquire ; and it has been used by alienists in the diagnosis of real mental disease, with conspicuous success. Its chief merit is, that it produces quick and accurate results, but these results are apt to be superficial ; they indicate emotions and repressed material, it is true, but only those which lie near the surface of the mind. In order to reach the deeper repressions and emotions of the complex itself, nothing can replace the prolonged and patient use of free association.

III

In the earlier stages of analysis, the watchword of the analyst must be—Leave the patient alone. If the analyst meddle, by giving premature counsel, even though he sees very clearly that it is needed, or by interjecting his own superior experience, he will thwart free association and dam the stream of facts which his patient is giving forth. A loquacious and " helpful " analyst will stultify analysis if he intervenes too soon ; his help in re-education will come

later but at first he should intervene only in the most un-
obtrusive manner, in order to assist the breaking down of
resistance or the building up of rapport.

Yet that does not imply that from the first the
Christian atmosphere should not pervade analysis. At any
preliminary interview it should be frankly stated that the
presuppositions of the analyst are those of the Gospel, and
that his Christian psycho-therapy is the only one, in contradistinction to all others, which can offer complete mental
health in readjustment not only to the world but to God.
As we shall see, suggestion plays a vital part in all analysis,
and such positive, Christian, and hopeful suggestion should
prevail from the outset, even though the analyst must
necessarily hold his peace while the patient is associating.
For example, if word association is being used, the
analyst's lists should contain, scattered through them, the
chief words of the Gospel—God, Christ, Faith, Joy, Church,
and so on ; words of which the average practitioner is
notoriously shy, and words to which he usually attaches a
very limited connotation. It should be made clear that
the religious instinct is as natural a part of life's equipment as
any other, and that the analyst himself, free, hopeful, and
able to help, is proof of that.

Resistance to religion, *i.e.* mental refusal to accord
full play to the religious instinct, is common to us all in some
shape or form, and is specially strong in the average neurotic.
Even in neurotics who are superficially obsessed by religion,
there is resistance to real religion, and their obsessions are
usually defence mechanisms to conceal a deeper complex ;
they find their freedom, not in escaping from religion, but
in finding it. As has already been said, far more mental
disorder has its root in starvation or thwarting of the religious
instinct, than has ever been realised ; a restlessness for God
is the true cause of many a psycho-neurosis which medicine

has tried to resolve into maladjusted sex or parent fixation. There is a great body of published analytical results along these latter lines, but there is abundant room for a parallel body of the results of Christian analysis to prove that a life which shuts down on the religious instinct, is *ipso facto* maladjusted, and to show what dire psychological results can follow the refusal of God.

Christian analysts have, therefore, a great and special opportunity before them in their clinical work, for they must learn to operate a new technique of analysis ; they must learn how to break down that obstinate resistance to speaking or thinking of religion, which sometimes colours every fibre of neurotic experience ; they must handle those associatings of their patient which reveal his spiritual strivings and needs, with reverence and knowledge ; and when the time comes, they must supply those suggestions which alone will re-edify him in spirit as well as in mind and body, and thus open the way for the Great Physician to complete the cure.

IV

These considerations open up the way to the examination of the next of the major instruments of psycho-therapy, namely, Suggestion. While Free Association is its main method, and is used from start to finish of analysis, suggestion is its constant ally, and indeed, without sug-gestion, readjustment and re-edification are impossible.

Apart altogether from analytical psychology, suggestion is probably the most powerful and generally applicable single method known to therapy. It succeeds in every department of medicine, on every occasion, from the simplest upward, and there seems no end to its range. Not only so, but it is an ever-present factor in life itself, for suggestibility is inborn in man, and is simply his innate plasticity, his native power of responding to the impacts of environment, under another aspect. Emotional suggestion, and our responses to it, are the commonplaces of daily life ; we react instantly to such things as charm of speech, or the appeal of music, or the attraction of personality in a friend, or the reiteration of clever advertisement. All dramatic art is built up on suggestibility ; when we are " lost in a book," we are so, because of our whole-hearted response to its suggestion ; and the present-day success of mass propaganda, in the press, and in the phenomenon of the dictator, is evidence that suggestion may be extremely dangerous.

Suggestion has been best defined as the acceptance of an idea by the mind, especially by the subconscious mind, independently of adequate logical grounds for such acceptance. This characteristic differentiates suggestion from persuasion ; for persuasion is a rational affair, and consists in proffering to the conscious mind such considerations as its reason will approve, in the hope of final acceptance. Suggestion makes no such appeal to reason, and it operates most forcibly when the mind has temporarily abrogated its critical and deductive powers, when opposing ideas have no chance of intruding, and the mind is made receptive, and entirely passive. The conditions, previously indicated, under which analysis is carried out, are peculiarly favourable to successful suggestion ; physical relaxation, freedom from distraction, and an atmosphere of hope and health, all contribute to that open quiescence which is so necessary.

For its success, suggestion depends not only upon mere acceptance, but upon sympathetic acceptance, whether that sympathy be conscious or unconscious ; that is to say, in its essence it is not an alien thing intruded upon the personality, but one which, consciously or unconsciously, is in line with the tendencies of that personality—suggestion is always tendencious. The theory has been advanced, that the suggested ideas are of themselves forcible, possessing the power of self-realisation, and that that fact explains the energetic response we make to suggestion from without ; but this " ideo-motor " theory ignores the fact that you cannot successfully suggest to any man ideas which are contrary to his own conscious or unconscious motives and desires. There is no injection, as it were, of outside energy from the operator ; the responsive energy aroused by suggestion is already in the mind to which the suggestion has been offered. In every case, when dissected, the power which makes the suggestion come alive, can be traced, not as McDougall traces it, to the submissive instinct, but to the far more fundamental Incomplete instinct. If, as we shall see, the essence of suggestibility is faith—faith in the suggestor, or faith (perhaps unconscious) in the consistency of the world, then response to suggestion is the venture of faith, and is simply the effort, instinctively made, to achieve the fuller completeness suggested. It is perfectly true, that in yielding to the influence of the operator or the analyst, there is an element of submission, but the answering power in the patient which energises the suggestion, can by no means be attributed to anything so passive as submission. If, on the other hand, having thus submitted, there is received a curative or ameliorative suggestion, then the conative energy of this greatest of all instincts is called forth, and the suggestion becomes powerfully effective. The power of suggestion is not, therefore, in the suggested idea, still less in the will or desire of another person ; its virtue and strength lie in the fact that it can penetrate beneath conscious volition and criticism, to the inhibited energy of an instinct, and, being in sympathy with the desire of that instinct, can release its energy in the suggested direction.

V

The key which admits suggestion, is Faith ; faith primarily in the suggestor as a bearer of help, and a person of superior knowledge ; and a faith, be it noted, which cannot be evoked, unless the suggestor himself firmly believes in his own suggestion. Unless there be implicit trust in the prestige and power of the originator of the suggestion, all suggestion will fail ; like Another, he can do no mighty works there. And in a sense, the path along which the energised answer to suggestion moves, is always the path of faith. The person to whom the suggestion is made, has no rational ground for adopting it, no empiric knowledge of that which he is about to do ; it is a swing out into the dark on his part, but he makes it on the threefold ground of his faith in the source of the suggestion, and because he knows that he lives in a world responsive to such acts of faith, and because he believes that he himself is truly capable of higher development—which things are faith for him.

There is thus a close relationship between religion and suggestion ; for religious faith is but the path along which we respond to the suggestions of God ; and by keeping this analogy in mind during analysis, it is an easier matter to merge ordinary suggestions of help or healing, into suggestions which open the mind towards God. Since all therapeutic suggestion wakens the desire for greater completeness, Christian suggestion ought to be competent to crown the process, and point to completion in God.

The capacity for faith is especially pronounced in the neurotic personality. The reason for this lies partly in the exceptional strength of the bond between such a personality and his therapist—any form of transference is a firm bridge over which suggestions pass from one to the other ; and partly by the fact that the neurotic personality is a dissociated one, and since its divided parts are necessarily weaker and less developed than the whole, they offer less resistance to the intrusion of an external suggestion. For these reasons, suggestibility is of the very greatest service in analysis ; but suggestion must always be used with the utmost caution, especially in the early stages. It is perfectly possible, for example, through hypnosis to suggest certain new ways so strongly to a patient, as to obliterate his old bad habits or symptoms ; but obliteration is not eradication, and his complexes may be still unreleased.

Suggestion, therefore, belongs properly to the later stages of analysis, when the new scheme of life is being prepared, and when sublimations have to be effected. There are no hard and fast rules for its application, and only experience can guide the use of a method so elastic. But wherever the necessary conditions are fulfilled, and the patient is quiescent and ready to trust, suggestion will always produce good results. Let the analyst make up his mind, on review of all the circumstances of the case, as to the curative suggestions which it most needs, let him offer them in a strong, hopeful, cheerful manner to a patient relaxed, uncritical, almost somnolent, and they will be at once accepted. And let the Christian analyst take full advantage of this " faithful " state of mind in his patient, offering reiterated suggestions of the power and willingness and love of God in Christ, and he will soon see them materialise, for such faith contains, as always, " the substance of things hoped for."

CHAPTER XIII

HYPNOSIS

Its history and nature ; foolish ideas regarding it ; its distinction from sleep ; its definition ; its induction ; its depths ; its use as a psycho-therapeutic agent ; what it can cure ; recovery of repressed memories ; Christian attitude to hypnosis ; use of religious suggestion.

I

THERE is one technique of suggestion, and one aspect of suggestibility, so striking in their accompanying phenomena and their therapeutic results, that they require separate examination. The phenomena of hypnosis have been observed and used in a sporadic way for thousands of years, and have been the handmaids of many strange and primitive faiths, but with the development of our psychological knowledge, they have assumed a new relevance, and now form a body of fact so impressive, as to be worthy of the name of a science. It has suffered much at the hands of charlatans, and much also by the crude popular ideas regarding its powers and its dangers, and has been slow in winning its way.

Mesmer, a Viennese physician of the late eighteenth century, was the first to perceive the necessity of synthesising these phenomena, and the first to attempt a scientific explanation of them. But his ideas of " magnetic fluid " have long been outworn, as are the common ideas which surround hypnosis with such words as " will-power," or " magnetism," or any such thing. The word hypnotism was coined by James Braid, a Manchester surgeon of the mid-nineteenth century, and to him, we owe the real foundations of the science. His work was followed up by Janet, Liébault, and Bernheim, the last two named being the founders of the great school of Nancy, which has still very many followers. Janet and Charcot, at the Salpétrière, have pursued the line that hypnosis is a species of disease, and the accompaniment of other neurotic symptoms ; and the school of Nancy maintain that hypnotism is suggestion and nothing more. Both of these are at fault, for the first-named ignore the fact that 95 per cent. of normal-minded people are susceptible to hypnosis ; and the second, the fact that the most evident phenomenon in hypnosis is not the power of the mere suggestion, but the amazing increase of energy released to carry out the accepted suggestions.

The result of the researches of the last fifty years has been to establish hypnosis as an exact science, and to make it one of the most productive and illuminating methods yet discovered for the study of the nature and functions of the mind, in health as well as in disease. It is to hypnosis that we owe a great part of our knowledge of the characteristics of the subconscious, its memory, its motives, and desires. Through hypnosis, we have learned much of what we know of the power of repression and the therapeutic value of suggestion. It has now become a major instrument of psycho-therapy, and in addition to the light it sheds upon mental processes, it has influenced pathology and physiology as well, by the information obtained through it on such questions as anæsthesia and the control of the involuntary nervous system. For our own specific purpose, it should be noted that its careful use, at the proper times and places, is productive of nothing but good ; and while there is much in it that is still mysterious and inexplicable, we know enough to say, that as a direct avenue of approach to the subconscious, it is unequalled.

Hypnosis is simply a condition of artificially
increased suggestibility, dependent upon a strong rapport
between the subject and the operator. It has been best
defined as a condition in which suggestions are not only
much more easily accepted, but are also realised with an
intensity much greater than is possible in the normal state.
There are two main elements in hypnosis which are met by
this definition. There is, first, the enormously increased
capacity of receiving external suggestion, an increase which
is quite peculiar to the hypnotic method ; and there is also
the equally extraordinary intensification of the power to
carry such suggestion into effect, a release of power which
often seems to border on the miraculous. One partial
explanation of these phenomena is the fact that in normal
life, suggestion has to run the gauntlet of conscious criticism
or inhibition, and is by them denuded of its powers, while
the response to it is, equally by them, prevented from its
fullest outlet ; but in hypnosis, these waking censors are
lulled, ordinary consciousness is dissociated, and both the
suggestion and its realisation in action are enormously
intensified.

II

Hypnotism, as we have said, has been slow in
winning its way, and even yet in the minds of many there
lingers the idea that in hypnotism there is an unwarranted
interference from outside with the sanctity of the personality,
the imposition of the will of another on an unwilling subject,
and the consequent weakening of his mental powers. Even
medical circles have been slow to admit its therapeutic
powers, and in Christian eyes it is often looked on as vested
with unnatural and diabolic influences, an evil and dangerous
thing. All such ideas may be definitely contradicted and
set aside. In the first place, no man can be hypnotised

against his will. The consent of the subject, and the fullest
possible rapport between subject and operator, are absolutely necessary before hypnosis. Not only so, but the
capacity to be hypnotised is no indication whatever of
weakness or inferiority in will or anything else. So far,
indeed, is that from being the case, that nearly everybody
of normal mind can be more or less easily hypnotised, but
the weak-minded are extraordinarily difficult, while the
lunatic are usually impossible. Nor again, is there any
question of permanent and possibly injurious control of the
subject by the operator, after hypnosis, and that, for two
reasons. No hypnotist can ever successfully make suggestions to a subject, when these suggestions conflict with
the latter's moral principles ; he cannot, for example, induce
him to commit a murder, or any gross sin—which last fact
wrecks the foundation of many a " thriller." The effort has
been made innumerable times, for experimental purposes be
it said, without any success whatever ; and the fact is an
interesting sidelight on the depth at which moral principles
root in the mind. In the second place, any influence which
the operator may have over the subject, is a secondary affect,
following on the success of his suggestions, and is, in any
case, evanescent ; it is but a temporary increase of rapport,
and the hypnotist can no more induce anyone to work his
will at a distance, or hypnotise a subject in his absence, than
he can fly to the moon.

Indeed, the results of hypnosis are effected, not
by the operator, but by the subject himself. It is from
him, not from the operator, that the energetic acceptance
comes which works the change desired. There is no in-
fusion of energy—it is his own ; and hypnosis, as we shall see,
in abrogating his consciousness, is but making his own subconscious free to use its strength in the desired direction.

Nor must hypnosis be confused with mere sleep.

Though the word "hypnosis" connotes sleep, and though many of its phenomena are akin to those of sleep, there are vital differences between it and ordinary sleep. In the lighter stages of hypnosis, for example, the subject, though apparently asleep, is quite aware of his surroundings, and he is, in all its stages, intensely responsive to the operator, and alert to his suggestions; while in ordinary sleep, there is complete oblivion. Yet if there be no suggestions offered, and the operator leaves the subject alone, the condition merges into sleep, and the subject wakes in a short time as if from ordinary sleep. There is another vital difference, in the power of the operator to recall at will the memory of what has happened during hypnosis. Hypnosis is a temporary suspension of normal consciousness, like sleep, and unless the suggestion is made to the contrary, the subject will emerge from it with no conscious remembrance of what has been said or done during the hypnotic period. This memory, however, can be evoked by the operator, and the subject be enabled to recall every detail, in either of two ways; he can suggest before the hypnosis that the subject shall so recall everything, or he can, by fresh suggestion after hypnosis, at once make him able to remember. Now, it is quite impossible under any circumstances to secure remembrance of what has happened during sleep—no path of communication with the outer world is left open, and the drawbridges are up; but after hypnosis, the subconscious memory can be quite simply brought to the surface, and the subject made conscious of all that has been done.

The hypnotic state may be defined as one of profound abstraction, with but one avenue of approach to the world left open, that which leads along the path of rapport, from the operator's mind, to the subject's. No notice whatever is taken of suggestions from a third party during hypnosis, unless the operator so desires, and the operator is the sole medium of communication. It is this narrowing down of all sensory perception, and all capacity, to one single channel, that existing between subject and operator, which constitutes the special characteristic of hypnosis, and differentiates it from mere sleep. All the knowledge and energy of the subject are enlisted to obey the suggestions which come along that channel, and this fact explains in part the intensity of the response made to them. The entire capacities of the subconscious, that great reservoir of power and experience, are at the direct service of the operator; since ordinary consciousness is waived, the operator has immediate and powerful access, and can make appeal to it, without obstacle or interference.

III

How, then, is hypnotism induced? Certainly not by any of the means associated in the popular mind with the science; the "mesmeric eye," or the "hypnotic power," or the "personal magnetism" of the operator are mere fictions, as are the mystic passes and wavings of the arm of which we read sometimes, nor is the process formidable or complicated in the very least. On the contrary, it is a comparatively simple matter to induce hypnosis, and practically everyone can do so; so simple, that it often seems incredible that results so great should be achieved in ways so direct.

Since very few people are sufficiently suggestible in normal life, certain preliminaries must be attended to, whatever the method used, in order to make them more open to suggestion. In the first place, the room should be nearly dark, not from any mysterious desire for darkness, but simply to keep the subject's eyes from anything which would distract his attention. Then also, the subject must be made completely comfortable, and told to relax utterly—no tension or voluntary muscular movement whatever. In addition, his normal suggestibility is appealed to by being told gently and persuasively what he is to expect; a gradually increasing sensation of fatigue—of comfort and warmth—of drowsiness—of heaviness in the eyes, and so on. Such preliminaries help to begin that fixation of attention, that inhibition of all rival claimants upon conscious perception, which is essential to the commencement of hypnosis; which fixation is further increased by the steady and monotonous stimulation of one of the senses. The really important thing here is, that by this mental concentration there is obtained that limitation of consciousness which is of the essence of hypnotism. All concentration tends to divide the consciousness, and since hypnotism is a condition in which the personality is dissociated, this limitation of consciousness for which we strive is a direct means to such dissociation.

The three important things are thus seen to be relaxation, fixation of attention, and monotony of sense stimulation; and it is in the induction of the last two that the methods used are so variable, each operator having his own favourite ways. Sidis, for example, monotonously strokes the forehead, saying, "Sleep, sleep, sleep," until a light hypnosis is induced. Liébhault and Bertheim used to make the subject gaze into their eyes, giving the same suggestions of drowsiness and sleep. Luys and others use revolving mirrors or an extremely bright light, at which the subject looks fixedly. It is indeed the sense of sight which is usually selected as a means for the fixation of attention, and for the purpose of that monotonous stimulation of which we spoke; and here is a simple and efficient method, selected from many, of using that sense for the induction of hypnosis. Experience alone, of course, will teach an operator his best method, and that method will vary slightly with

15

each separate case, but this one has the advantages of simplicity and general applicability.

See that the subject is relaxed and resting, and begin by explaining to him something of the power of suggestion and the process of hypnosis. Then make the initial suggestions, as mentioned above, of drowsiness, heaviness of the eyelids, fatigue, and comfortable warmth, which he will increasingly feel as you proceed. Then take a tiny pocket torch and hold it about a foot from his eyes, and in a line a little above his usual line of vision, and continue the suggestions of drowsiness and heaviness of the eyelids, gently and monotonously. Tell him to pay no attention whatever to what the operator is saying ; this is important, because the personality of the operator must not obtrude between the subject and his sleep. Tell him also to blink as much as he likes ; that his eyes are becoming too heavy to hold open ; and continue so, till you see that the eyes are indeed almost closed. Then say to him that you will count ten, and that when you have done so, he will be asleep ; and it will be found that in the very great majority of cases, a fairly deep hypnosis has been induced.

The depth of hypnotic sleep varies very greatly, and attempts have been made to gauge the various stages in it, and to classify the phenomena which accompany each stage, but the process of slipping down into this sleep is so gradual, that no hard and fast lines can be drawn. All that can be said is, that there is a gradation from the light but very suggestible stage of drowsiness and unwillingness to move, to the deep stage in which the whole muscular and sensory apparatus can be made to obey the suggestion of the operator, when, for example, anæsthesia can be produced at will, and any organ or muscle of the body influenced. All share the universal characteristic of greatly increased suggestibility—but only as regards suggestions from the operator—and of greatly increased intensity in the response to such suggestions ; and innumerable experiments of great interest and value have been made, to determine the duration and the limits of both those increases.

IV

But the paramount interest and importance of hypnosis lie, not in such " laboratory " work, but in its use as a psycho-therapeutic agent, in the cure of physical as well as psychic disorder ; and in most cases, it is noteworthy that a comparatively light stage of hypnosis is sufficient for therapeutic purposes. It is impossible to avoid the con- clusion that this field has not been worked as it ought, either by the ordinary physician or the psycho-therapist. The accumulated clinical and experimental results form a most impressive body of evidence, all tending to prove the case for hypnotism as an instrument of immense potentialities for the exploring of the subconscious, and for the readjusting of bad habits of every conceivable kind, and to show that even yet we are only at the fringe of its powers. No one, however, should attempt hypnosis, without a comprehensive and detailed study of the whole subject, and it is obvious that so potent a method must be used with extreme care.

The list of disorders which have proved themselves amenable under hypnosis is an exceedingly large and import- ant one. Here is a short list, selected from many, of some of the better known, a list in which nearly all are functional nervous disorders in which no organic lesion can be traced ; a qualification always necessary to remember, though, as we shall see, even there, hypnosis can alleviate by acting as a pain controller in cases of incurable or malignant disease.

Insomnia.
Somnambulism.

Pain of every kind ; neuralgias, facial tics, nervous headaches, or toothaches which are not produced by abscess, etc.

Functional paralyses and contractures, as well as alleviation of organic paralyses and contractures.

Nervous dyspepsia and disturbance of appetite.

Constipation and diarrhœa ; if, in the latter, there is no focus of poison.

Impotence, and all forms of sexual disturbance or perversion.

Drink and drug habits ; and such minor habits as nail-biting, for example.

Muscular and arthritic rheumatism, and lumbago.

Hay-fever, certain asthmas, and the early stages of the common cold.

Disturbances of speech, hearing, or vision, from nervous causes.

Nausea and sea-sickness.

All types of hysterical and neurasthenic symptoms ; phobias, obsessions, petit-mal, enuresis, etc.

It is obviously impossible here to examine in detail such a list as this, and a few of the simpler examples must suffice. Take insomnia, for example. Sound and natural sleep can usually be easily induced by suggestion made in a light hypnosis, a few hours before bedtime. Suggest that the subject will fall asleep in five minutes, and not wake at all till morning, and it will always work. It will again seem matter for incredulity that such things as hay fever, asthma, and the common cold, are curable under hypnosis, but the

facts are certain. At the outset, the common cold can be
aborted, and, at its height, relieved and ended in a few hours,
in a light hypnotic sleep. In both hay fever and asthma,
there is, as is well known, a large psychological element,
and both of these troublesome complaints have yielded to
hypnotic suggestion. Air-sickness and sea-sickness can be
similarly dealt with; and the response to suggestion in
cases of obstinate constipation is immediate, regular, and
lasting.

The anæsthesia induced by hypnosis has none of the
dangers or after-effects of ordinary anæsthetics. It has been
widely used in dental treatment, for example, in neuralgias,
headache, and toothache, and even in confinements, with
complete success. While pain is often the finger-post to
diagnosis, and the red lamp of Nature, suggestion can play
a great part in minimising the distress of pain, and in sub-
duing its effects. In pre-operation nervousness, and for
inducing post-operation rest, it has proved invaluable;
and even the agonies of incurable cancer can be changed, if
not to hope, at least to new peace and courage.

One psychological fact emerges here with great
clearness, namely, that such phenomena still further obliterate
the line that has been arbitrarily drawn between the psychic
and the physical. In hypnosis a purely mental control is
exercised, not, of course, by the operator over the subject,
but by the subject himself over his own habits and disabilities;
and the comprehensive results of this psychic control upon the
entire organism, including even such recondite parts thereof
as the circulatory and the so-called involuntary nervous
systems, clearly indicate that in that organism, the psychic
element is dominant, and can accomplish on the flesh that
which it pleases. And striking as are the curative results of
hypnotism upon such disorders as we have seen, where the
greater part is physical, it naturally follows that they are

yet more striking in disorders of a more purely psychological type.

In cases of alcoholism and drug addiction the effects of hypnotic suggestion are immediate and lasting. Such cases are found to be peculiarly susceptible to hypnosis, and suggestions that they shall have no more cravings, that they shall not tolerate the smell of drink or the taste of drugs, are powerfully and continuously acted upon, and the habits of years can be broken in a manner which appears miraculous. Each such case, however, requires cautious and individual treatment. The sudden stoppage of alcohol, for example, in cases of true dipsomania or chronic alcoholism will have dangerous results, and the ban on alcohol must be gradually imposed ; and, similarly, in many cases of drug addiction, total abstinence must be reached step by step. It must also be always remembered, in such cases, that the mere breaking of the habit is not enough. Search must be made, through hypnosis or otherwise, for the root cause which instigated the habit, and that must be treated also. The temptation, in such cases, to rest content with the sudden success of a hypnotic treatment, is one that is not always resisted, but it must be, lest the last result be worse than the first.

It is, however, in the recovery of repressed and subconscious memories, that the hypnotic method is the most completely successful of all known methods. It does not, indeed, supersede the analytical method, but if the two be used together, there is no repression that will not, in time, yield up its secret. As in the cases mentioned in the preceding paragraph, a hypnotic suggestion alone will not cleanse the mind ; it will recall the repressed memory, but where, owing to that repression, all the ramifications of a complex have spread through the unconscious, a further analytical process is necessary to readjust the mind. Practically all the phobias—agoraphobia, claustrophobia, and so on—

all obsessions and hysterical symptoms wherever manifested, are due, as we have seen, to the outflowing energy of a repressed and forgotten traumatic experience ; and when, in hypnosis, the suggestion is made that the subject recall something which will arouse just those sensations experienced in his symptoms, he will, sooner or later, inevitably recall the exact incident which is at the root of the whole trouble. It may take several sittings and be recalled bit by bit, but it will certainly be recalled and its attendant stress of emotions dispersed, perhaps with accompanying bad dreams and nerve storms, yet in the end, dispersed and lost.

There seems to be almost no limit to the powers of recall under hypnosis. Cases are on record in which events of remote infancy have been recalled, buried deep in the first layers of memory, and there are innumerable records of cases in which memories have been recovered from the third year onward. The whole method was brilliantly exemplified in the war hospitals, during the later years of war, where hundreds of cases of shell-shock were cured in an hour or so by hypnotic means, which at once uncovered the memory of those terrific experiences whose repression was wounding and straining the mind. It can with confidence be said, that, in every case in which the analyst is confronted with an obvious repression, hypnosis is the most certain and immediate method of recovering the lost memory. In cases where a prolonged analysis is, for any reason, impossible, the hypnotic method ought always to be used. It is an indispensible short-cut to the recesses of the mind, and, when perseveringly and gently used, in conjunction with other methods, it never fails.

V

Here, then, we have a psychological method of signal and proved value, reasonable and reliable ; and the question at once arises, what is the Christian attitude towards it ? It ought to be the same as to any other method which does no despite to the dignity and value of the human personality, and whose therapeutic powers are vouched for by clinical experience. It is only where the popular delusions regarding it linger and distort the truth, that any doubt can be entertained as to its suitability for us here. There is no invasion whatever, of the rights of the individual ; there is only the endeavour to free that individual, by his own energy, from his chains, and to give his personality room to grow as it ought.

Any method of psycho-therapy in Christian hands, must be used in the light of the Christian axioms regarding the sancity of the individual, his innate right of free access to his Maker, and his power to grow in likeness to the ideal revealed in Jesus Christ ; and this can be true of hypnosis. The hysterical symptoms of later life are caused as much by early trauma of the religious instinct, as by any other cause ; the experience of Christian analysts is conclusive on that point. Infantile terror of God, years of childhood and adolescence spent with the channels of that instinct blocked, sudden calamity or grief unrelieved by any of the hopes or truths of the Faith, have been proved to warp the personality as disastrously as any of the inhibitions of the sexual instinct, so assiduously displayed by Freud ; and only the fact that nine-tenths of analytical research has been left to non-Christian hands, prevents the proofs of these things from being as public and as manifold as the results of the other research.

Hypnosis, therefore, to the Christian analyst, can reveal the atrophy and the misuse of the religious instinct, just as much as of any other. Religious desire and motive can be repressed into the unconscious, and forgotten, equally with any other desire or motive, and only a Christian mind can give due weight to such repression when it is revealed under hypnosis. Two things may, therefore, be said regarding the Christian use of hypnosis. In the recovery of such repressed and lost religious emotions or experiences, and in the recall of any past trauma of the religious instinct, as of any other instinct, hypnosis may be freely used. And also, suggestion can be fully given for the release and the proper use of that instinct, in the legitimate expectation of a response as energetic and intense as that given to any suggestion on other lines.

Such suggestion is no implantation, as many think, of an alien and unnecessary element into the personality. Religious suggestion is as potent and as necessary to the full expression and development of that personality as any other, and has as much right to be given. Nevertheless, one stipulation, peculiar to the Christian system, must be made. Religion is built up from two influences, man's desire, and God's power. We can but educate and release the first ; we cannot command the second. Therefore it is illegitimate to suggest to a man under hypnosis, "When you wake up, you will believe in Christ " ; that is altogether outside our province, and in God's. What we can and ought to do, is so to open up his mind, so to give play to his religious instinct, so to clear the channels, that a new perception of God's presence may do the rest.

A therapeutic instrument of such power as hypnosis can obviously do great harm in the hands of ignorant or unscrupulous operators ; itinerant showmen, for example, practitioners of the art, are known to have done much damage to nervous subjects. But the same is true of any strong medicine, and hypnosis should be given with the same knowledge and the same care in preparation as are devoted to the giving of anæsthetics. Enough, however, has been said to prove that hypnosis is a method worthy of the

closest study by all psycho-therapists, and not least, by
those that are Christian. In this case, at any rate, there
will be no danger of suggestion that would weaken or further
divide the personality. And when hypnosis is used in the
process of analysis, its results are literally unique, for,

> "only its relieving and strengthening suggestions,
> and its penetrative discoveries, can dissolve away the
> mortal matter when the mysterious nexus where the
> physical and psychical forces intercross, becomes a core
> of anguish and corruption ; can unravel the twisted
> knots of insubstantial yet intolerable pain in the dangerous
> net of the nerves, and harmonise those discords between
> bodily and spiritual life that beset a highly artificial and
> complicated state of civilisation. When the senses
> practise strange tyrannies over the will, or when the
> imaginative and intellectual powers maltreat the body
> into supposed treacheries and revolts, psycho-analytic
> suggestion alone seems able to interpose in the con-
> fusion of consequent suffering. The dualism of the
> remedy matches the dualism of the malady ; it is an
> instrument of which the peculiar nature and the full
> consolatory virtues are not yet completely realised." [1]

[1] Wingfield : *Introduction to Hypnotism*, p. 290.

CHAPTER XIV
DREAM ANALYSIS

Superstition and the dream ; a radical change ; dream interpretation a psychological science ; the dream and the cartoon ; everyone
dreams; (i) Structure of the dream ; surface and latent content ; rules of
Representation ; simultaneity, casuality, etc. ; wit in the dream ; rules
of Condensation ; displacement in the dream ; (ii) Function of the dream ;
the dream as wish-fulfilment ; the dream as picture of a psychological
state ; as compensatory ; (iii) Analysis of the dream ; mere association
not enough ; find the context of each dream idea ; symbolism in the
dream ; the prophetic dream ; the Divine in dreams ; the wide kingdom
of the dream.

I

FOR ages, man has been uneasily conscious that in
his dreams and visions of the night, some voice,
alien to those of his daily life, was speaking, and his efforts
to interpret its unknown tongue have been various and long-
continued. In the main, they have been inspired by the
notion that through the dream, some outside power was
striving to manifest, some message from another world
struggling to get through, in order to warn, to encourage,
and to foretell the future. It seemed to be the only rational
explanation of what was so incongruous to ordinary experience, so whimsical and so irrational as a dream ; and till
recently, all the dream analysis of men has been conducted
on this primitive level. Elaborate lists of dream objects
and appearances were prepared, and related symbolically to
what had happened, or might happen, to the dreamer, and
so a vocabulary of dreams was constructed that might be

translated into the common tongue. In spite of unvarying failure, this more or less puerile effort at analysis continued long, for the double reason that dreams were always with mankind, and always puzzling, and that such attempts ministered to the superstitions of the uneducated mind in a very easy way. Popular folk-lore still abounds in such foolish interpretations, and for that reason, science and philosophy have passed by the dream, and have been content to leave its discussion to the gypsy, and the amateur of the occult.

A radical and permanent change in this state of matters has, however, been wrought by the work of the analytical psychologist. It was Sigmund Freud who initiated the change in 1900, by the publication of his epoch-making work, *The Interpretation of Dreams*, and though here, as elsewhere, his successors have found it necessary to differ widely from him in various ways, the basic principles he evolved are still unassailed. Research and understanding have revealed the dream, still mysterious, still but partially unravelled, as one of the most important of mental phenomena, and its analysis as one of the greatest instruments in the hands of those who disentangle the roots of mental disorder. It is now seen that the dream is the vehicle of the purposes of that unconscious we have learned to respect so much, that there is therefore no such thing as an " idle dream," and that there is no excuse for ignoring or belittling its function. Under the light now shed on it, the dream stands forth as an eminently purposeful activity, speaking a language whose rudiments we begin to understand, having its own well-defined place in the life of the psyche, and fulfilling a function of great importance in ordinary life, and of vital importance where mental disorder is being investigated.

The old idea that the dream is ministered to us

by a visitant from without, is departed from, and the ordinary dream is seen to be purely psychogenetic, produced and elaborated by the dreamer himself, using his own individual equipment of experience and memory. Certain well-authenticated, though infrequent types of dream, however, fall outwith the category of " ordinary." No one who acknowledges the power of telepathy and the possibility of direct revelation in spiritual things can doubt that dreams in which, say, apparitions are manifested of those who at the moment are passing over into the next world, or in which, again, some influence or message is discernible that no analysis can possibly relate to the life and work of the dreamer, come to man at the bidding of some power not himself, borne to him on the wings of an energy he himself has not put forth. Such dreams are established facts, but their interpretation is outside our purview at the moment, and they are the exceptions which prove the rule. Apart from these, every dream is a message from the unconscious within the dreamer himself, and is to be understood as such.

Till recently then, the dream, with its vagaries, and its inchoate structures, was regarded as something totally unrelated to the rational, causal world of ordinary experience. It is now seen to bear a close relation to our desires, and to express our psychological state in a language closely akin, in some respects to one we use in waking life, namely, that of symbol. The general use of symbolism in ordinary life needs no illustration ; the very words we use in speaking of it are themselves symbols of the ideas they represent. But we have seen one particular symbolism in previous chapters which bears an intimate relation to the symbol mechanism of the dream, and which enables us to begin to understand one purpose of that dream, namely, the disguise mechanism employed by the repressed emotion or instinct in order to get past the repressing force which holds it

down. Every symptom, every mechanism we have enumer-
ated, is a symbol ; and when the waking life is in abeyance, a
similar process goes on. The repressing force is wakeful,
though we are not, and the duel between it and the thing
repressed is incessant. Once more the well-used language
of symbol is resorted to, once more, though in primitive
manner, a distorting mechanism is evolved in order to get
the forbidden thing past the censor into expression, and the
dream thus becomes the vehicle of a message straight from
the unconscious mind of the dreamer.

II

Before proceeding to look at the structure and
function of the dream, three preliminary observations may
here be made.

(i) It is of great assistance when beginning the
study of the dream to bear in mind the idea of the Cartoon.
If one were given, say, a political or psychological truth, and
asked to express it in pictorial form, how would one set
about it ? In one way only, by using the well-known
method of the cartoon, which, like the parable, expresses a
meaning totally different to the structure of figures and
places employed, but which is yet a unity, for the idea and
the picture are linked in the bond of symbolism. Regard
your dream as a cartoon, and light begins to dawn upon its
vagaries, and a meaning begins to emerge beneath its surface
impossibilities. The more we study dream analysis, the
more we respect the ingenuity, the humour, and the inventive
power employed by the unconscious in getting its message
through, and speaking its mind, in spite of the watchful
censor of repression. A very simple illustration may suffice.
A spinster dreams of a man she has not seen for years, a
practical stranger who yet approaches her, kisses her, and

proposes marriage ; and she wonders what on earth she means by dreaming so. But when it is found that the man is remembered as wealthy and grasping, turning all he touches into gold, and furthermore, that the dreamer is fond of power and has little, the dream, in one surface aspect, becomes a very neat compendium of thought, stating clearly the desire of the unconscious for power (symbolised truly by money), a desire which the conscious life respectably buries and ignores ; to say nothing of that side of the dream which reveals the thwarted life of spinsterhood. The man is a cartoon, and expresses a hidden desire, both in his wealth and in his person.

(ii) Everybody dreams ; and this statement can be confidently made, in spite of vehement denials on the part of those who do not recall their dreams. That they do not remember them is but evidence of the strength of the repressive force which wipes clean the slate on waking : and the very vehemence of denial, (usually made with that familiar half-smile which is so significant a symptom of underlying tensions to the eye of the analytical psychologist) is a reflection of that strength. In the course of analysis, dreams begin to be vaguely recalled, even by those ; and the man who never dreams has yet to be born. The student of dreams will be well advised to have pencil and paper at the bedside, and to write down at the *instant* of waking, what he remembers of his dreams. Thirty seconds after may be too late, for erasure is swift, and is swiftest with the very details which matter most ; and the effort of recalling the last dream will often unveil the penultimate one, and even those further back than that. Always watch for the detail which tends to be forgotten ; it is usually that which is wanted to be forgotten, and may be the clue to the whole.

(iii) The pioneer of dream interpretation is, as has been said, Freud, and his distinction is closely shared by Jung, whose conclusions differ in several vital respects from those of Freud. Here, too, Freud has overstressed what he is pleased to label the sexual root, and finds it in all dreams. While, indubitably, hidden sexual desires are discernible in very many dreams, as we might expect, they are by no means omnipresent, and Jung, in limiting this element of the dream to its proper place, and evolving the concept of the compensatory function of the dream (which often asserts, and tries to make up for, some lack in the dreamer's waking life) is nearer the truth. Nevertheless, as we shall see, that part of the work of Freud which deals with the content and structure of the dream abides, and is permanent. What follows is, therefore, a synthesis of these permanent elements, with those stated by Jung ; and where needed, Christian truth is drawn upon.

In order to clarify and condense what is a tremendous subject, and one of the most fascinating in all psychology, we divide our survey into :

(1) The Structure of the dream.
(2) The Function of the dream.
(3) The Analysis of the dream.

III

(1) The Structure of the Dream

It is obvious from what has been said, that the appearance of a dream may be very different from the meaning hidden behind it, and that therefore, a dream has both a surface and a latent content. It is the task of analysis to discover this latent content, and in this task, the analyst is aided by certain rules, which, it has been discovered, are obeyed in the " dream-work," or the formation of the dream. The dream, this pictorial effort on the part of the unconscious, by which it gets its disturbing ideas past the threshold of consciousness in disguise, follows well-defined methods in building up the structure and sequence of its events. To the eye which regards surface content alone, these are often ridiculous, inconsequential, and unmeaning ; but when we begin to analyse, we find that even these apparent meanderings are purposeful, and behave according to rule. Some of the more important of these rules follow, and if they seem to be stated briefly and dogmatically, let it be remembered that behind each, there is a vast background of patient scientific research, conducted by psychologists of all the schools, in the course of which, multitudes of dreams have been skilfully sifted, unravelled, and observed to obey this or that rule.

(a) Rules governing *Representation*.

A cartoon is a static affair, and a dream is a progress, more or less direct, a sequence of ideas apparently unconnected, but still a sequence. Is there any clue which can relate the parts of this sequence to one another, and make the pictorial parable declare itself ? In other words, how does the dream represent the ideas it intends to convey, abstract as these often are, using only the limited syntax and language of picture ? As Freud himself has said :

" Dream-thoughts commonly reveal themselves as a nexus of thoughts and memories, of the most intricate possible construction, with all the characteristics of the thought processes known to us in waking life. . . . The individual parts of this complicated structure naturally stand in the most manifold logical relations to one another. They constitute foreground and background, digressions, illustrations, conditions, lines of argument, and objections. When the whole mass of these dream-thoughts is subjected to the pressure of the dream-work, during which the fragments are turned about, broken up, and compacted, somewhat like drifting ice, the question arises,

16

what becomes of the logicalities which had hitherto provided the framework of the structure ? What representation do ' if,' ' because,' ' as though,' ' although,' ' either—or,' and all the other conjunctions, without which we cannot understand a phrase or a sentence, receive in our dreams ? " [1]

Just as the art of painting finally succeeded in depicting, in the persons represented, at least the intentions behind their words—tenderness, menace, admonition, and the like—by other means than by floating labels hung from their mouths, so also the dream has found it possible to render an account of certain of the logical relations between its dream-thoughts, by an appropriate modification of the peculiar method of dream-representations. What, then, are some of those modifications ?

(i) It represents logical connection in the form of simultaneity : like the famous curtain of the London Coliseum, which depicts all the great ones of the stage in one grand group, the dream-groups, impossible though they seem, are logically connected in the dream-thoughts which inspire them ; that is, whenever two things come close together in a dream, their logical connection is implicate.

(ii) Causation is represented by succession ; sometimes by a succession of two or more dreams, sometimes by the immediate transformation of one image into another. When, say, a brief dream prefaces a longer one, or a figure changes while we watch it, " because " is the key-word to remember. In this connection, it is worth while noting that all dreams of the same night are parts of one whole ; their divisions, their sequence, their relationship to one another, are rich in significance, and this significance usually becomes more and more plain, as the series unfolds.

[1] Freud : *Interpretation of Dreams,* p. 298.

(iii) When the dream wishes to present alternatives, it puts the two side by side as equal. Hence many apparently exclusive and contradictory elements of the dream, simply mean " either—or."

(iv) " Like," or "Just as," are expressed by the dream, through contraction into a unity of the elements that are similar ; that is similar things or persons are just folded together into a kind of composite picture, bearing some of the characteristics of each component. (This we shall see later, under Condensation.)

(v) Moral ideas of right and wrong are frequently interpreted as the right or left hand of the dreamer ; and importance is often shown by the size given to the person or object in the dream.

(vi) The real wit of the unconscious is very obvious in the dream. Punning allusions abound, as might be expected where two ideas are often slid together into one ; sly digs at peculiarities or shortcomings of the conscious life, such as self-conceit; warnings in jocular form; and, of course, perfect frankness in all matters on which we are usually reticent. Look, for example, at the perfect maze of puns in this dream, recorded by Dr. Ernest Jones and Dr. Yellowlees :

> " The patient dreamed of the scriptural character *Lysanias*, who was spoken of as the Tetrarch of *Abilene*. On analysis, the patient recalled that at his school, which was called the *Lyceum*, he had indulged in *licentious* practises in an old *abbey* with a boy named *Leney*."

In addition, too, arithmetic is freely and amusingly used, numbers found in dreams, such as dates or sums of money, revealing themselves as mines of information on analysis ; one number often unfolding into three or four most significant dates, or financial transactions.

(b) Condensation in the dream.

This is one of the most remarkable properties of the dream, one of its main characteristics being its economy, its habit of expressing in the briefest possible images, the greatest possible number of ideas. When analysed, one dream-image will produce many dream-thoughts, and a dream which occupies a sentence or two in describing will reveal a tremendous aggregate of thoughts behind an apparently simple structure. In order to get through at all, that dream has to compress, otherwise, if it were to say all it has to say, it would need to be of inordinate length, and therefore, these " portmanteau " images are very common. We dream often of a person with the face, say, of one man we know, the clothes of another, and the speech of another ; or of a house which is a jumble of several we know in waking life ; or we hear a sentence, or see it written in a book, containing elements of half a dozen thoughts we recognise ; and each such element, when separated out, provides a valuable clue to the analyst. In addition, it can usually be said that the greater the vividness of a dream-image, the more condensation has been applied to its composition.

Even if we search no further than the surface content of a dream, this power of producing a composite photograph, of telescoping ideas into one another, explains many an apparent incongruity ; and if the layers be stripped, the process goes far to unveil the latent content and purpose of the dream.

(c) Displacement in the dream.

Where resistance has to be reckoned with, displacement is inevitable. Whether or no we personalise the inner Censor, the watcher by the threshold, as Freud does, the more we study the dream, the more we are conscious of the repressive forces it has to contend against. Here, again, analysis reveals a distorting mechanism of great ingenuity in the power a dream possesses of altering proportions entirely, making mountains out of molehills, and weaving a mirage of unimportance round its treasures, in order to get them through. Like the cartoon, the dream may centre, not upon what looms large in the foreground, but upon some apparently trivial detail. To emerge at all, it has had to change its centre of gravity, and overweight the unessential, that beside it, the really important thing may slip in, disguised obscurely. No sooner does analysis touch a dream, than the proportions of its surface content begin to shift and dislimn, and unsuspected depths appear where we should least expect them ; and where we did not expect, neither, obviously, did the censor.

There is a half-truth, too, in the old adage that dreams go by contraries, for Inversion, or the representation of a thing by its opposite, is one of the instruments the dream uses, to create its illusion of complete harmlessness. The reason of this at first sight meaningless proceeding is, that if the dream be a wish fulfilment, it is here only translating the familiar phrase we use in waking life about anything we hate remembering, " I wish it had been the other way about ! " ; and in the dream, accordingly, it *is*. Quite often, a dream which refuses to yield its meaning to any persuasion, becomes crystal clear on being thus turned upside down.

IV

(2) FUNCTION OF THE DREAM

Whatever the material which the dream impulse seizes upon as vesture for its parables (and very often it is that which lies closest to hand, namely, the events of the previous day), it is subjected to the processes of disguise already surveyed, and passed on, but passed on with a purpose which has little or nothing to do with the events chosen. They are made the vehicles of a hormic urge which creates the dream pictures, and insinuates them without disturbing sleep, and which always has its own ends in view. This essential function of the dream has been described in two very different ways by Freud and Jung ; neither of these ways is an exclusive right-of-way, and both are most valuable, but that of Jung leads much further.

(i) According to Freud, every dream is a wish-fulfilment, a declaration of the imaginary satisfying of some desire to which conscious life denies expression. That wish is the direct voice of unconscious life, and gives, therefore, a clear idea of the forces at work there. When clarified and reduced to its elements, the dream always reveals repressed desires, and it is thus of the utmost value as a guide to the site and nature of the complex. The dreams of a psychopath relate the complexes of the psychopath, and by their dreams ye shall know them. Were this more generally known, there would be far less eagerness on the part of the readers of certain newspapers to rush into print with their " odd " dreams.

To shadow forth such wishes, the dream uses a number of symbols, objects that are found to be universal, and independent of language, time, or race. Freud has made an exhaustive study of such symbols, and while it is impossible to agree with him that they are nearly all sexual, there undoubtedly is a strange series of dream symbols, not yet catalogued, closely related to primitive myth and universal folk-lore, and independent of the dreamer's own personal experience. By means of these symbols, the wish can be put forth into consciousness, because consciousness does not know the meaning of them, and the unconscious through them can speak freely.

(ii) In the hands of Jung, the dream becomes a statement to the dreamer of his own psychological needs. Factors in the life of his psyche which may have been neglected, as well as those which may have been repressed, are presented by the dream, which thus becomes a declaration of omission, a warning of need, a call for attention, as well as a statement of desire.

"The dream gives a true picture of the subjective state, while the conscious mind denies that this state exists, or recognises it only grudgingly. It has no respect for my conjectures, or for the patient's views as to how things should be, but simply tells how the matter stands. It is the way of dreams to give us more than we ask. They not only allow us an insight into the causes of the psycho-neuroses, but afford a prognosis as well." [1]

Freudian interpretation is therefore permissible, but only partial, and must be widely extended. Just as the daylight consciousness comprehends vastly more than mere desires, so that infinitely greater realm whose borders we are treading contains forces and fears, truths and plans, anticipations and telepathic powers, and is wider far than just a residence for complexes. The dream, therefore, which is the authentic voice of the unconscious, to whose production, by the way, at least one-third of life is given in sleep, cannot be denied its right to appear as the herald of these other elements, and not alone as the speech of repressed desire.

There is deep wisdom in the view which regards the relations between conscious and unconscious, as self-adjusting, and manifesting, like all the rest of the organism,

[1] Jung : *Humanity in Search of a Soul*, p. 5.

a purpose towards balance. When any one part of life goes out of gear, a compensatory activity is set up to endeavour to adjust the whole, and keep the peace ; and this is abundantly clear in mental life, for, as we have seen, it is when repression has taken place that the unconscious begins to strive, with " groanings which cannot be uttered." Similarly here, the dream is caused by something which has actually happened in the life of the psyche to upset the equilibrium, and is an endeavour to compensate therefor. Viewed in this light, the dream becomes one of the most illuminative and far-reaching of mental phenomena. It reveals hidden and neglected factors, speaks unwelcome and forgotten truths, and utters in prophetic accent what must happen should a certain course be taken.

V

(3) THE ANALYSIS OF THE DREAM

In order to reveal itself, and fully to declare its meaning, the dream must be analysed. All interpretators of the dream, save analysis, have failed, because they have dealt with surface content only ; and the dream picture is a highly imaginative and elaborated complex of ideas, which require to be separated into their component elements, probed, and dissected, before the dream can fulfil its purpose as a messenger of the unconscious. Even through analysis, the interpretation of a structure so manifold, so condensed and introverted as the dream, is a matter of extreme difficulty, and one whose technique can only be acquired by long psychological experience.

Broadly speaking, the method used is a variant of the free association method already described. Mere free association on a dream, does not take us far enough ; it

is not sufficient simply to take the dream fibre by fibre, and
to associate freely upon each. To do so, ignores both the
meaning of the dream " cartoon " as a whole, and the purposive character of the dream itself. One might as well,
with equal success, associate upon the first images which
floated into the mind at the interview, irrespective altogether
of the dream. We shall begin to perceive the purpose of a
dream, only by taking each separate image therein and
subjecting it to minute examination, in order to discover the
exact connotation which surrounds that image in the patient's
mind and experience. There is a nimbus of ideas surrounding it, as well as an associative train or trains ; and it is this
nimbus of ideas which gives the real clue to the meaning of
the dream. In that halo, that aura, there will always be
distinguished something, underneath the inversions, the
condensations and so on, of the dream-image, which will
form, perhaps, a word in the complete dream-sentence.
And if there be darkness round the dream-image, no halo, no
response to the request for connotations, this is, in itself, a
pointer in a suspicious direction ; for, in analysis, silence can
often speak louder than words.

When each image in the dream has thus been placed
in its appropriate setting, and related not only to the remembered experience of the patient, but to the tendencies and content of his mind, as well as to his heredity, the latent content
of the dream begins to dawn upon the analyst. Since,
also, the psychological state of a patient, his psycho-neuroses,
and his unconscious wishes, do not greatly vary from day to
day, it is natural to suppose that his series of dreams on
the same night, or his dreams on successive nights, may be
presumed to be variants of the same, or similar messages ; and
the analyst will be wary of coming to a premature conclusion
regarding the meaning of a single dream, without putting
it in relation to its neighbour dreams, either of the same, or

of other nights. This fact alone delivers the analyst from the necessity of troubling overmuch about the immediate bodily condition, or the external stimulus, which may have made a dream especially vivid, or have cast it in a particular mould, related, perhaps, to an immediately preceding event which has been reacted to with great intensity. There is no doubt that digestive disturbance, or external light, sound, and so on, have their effect on the format of a dream and its clarity ; or that this format often tends to relate to the most recent events. Such surface trivialities have no effect whatever on the particular message which the unconscious may be striving to get through, and the unconscious, as usual, is swift to seize any instrument, even a passing dyspepsia, to fulfil its purpose.

The one instance in which dream analysis borrows from popular dream interpretation, may be said to be the suggestion that certain dream-images always represent the same thought, and are, therefore, universal symbols of that thought, wherever they occur. As might be expected, Freud, in his comprehensive catalogue of dream-symbols, has reduced the image in nearly every case to a sexual root ; and Jung has, with more probability, worked out another list, founded on the universal symbols of mythology and folk-lore, suggesting that, in such dream-images, the " collective unconscious," the inherited race memory of the individual is speaking. But the analyst should be wary of accepting as hard and fast any list of symbols and their equivalents, however authoritatively laid down. It is indubitable that in a great many instances, certain dream-symbols can be dearly referred to the sexual instinct, and equally, that others can be interpreted as mythologies are interpreted, speaking from the archaic depths of the unconscious mind ; but it is not possible to say that such symbolism is of universal application. Dream-symbols can only be interpreted in the light of the fullest knowledge of the mind of the individual patient, and that mind has in it, religious and moral elements, which, when repressed, cry aloud with full voice in dreams and symbols. It is exceedingly unfortunate that the vast majority of the research upon the subject has been done by men whose presuppositions were not Christian. Freud especially, and Jung in a lesser degree, seem to exclude in their interpretations, all possibility of a religious content from the symbols, as from the structure of the dream ; and it is plain fact, verified in the more limited, but as authentic, analytical experience of the writer, that when religious repression has taken place, or conscience has been aborted, the dream is not slow to tell us so. It voices the hidden yearning for the spiritual ; it declares the mutilation of the religious instinct ; and it can be interpreted more authoritatively and clearly, from the religious angle, than from the Freudian or any other.

Another consideration supports this view, because no account of the dream would be complete, which made no mention of that well-authenticated and disturbing phenomenon, the prophetic dream. When every possible allowance has been made in such dreams for unconscious wish-fulfilment, for symbolism, and the rest, there remains an irreducible residue of evidence, which is inexplicable on any other hypothesis than that, in obedience to laws of which we are in ignorance, the curtain has been lifted for a moment. It may be something urgent which is spoken of, such as accurate warning of impending death, by catastrophe, be it noted, and not by illness ; for, in that latter case, the unconscious deeps have been proved to have foreknowledge of organic trouble, long before the conscious is made aware of danger. Or, as is most usual, it may be something completely trivial, a detailed vignette of some unimportant scene or event, which occurs in minute reproduction weeks or

months later. In either case, they are deeply disturbing to
such as believe in the free choice of man to determine his
actions, and they, at the very least, represent an aspect
of dream activity, far removed from the ordinary powers of
the mind.

They are not mentioned here in order to suggest
their interpretation, or their origin, for nobody as yet has
been able satisfactorily to do either ; but to suggest that in
them, the spiritual may be at work, moving in quite other
dimensions than those of space and time. And the testimony of such dreams is amplified by Christian experience,
which declares that time and again, it has been " warned of
God in a dream," and that in sleep, a visitant from another
place has spoken. That deep Incomplete Instinct, which
is the dynamic of so much of our waking life, can speak in
dreams, and, what is more, be spoken to, in a language which
is not of earth ; and, since it can translate the message only
in symbol, or parable, it puts forth a dream, and makes the
dream God's herald. When all conscious sense is shut off,
who shall say what avenues are opened ; and though exact
knowledge or interpretation are not yet possible, they will
be more possible when Christian analysis has concentrated
upon the dream.

Waking consciousness is, after all, a limited affair,
narrowed by the immediacies of the five senses, and concentrated at every moment on but one moving point. In
dreams, we seem to enter a wider kingdom, freed from the
fears and restraints of normal life, a field where earthly
forces and laws are set at naught, and where the whole
immensity of the subconscious can have freer speech, and,
like a rising tide, submerge the petty logics of our daily life.
We have not yet discovered the laws and the proportions
of that wider field, but at least, we are conscious that in
dreams, we often touch the edges of our Paradise, and fulfil

the good desires which the world can never gratify. And since these things are so, a Christian analyst can approach the dream with greater readiness and reverence than any other. The dream, when better comprehended, may yet prove to be not only the authentic voice of the subconscious, but a path towards fuller knowledge of the unseen world in which our finite life is set. When thus analysed, and not subjected to materialist axioms, or straitened by Freudian presuppositions, every fibre of the dream may be found to point to the central fact of all creation, and our dream-life may thus become an index to Eternity.

CHAPTER XV

CHARACTER AND TRAINING OF THE THERAPIST

Analytical psychology not for the disordered only; creative energy of the unconscious; influence of this on Christian doctrine; sublimations of a Christian psycho-therapy; (i) Character of the therapist; vitally important; reverence, humility, and selflessness; rooted in Christian love; (ii) Training of the therapist; Christian experts needed; should be available for all; three elements in training; a threefold knowledge of psychology, psycho-therapy, and analytical psychology; they must themselves be analysed; clinical experience more than books; and in the end, only Christ can crown the work.

I

WE are now in a better position to see the meaning of analytical psychology and its applications to therapy. Our survey has led us first, to the examination of the unconscious mind and its resident powers and instincts; then, to the various ills induced by the maladjusted mind, all of which can be traced to unconscious origins; then, to the aims of psycho-therapy; and lastly, to its methods. And in the course of that survey, it has become abundantly evident that this book is justified in its purpose. There is a wide door and effectual before the Christian analyst who will learn to infuse this new therapy with the breath of Christian love.

Yet it would not be right to assume that the message of the new psychology began and ended with this ministry to minds diseased. Analytical psychology has made a twofold contribution to knowledge ; it has taught us when and how to use the instruments which we have been describing ; but it has also taught us a new attitude towards the creative mind of man. If we regarded the new psychology simply as a therapeutic agent, we might be pardoned for thinking of the unconscious merely as a limbo for repressions, and a restless home for all those elements of experience which are repugnant to the ordinary consciousness. To do so, would be to ignore the truth, that it is precisely because of the very powers of the unconscious that such repressions have endured, and that such complexes have had an autonomous life and energy. That energy, instinctual and emotional, is a permanent endowment of the unconscious, and it is the dynamic of all the normal creative work of the mind, as well as being the temporary power-house of the complex. Rightly viewed, such complexes and repressions are merely incidental to the unconscious, whose normal function is creative.

Something of this, we saw, when we considered the nature of inspiration, and the manifestation of genius ; but from this point of view, there is something inspirational about even the simplest action. Our lightest wish, our most habitual reaction to life, may be dictated to us, not by consciousness, but by imperatives of whose power we have no knowledge. Ordinary consciousness is but the servant of a very large house indeed, and, in this regard, only sets open the chamber door to the coming and going of the masters of the house. Our reaction to circumstances may seem, on the surface, immediate and uncomplicated, but behind it there is a whole constellation of directing powers, most of them unconscious.

We have therefore learned to regard the unconscious as the constant seat and source of all energy, the sphere in which all mental processes are prepared, before being brought to light, and by means of which, they may be profoundly modified after they are thus brought to light. No power of the conscious mind, volitional or any other, can deny right of way to the demands of the unconscious when they surge up and cross the threshold ; it may qualify, and repress, but it has to acknowledge receipt, albeit sometimes with pain and suffering. And not only is their knocking at the doors insistent, but such powers have a quality all their own, outside the bounds of sense, and unfettered by the time-space limits of consciousness. When a concept or an impulse thus enters consciousness, it at once encounters the inhibitions of time and space, but till then, while it was with the unconscious, it was fourth-dimensional ; and this other-worldly, quasi-eternal element in the unconscious, makes it the natural recipient of the truly eternal, because it is from the unconscious as a seed-bed that spiritual principles root and blossom into conscious religious life.

The influence of this upon Christian life and doctrine is at once apparent. Sin, as we have seen, has roots in the unconscious ; why not righteousness as well ? Through what door will the powers of God enter a man, entering, as they often do, long before he knows them, if not through the portals of the religious instinct, deep down in the unconscious with its neighbour instincts ? This is, for example, the only explanation of the strivings and wrestlings of, say, Paul, or Augustine, before conversion ; the hand of God was on them, but they were not conscious of it. It is literally deep answering unto deep ; the power of the external and unseen God, being met by the power of the internal and unseen instinct, reaching up towards Him. If, therefore, the simplest action may, as we saw, have deep roots in the unconscious, some at least of those roots may be spiritual, even though consciousness be unaware of the fact. It is in the unconscious, that the creative work of God joins the

creative impulse of man ; and here psychology unites with
religion, in the endeavour to find new ways in which these
unconscious powers may be expressed.

II

In this endeavour, analytical psychology can
assist in a manner peculiarly its own ; for it not only shows
the way to the relief of unconscious repressions, and the cure
of mental disorder, but also, in the process of analysis, it
has proved itself capable of releasing energies hitherto misused, and of re-educating them.   The energy spent in holding
down a repression, or vitalising a complex, can, after analysis,
be spent in creative and useful ways, and this educative
aspect of analysis is closely analogous to the work of religion.   Indeed, it is true to say that analytical psychology is
the only means yet known to man, apart from the assistance of
the Divine, of reaching and redirecting instinctual and
unconscious energies.   But, as is only too evident in the
works of the leading analysts, this part of the field is poorly
and most ineffectively worked ;   many of them shirk the
creative part of their task entirely, and when they do con-
descend upon advice, the channels they suggest for creative
energy, after analysis has done its work, are ludicrously
shallow.   You cannot, as they seem to suggest, offer outlets
in literature, or art, or athletics, or community service,
wholesale, as universal panaceas, to minds which have neither
endowment or predilection for such things.   But what you
can do is to link such minds, with their released creative
energies, consciously to the Divine, and let them find their
fullest scope in learning to love God, and their neighbour
as themselves ;   and you can, in literally every case, endeavour
so to present the beauty of Christ, that the patient will turn
to Him, and learn to love God and man, by learning to love

17

Him, who is both God and man. Not only so, but you can reveal to him the unconscious in every action, even the slightest, and show him, that, even when he does not know or regard God, God may nevertheless be at work on him.

It is here, therefore, that, as we have said, psychology unites with religion, and it is in and through religion alone, that analysis can find its completion and its crown. It must therefore be obvious that there is no higher work known to man than the work of a Christian analyst, who has the supreme task, not only of cleansing and reorientating the wayward minds of men, but of releasing the energies of their religious instinct and making them conscious of God. It is a work which ought to be approached with the utmost reverence; and it demands a twofold equipment of character and training which we may well examine now.

The character of the therapist himself is of the very first importance; for, when one asks the question, " What is it that does the work in psycho-therapy ? " the answer is, not so much the method, as the character of the man behind the method he uses; not so much the probe, as the hand that impels it. It is on the rock of personal character that both amateur and professional analysts have split, for, in all too many, it is their motive and not their character which dominates their work; motives, in the case of the amateur, of curiosity or love of power, and, in the case of the medical psychologist, motives coldly scientific and often worldly. Success in psycho-therapy depends, of course, on accurate knowledge of the mind's disorders, their symptoms and their cure, but much more, upon what the patient sees of strength and rightmindedness in his therapist. There is no one so sensitive to atmosphere as your neurotic, and good character is its own infection; you cannot cleanse a wound of the mind, as of the body, unless you yourself are

aseptic. There is a noticeable reluctance in many quarters
to face this issue, and to regard analytical psychology as
simply another medicine, a little more intangible than most,
but as reliable in its effects as a drug, no matter who
administers it.

The most formidable, therefore, of the difficulties
of the therapist, lies just here. Anyone who wishes, can
acquire the jargon of analytical psychology, and dabble in it,
with deplorable results ; and anyone who applies his mind
can learn the scientific facts of mental disorder and of psycho-
therapy ; but not everyone has the courage to act upon the in-
junction, " physician, heal thyself "—yet that is the indispensable prerequisite of all healing of other men. This is all
the more strange, because the instant you begin to touch
analysis, if your mind be sensitive at all, there comes the
swift perception that you yourself are mirrored in the needs
and faults of your patient, that there, but for the grace of
God, go you, and that, in the presence of his psycho-neuroses,
you stand self-confessed. Such perception is literal sympathy,
a suffering with and beside the sufferer, and without it, there
is no therapy ; it may be shocking to be so revealed in the
image of another, and that a neurotic, but self-knowledge is
often shocking, always salutary, and much needed to prick
the bubbles of self-esteem and love of power, that are the
special temptations of the analyst. It has all along been insisted upon here, that to set one's hand to so delicate and far-
reaching a task as the therapy of the mind, needs a self-
preparation of the highest possible kind, and this demand is
strengthened by the consideration we have just stated.

III

There must first be reverence, deep and strong,
in face of the manifold powers and capacities of the kingdoms

of the mind. To be able to touch even the fringe of a thing so wonderful is, even from the scientific point of view, a thing to marvel at and to be grateful for; but when as Christians, we remember that that mind is the cradle of Divine purpose, and enshrines a character and a personality that may live for ever, and that what we do to it may have repercussions, not only in time but in Eternity, it may well give us pause before we lay hand upon the Shekinah. Still more should we be hesitant when we consider the healing of its ailments, for our hasty touch may deepen and not heal the wounds, our meddling may hinder God's purpose, and our opening up the unconscious may wreck the balance of the whole. A hesitant and prayerful reverence, first, last, and always, for the mind of man, the acme of creation, the vehicle of God to earth, and the heir of immortality, is the mark of the character of the Christian analyst.

And with reverence goes humility ; and that for three reasons. In the first place, with all our knowledge of the mind, we are only at the beginnings. If we had learned the laws that would enable us to control and organise our own natures, as we have learned those with which we control and organise the world for ourselves, the catastrophic events of the last thirty years would not be happening. It is we ourselves who are maladjusted, and not only the neurotics ; we live like strangers, in a new earth, with new heavens above us. Scientific knowledge is creating a hostile environment round the mind, one to which the mind reacts in terms of overstrain and breakdown, simply because we have not begun to know ourselves one hundredth part as well as we know the forces of nature and the face of the stars ; a humiliating thought. If our endeavour be to understand and build up that overstrained mind, let us be very humble about it, for there is a good deal of the " pious hope " in our work ; psychology is only rudimentary, in spite of its advances.

Freudian cocksureness is no passport here—it is a puerile reaction to the majesty of the mind.

In the second place, if we have to receive, and deal with, the very worst in our patients, without flinching, we have to be ever mindful of our own dark spots, and walk humbly side by side with him. Too many analyses have been spoiled because analyst has dealt with patient " de haut en bas " ; judge not, because your patient is your judgment, and if you fail with him, you fail with yourself. And in the third place, if we believe that we are making straight the way for the Creator to come and deal with His creature, we must, like the Baptist, decrease, that He may increase. A Christian analyst, above all men, must keep down, lest he get between God and His ailing child, must be humbly careful of stating his own conclusions, in case his voice overpower a certain still, small sound.

Akin to this humility is the third great quality needed in the analyst, namely, selflessness. It is one of the subtlest of his temptations, to feel himself to be leader and guide, to indulge in a priestcraft of the mind, and to magnify the transferences of his patients for his own greater glory. Over against that, there is his other major temptation, which is, in reality, a short-cut, that of being the cold scientist, acting with a watchfulness so impersonal, as to be, in a wrong sense, selfless. True and enduring results can only be achieved when the analyst follows the example of the greatest of all, and, in his own little degree, "empties himself of glory," that he may redeem ; when he feels himself to be an instrument in Another hand, knows his knowledge to be only a medium for Another's wisdom, and his analysis only a prelude to the far more searching and life-long Analysis, which his patient must be made to welcome. It is, no doubt, a noble enough aim which the Freudian or the Adlerite analyst has, that of restoring a man to his optimum, and his rightful place in society, but it is an aim which redounds to the praise of the Freudian or the Adlerite. Ours is a simpler and a better one—to break the barriers of habit and of illness, and reconcile a man to his God ; and, in that service, the less of self there is, the more there is of God.

These three great qualities are easy of attainment if the whole analysis, and indeed, all psychological work whatever, be set in the atmosphere of constant dependence upon God. He who made the mind, will teach the healer of the mind ; and if that healer's work be begun, continued, and ended in prayer, and the healer himself be conscious always that under overshadowing guidance, he fulfils Another's purpose, his Christian psycho-therapy must succeed. His mere knowledge is not enough, though he must " to his faith add knowledge," nor is his technique ; in this, as in every sphere of Christian work, all hinges upon close rapport between the disciple and his Master.

Other qualities there are, no doubt, which are essential to the analyst ; leadership, understanding of men, tact, and so on. Such things are added to the man whose work is rooted and grounded in the greater qualities ; and the crowning glory of these greater gifts of reverence, humility, and selflessness is, that they are not, like genius, for the few, but are for all who truly seek to have that mind in them which was also in Christ Jesus.

IV

For the proper application of these therapeutic methods, adequate training is clearly necessary, on a scale, and with a thoroughness, not yet attempted. Christian analytical work has sometimes been justly suspect, because of the lack of this systematic training in those who attempt it ; here, of all places, a little knowledge is a dangerous thing.

But that is by no means the most dangerous thing with which
we have to deal. Far more dangerous to a Christian psycho-
therapy, is the doctrinaire attitude of medical psychiatry,
who deny its right to exist, firstly, because it conflicts with
their short-sighted views on the validity of experience, and
also, curiously enough, because Christian psychologists have
made mistakes which were due to insufficient training.
Lack of clinical training is no disproof of a science, and reality
has lately shown them a disconcerting readiness to discard
the swaddling bands of materialism ; and one can only suppose
that the very vehemence of the desire expressed, that this
knowledge should be confined to medical circles, is itself a
testimony to the force of these two facts.

When we turn to the training necessary for a
Christian psycho-therapist, we are, of course, dealing with
futurities. There can, naturally, be no suggestion that the
average minister or Christian worker should be an analyst
or an expert psycho-therapist ; he has no time to specialise,
even if he wished. But every minister or worker ought to
know the broad principles of psycho-therapy, as they have
been outlined in this book, in order that, at least, he may
know the symptoms when he sees them. He ought to be
able to direct the sufferer to where he ought to go, in order to
receive proper treatment at Christian hands, but that possibility is not yet. At present he can only direct the very
few who have the money or the time to the nearest psychiatrist, and hope that he may not be a Freudian, who will
send him back to life with his religious instinct well battened
down and his spiritual experiences explained on sexual
grounds. Others, who can afford neither time nor money,
he may help a little, if he knows the principles of Christian
psycho-therapy, but he dare not go very far, lest he do
irreparable harm.

In suggesting some of the elements which ought

to enter into the training of the Christian psycho-therapist, it must not be thought that we deal in theories. These principles are the outcome of practice, not of theory ; and the suggestions for this training meet not only the need for the cure of the disorders we have been examining, but also the widespread desire among ministers, Christian workers, and students for the ministry, for greater practical knowledge and help in this regard. This desire is far from being met by any of the " popular " books on psycho-therapy, including those written from the Christian angle ; such books often do greater harm than good, by whetting a slightly morbid curiosity, and tempting men and women to dangerous and illegitimate experiments on others. A much more arduous apprenticeship is needed than that, and the training to be envisaged is entirely divorced from " popular " psychology.

In examining such a training, it may be convenient to divide the matter by asking two questions : To Whom is it to be given ? and How is it to be given ?

(1) It must be obvious that so highly specialised a study ought to be in the hands of specialists. In the future, it may be devoutly hoped that the Church will be guided to set apart certain duly qualified men and women for this vital and urgent work. The haphazard methods of the cure of souls ought to be scrapped, and a careful training, along the lines we shall indicate, given to those who are judged fit to take up the work in a Christian and scientific way. Such a corps of Christian psycho-therapists would be at the free service of their maladjusted fellow-men, in clinics or working singly ; and wherever a minister or other Christian worker diagnosed a case of clamant need, he would be able to direct the patient to the nearest expert. Christian psycho-therapy would thus be delivered from the reproach of poverty and insufficiency under which it lives at present, and

a body of Christian psychological clinical material would be built up, comparable to the results of medical psychological research, and of the utmost value theologically as well as psychologically.

In default of such an organised and definite attempt on the part of the Church to deal with this pressing need, the field must continue to be occupied, as at present, by isolated men and women, some more, some less qualified, without standards of training or recognition by the Church, and working sporadically in the intervals of other work. Hitherto, the Parish and the pulpit have been the only approaches of the ordinary ministry to the disorders of mankind ; but in view of the knowledge we now possess, and of the overstrain of the world, a new ministry is very clearly indicated.

To whom, then, is such a delicate and highly specialised ministry to be entrusted ?   Clearly, to those who are fitted ; and by that is meant, not those possessed by the superficial curiosity which is so rife to-day, but those whose strength of character and consecration are sufficiently great to create in them a deep spiritual desire to do this work in the name and in the spirit of Jesus Christ.   Then, and then only, can scientific training begin ; in far too many schools, scientific training is separate from character, and the results are obvious to the Christian eye.   What has already been said on the Christian characteristics of the psycho-therapist ought to be sufficient to make the point that here, as always, works without faith are dead.   To this foundation of character must be added clear-headedness and a truly scientific spirit of inquiry, discriminative and critical. These given, we can begin to work out the necessary elements in the training and equipment of such men and women.

V

(2) How is such training to be given ?   When the Church sees fit to set apart these men and women, her colleges will have to make room in their curricula for their training.   At present there are on their staffs none qualified so to train ; academic psychologists or lecturers on pastoral theology cannot, and medical psychiatrists will not, and therefore any training there is, is self-imposed and un-regulated.   Even so, however, it is easy to see that in any scheme of training, systematised or not, three main elements are essential.

(A) First and clearest, there must be a working knowledge of psychology in each of three realms.

(i) To commence with, a study must be made of academic and experimental psychology, in order to under-stand something of the natural working of the mind itself. It is necessary to know the phenomena of perception and of reaction to stimuli, and the behaviour of the mind in health, before any effort can be made to understand that mind in ill-health.   Some norm of health must be established, and in that norm, the spiritual elements of the mind must have their proportionate place.   It is for precisely this reason that no existing department of university psychology is quite adequate for us here, because we have to include tran-scendental and inspirational material in their influence on behaviour, and to work, therefore, on a broader basis.   Every single phenomenon of the mind is coloured more or less for us by the facts of revelation and of communion with the unseen ; and for us, the properly developed mind is that which lives in the constant practice of the presence of God.   Re-action to the world is only the half of behaviour ; reaction to God is the complement.   A Christian psychology is therefore dual, and recognition of, and training in, that truth is fundamental.

(ii) Following upon this, there ought to be a detailed knowledge of the disorders of the mind, the psychoses and neuroses, as well as the psycho-neuroses, in order to understand where the domain of the psychiatrist extends, and where it touches those of the alienist and the neurologist. Such knowledge is at once a safeguard against presumption, and a necessary foundation for all psycho-therapeutic work. To touch mental disease would be to go outwith our province, as it would be to try to cure a mental disorder which had a clear organic source. The limits of our kingdom have already been pretty clearly outlined in this book, and within them there is great and increasing opportunity for the Christian psychotherapist. He must read and know all he possibly can on the disorders within his province, but he must do more. He must, on every page, qualify and add ; qualify the diagnoses which seem to him to be based on material grounds, to the exclusion of the spiritual, and add his own explanations of such symptoms as may conceivably be the outcome of denial and repression of the conscience, or of inhibitions of the religious instinct. In this alone, there is a life's work ; for a Christian psycho-therapy must build itself up on quite other concepts of behaviour and derangement than those of medical or academic psychology.

(iii) And again, he must know intimately the work of the founders of his science, especially those of Jung and his school. Freud is, of course, the pioneer, but he must be read with a reservation and a criticism which are not possible to beginners, and he, like Adler, has to be supplemented and corrected at many points. It is, on the whole, safe advice to begin one's study in this part of the subject with Jung, who, though not orthodox, as we know the meaning of the word, is far nearer to the Kingdom than the others, and always open to the spiritual. To such reading must be added a far closer study of the methods of psycho-therapy than has been given here. Each of them, analysis, hypnosis, suggestion, dream analysis, and so on, is a separate department in itself and needs a library ; and knowledge of each is vitally necessary. Such study links his knowledge of the first two aspects of psychology mentioned above, to the work he hopes to do. It gives him, as we know, an entirely new outlook on the mind and its disorders ; but, as we also know, it imposes on him the necessity of adding and subtracting as he studies, at the dictates of his own knowledge of the greater things of God. Some of that spiritual arithmetic we have endeavoured to do here, but only in outline. That outline must be filled in in detail by students, who require to be critics as well as students, and who are prepared to alter or delete whatever conflicts with the truth of the Gospel.

(B) To such study must be added one thing vitally necessary and frequently overlooked, perhaps because of its stringent character. Its mere statement will make apparent what a barrier it places before the amateur and the dabbler, and the writer makes it with full conviction and knowledge. It is this : every aspirant to the high office of a psycho-therapist must himself have undergone analysis, in some shape or form—it must be regarded as an absolutely essential part of his equipment. He can, of course, do some little good to others without it, but he cannot be a psycho-therapist. There are two reasons for this demand, and they ought to appeal with double force to the Christian mind. For, if the medical psychologist submits himself to analysis before taking up his therapeutic work, much more should the Christian, whose conceptions of mind are broader, and whose ideals of healing are higher.

(i) In order to know others, one must know oneself ; and (advisedly be it said), the vigorous probing of analysis is the only means yet devised of attaining full and true self-knowledge. Analysis is no medicine for the sick alone ; it is a necessary tonic and cleanser for the so-called healthy as well ; and indeed, in the ideal state of society, it may well be that it will have a place at some stage in every life. Book knowledge of analytical methods will carry one only so far ; and it is because the knowledge of most Christian practitioners of this science rests on books alone that it *has* only gone so far. To have undergone the stark and searching necessities of an analysis is unforgettable experience. No man can ever know his depths until another hand has guided the exploratory light to shine upon them ; of himself, he has not the courage, nor will his conscious censor let him see them. Nor can he know his powers and his desires, till his resistances and his repressions have been shown to him, and until he is made aware of the full strength of the instinctual life within. Such full and searching self-knowledge is indispensable to him who would put out his hand and mould another's mind.

(ii) And again, in order to understand the reactions of another to his analysis, the therapist himself must have been there also. If not, he will pass over innumerable tiny signs, misunderstand many danger signals, and bungle where he ought to be firm. Books alone can never teach more than the fringe of a technique which is literally unutterable ; it is the living word, and not the written, which is effective here. He has no right to ask others to submit to a process which, for him, is entirely theoretical ; for, in this respect, mental disorder differs absolutely from bodily disease. The latter can be, and is, dealt with by drugs and methods which are outside the personal experience of the doctor ; but the analysis of the former can be rightly done only by a mind which has itself been through the mills of analysis.

(C) And lastly, the training of the psycho-therapist can only be half acquired from books ; his practical training must be clinical. Till Christian clinics exist in greater numbers, this, of course, can never be fully given, but something at least can be done by enlisting the services of the few Christian psycho-therapists who have, often at the cost of mistakes and set-backs, evolved a practical technique for themselves. Although, of course, analysis is usually private to the analyst, it ought sometimes to be possible to allow a listening student or students. Hypnosis, for example, can be observed outside the consulting-room, and, in view of the invincible readiness of people to retail their dreams, dream analysis can be practised apart from analysis itself. Something too may be learned from the observation of everyday behaviour, for, as we saw, the ordinary mechanisms of daily life shade off without a break into the more elaborate mechanisms of the neurotic.

All these, however, are but second best. Nothing can take the place of first-hand clinical knowledge, and just now that is far to seek. Till it can be systematically obtained our training system is truncated. Only when in every large centre there are free Christian psychological clinics such as The London Clinic for Religious Psychology, or the psychological clinic at Whitefield's Tabernacle, will we be able to offer a complete scheme of training, and not have to depend as at present on a system of individual trial and error to supplement our book knowledge.

VI

With that practical vision of the future, we may well conclude. Our whole endeavour has been towards its realisation, towards the equipping of men and women within the the Church with new knowledge and new hope, in face of world-wide tension and overstrain. In these last days, fear and darkness have suddenly and ominously increased.

New fetters are everywhere enchaining the mind, and new repressions on a world scale must be the consequences. We are right to fear the results, political and economic, of the tyrannies and competitions of the day ; but we need to fear far more their results on the delicate machinery of the mind. It is all to the good that medical psychology has stepped in to endeavour to repair the damage and restore the balance ; but more than that is needed if the mind is to be made whole. One Psychiatrist alone can do that, and Christian psychotherapy can but humbly proclaim His power. If that power be ministered through new channels, His is the glory, and under Him alone can we deepen and enlarge them. What a field is here for study and research—how varied and how great ! The imagination rises at the thought of walking there with Christ.

INDEX

18